God's
POLITICIANS

God's
POLITICIANS

THE CHRISTIAN CONTRIBUTION
TO 100 YEARS OF LABOUR

GRAHAM DALE

HarperCollins*Publishers*

HarperCollins*Publishers*
77–85 Fulham Palace Road, London W6 8JB
www.**fire**and**water**.com

First published in Great Britain in 2000
by HarperCollins*Publishers*

1 3 5 7 9 10 8 6 4 2

Scripture quotations are taken from the
HOLY BIBLE, NEW INTERNATIONAL VERSION.
Copyright © 1973, 1978, 1984 by International Bible Society.
Used by permission

Graham Dale asserts the moral right to be identified
as the author of this work

A catalogue record for this book
is available from the British Library

ISBN 0 00 710064 7

Printed and bound in Great Britain by
Creative Print and Design, Ebbw Vale (Wales)

Contents

Acknowledgements

This book represents the work not only of the author but also of all those connected with him during the winter of 1999/2000. First and foremost I need to thank Pete Moorey, who did the research and provided me with excerpts from the extensive bibliography at the back of this book. Arguably Pete knows more about this subject than I do and he was essential to the project's success – I simply could not have done it without him. We are both now convinced of the centrality of the Christian contribution to the Labour Party and it has reinforced our own commitment to continue to serve the party.

Next I need to thank my wife Gillian and our children, Nathan (3) and Joseph (1), for putting up with this project and their angst-filled dad and husband. Gillian took some convincing, but when the green light was given she supported me through the good times and the bad. I also want to thank Stephen Timms MP, for the practical and thoughtful support he has given to this project. Stephen believed in the idea from day one and I am delighted that he was willing to write an introduction for the book. His own story of faith within the Labour Party is the latest in a long line of similar politicians, some of whose work this book has sought to record.

The Officers and Executive Committee of the Christian Socialist Movement are also to be thanked. They magnanimously gave me a sabbatical just one year into my new job as director. One year on and three months off is a pattern I would like to continue. Special thanks must go to Bev Thomas, CSM's interim director, who served excellently at such short notice alongside Emma Antoine in the CSM office. Thanks also to James Catford at HarperCollins, who believed in this book from the original idea, and to Gordon Marsden MP, who encouraged me to approach a publisher in the first place. Thanks to all those who sent me their personal stories, some of which I have included – with apologies to those I have not. Thank you also to those who have prayed for me during this demanding time.

The characters whose stories are told in this book are only some of the many wonderful people I could have mentioned. It has been a demanding privilege to write about them and one that has changed my life. I am conscious, however, that many more have not been mentioned, wonderful people who have served anonymously and faithfully. For these people the quote from George Eliot which Stephen Timms includes in his introduction sums everything up so well: 'For the growing good of the world is partly dependent on unhistoric acts; and that things are not so ill with you and me as they might have been is half owing to the number who lived faithfully a hidden life and rest in unvisited tombs.'[1]

Foreword

by Tony Blair

I am pleased to provide the foreword to this book celebrating the 'Christian contribution to 100 years of Labour'. The Labour Party has always included people of different faiths as well as people with no religious faith and this diversity is its strength. Christianity is one of the many forces that have influenced Labour during its first hundred years and it is not a faith the party claims a monopoly on – Christians have served and continue to serve in other political parties. However, as this book shows, many Christians have played a significant role in the development of the Labour Party and it is appropriate that we acknowledge the impact these people have had.

The Labour Party and the nation are indebted to people whose Christian faith motivated their political service: individuals who were outraged by the social injustice they saw all around and believed that it was their duty to stand up for the downtrodden; individuals who wanted to show compassion towards their neighbours and saw the Labour Party as a means by which this could be done; individuals who saw a connection between the values of Christ and the values of Socialism, and who chose to work out these connections in the rough and tumble of party politics.

It was the Christian values of these people that informed their political thinking. They believed in community, in equality and in individual responsibility. Their beliefs forced them to take political action when faced with the great need around them – the need for jobs, the need for homes or the need for health care. They believed that legislation, not just charity, was needed to transform the inadequate present into a better future. In 1906 the Labour Party had just 30 MPs, 18 of whom were Nonconformists, so it is easy to understand why some say Labour owes more to Methodism than to Marx. But there were Anglicans and Catholics too, people from other faiths and people of no religious faith, all of whom were united in their belief that politics has a moral purpose. For all these people the Labour Party was a means through which their values could be put into action, and this is the nub of the issue. Neither faith nor politics can be simply about believing – it must be about action. Religious beliefs and political beliefs will achieve nothing until people are prepared to act on those beliefs. It is on what politicians do and not just what they believe that they are judged. Just as it is on what this Labour Government has done – on jobs, on education, on the NHS and on the National Minimum Wage – that it too will be judged.

I warmly commend this account of the men and women who built the Labour Party and whose faith informed their political action: from Keir Hardie (a Nonconformist), often described as the father of the party, through to Arthur Henderson (a Methodist), who gave the party its original Clause 4; John Wheatley (a Roman Catholic), who gave the nation its first housing programme and Ellen Wilkinson (a Methodist), who walked with the men of Jarrow in their dignified protest for work; George Lansbury (an Anglican), a Labour leader and pacifist who argued with Hitler, and Stafford Cripps (an Anglo-Catholic), a Labour chancellor who helped secure Russian support in the fight against Hitler; and more recently Harold Wilson (a Congregationalist), who caught the mood of the nation in the 1960s and John Smith (a Presbyterian), whose untimely death denied him his request of 'a chance to serve'. It is to recognize people like these, both those recorded here and others unknown, that this book has been written. We are grateful to them for the service they have provided to their party and to this country.

Introduction

BY STEPHEN TIMMS MP

If you walk north from Cambridge along the banks of the River Cam to Ely, it is a distance of about 15 miles. I have done the walk on a couple of occasions and you can see Ely Cathedral within a mile or two of starting out, rising up from the flatness which spans the horizon in every direction. It stands on the only high ground for miles and you would be able to see this even without a cathedral on top of it, but, with the vast cathedral tower pointing skywards, it is an awe-inspiring sight. Walking from Cambridge, you spend the entire day, one footstep after another, drawing closer to this extraordinary building, until finally you climb away from the river, up the hill through some orchards, and at last enter the huge cathedral doorway. That cathedral occupied the skills of innumerable craftsmen and has been a place of worship for countless believers throughout most of the past millennium.

About half way along that walk, on what is in one sense a rather dreary journey through the Fens with just that cathedral to draw you on, you come across – just alongside the river, apparently in the middle of nowhere – another, more recent place built for worship. It is an abandoned Methodist chapel. Once in that place, a group of ordinary farm labourers, perhaps following a visit by John Wesley himself, had set out to follow Christ and had decided they wanted to build a chapel where they could meet to worship and express their new-found faith together. The building – though not used now – is a reminder of the change in the lives of that group of people when they came to believe.

I used to wonder which of those two buildings for worship was the more impressive. In one sense the answer is obvious, and yet that chapel has a claim to the accolade too, absorbing as it did the faith and

xi

commitment of people who had never done anything out of the ordinary before. It testifies to the change which occurred in their lives, a chapel built not by royal decree with all the resources of the medieval Church, but through the determination of a little group of ordinary people. George Eliot put it like this in the finale to *Middlemarch*: 'For the growing good of the world is partly dependent on unhistoric acts; and that things are not so ill with you and me as they might have been is half owing to the number who lived faithfully a hidden life and rest in unvisited tombs.'[2]

Certainly, as far as the history of the Labour Party is concerned over the past century, the movement represented by the people who met in that chapel, and in chapels like it all over the country, has had much the greater impact. It was through the experience of conversion, of groups of ordinary people taking responsibility for organizing their own worship, that the infrastructure which led on to the grass roots of the Labour Party came into being. Ordinary people, to whom the idea had never previously occurred, discovered that they could take on and succeed in positions of leadership. They did not simply have to wait for their betters to decide what happened – they could make things happen themselves. They discovered from the Bible that there was no such thing as their betters anyway, and they applied that discovery to the ordering of their lives, not just in the chapel but outside it too.

They learned what Paul had told the Christians at Corinth: 'Brothers, think of what you were when you were called. Not many of you were wise by human standards; not many were influential; not many were of noble birth. But God chose the foolish things of the world to shame the wise; God chose the weak things of the world to shame the strong' (1 Corinthians 1:26–7). Their lowly status was no obstacle as far as God was concerned. Their experience of faith changed their lives.

Among the results of this were the Labour Movement and, after a few generations, just 100 years ago now, the formation of the Labour Party. Of the 30 Labour MPs elected in the mould-breaking General Election of 1906, 18 described themselves as Nonconformists, and right through the party's early decades it was the chapel influence which provided the inspiration for very many of those who were involved.

The nationwide movement which that chapel by the Cam represents was profoundly and vitally important as a source for the development of the Labour Movement and the Labour Party. It was Nonconformist

Christianity which provided the infrastructure and much of the inspiration at the grass roots for the party, and in doing so it shaped the character of the whole movement. It was more influential in that respect at the grass roots than anything else. Its adherents imparted a set of ethical principles to the party. They believed there should be a moral basis for the party's policies, and specific policies were drawn from the set of values which was the result. It led to a broad moral basis which contained elements of personal as well as social morality. It stressed the need for personal discipline, self-improvement and responsibility as well as equality and social justice.

You can see the scale of that influence in the party's leading figures, whose lives are documented in the chapters which follow. Keir Hardie was first elected as a Labour MP before the party was founded, for West Ham South in 1892. He was the party's first leader. He said of his inspiration: 'The impetus which drove me first of all into the Labour Movement and the inspiration which carried me on in it, has been derived more from the teachings of Jesus of Nazareth than all other sources combined.'[3]

Hardie was a Nonconformist from his conversion and maintained a keen distinction between institutional Christianity, which he saw as organized hypocrisy for the benefit of the ruling classes, and 'real religion', which emanated from the hearts of the people. He closed a chapter in his book *From Serfdom to Socialism* with the words:

> *My purpose in writing this chapter will have been served if I have succeeded in showing that the Socialist ... is in the true line of apostolic succession with the Old Testament prophets, with Jesus himself and with the Early Church Fathers who maintained even to their death the unsullied right of their religious faith to be regarded as the Gospel to the Poor.*[4]

In Parliament Keir Hardie fought hard to draw attention to the evil of unemployment and came to be known as the 'Member for the Unemployed'. Kenneth Morgan has written, 'He directed attention, as no politician had before, towards a fundamental social evil in the late Victorian economy. Unemployment became, and long remained, a social and political theme of primary concern, despite the political impotence of the unemployed, almost all of whom were disenfranchised or unregistered. For this Hardie deserves much ... credit.'[5]

Another intriguing figure from that time is Will Crooks, the victor of a famous by-election in 1903 which foreshadowed the gains at the General Election of 1906. He was based in Poplar and regarded the Labour Party as a religious force. He was a keen advocate of the adult school movement and ran a series of winter addresses at the town hall on Sunday afternoons with the rector of Poplar. In his 1908 autobiography, *From Workhouse to Westminster*, he wrote this of his Sunday addresses:

> *The gatherings are not religious in the orthodox sense, nor is any attempt made to teach religion, but I venture to say that they have as much influence for good on the workpeople of Poplar as many of the churches. We nearly always begin with music by singers or players who give their services, and then we have a talk, generally by a public man, on social questions, on education, on books, on authors, and citizenship. Some of our speakers take Biblical subjects ... the presence of the rector has convinced many, who were formerly hostile to all parsons, Anglican and Nonconformist, that the churches and Labour can work in harmony.*[6]

I recently took the opportunity to discuss all of this with one of my constituents, Jack Hart, who was the leader of Newham Council when I was elected a member of it in 1984. He joined the party in East Ham in the 1920s, was first elected to the Council in 1936 and stayed a member for 54 years.

In 1927, aged 14, he attended a Socialist Sunday School at the old Labour Hall in East Ham. The emphasis there on the part of Mr Rawlinson, who led the school, was on doing your duty by your neighbour – holding the door open for the next person when you went into the Co-op, giving up your seat on the train. There were only about 20 young people present. It was more about politics than worship, although there was always a Bible reading, a hymn from a sheet – 'Jerusalem' was a favourite – and the Lord's Prayer. Jack did not find this too inspiring. He found greater spiritual sustenance from two other sources – from his ward meeting, where the powerful women members were particularly impressive, and from the Methodist Central Hall, East Ham, where Jack was part of the congregation until it was demolished in 1975.

When Jack became a councillor in the mid-1930s there were eight or nine other councillors who were also members of the Central Hall. It had a capacity of 2,400 and on Sunday afternoons it was full. At five minutes to three, a hush fell on the congregation. On the dot of three o'clock, the minister appeared and called on someone to pray. There was a rousing hymn, led by a choir of 30 and an orchestra of 50. Then came the speaker – Donald Soper was very popular, along with Lax of Poplar, who used to say, 'If Jesus came today, he would come to Poplar.' For Jack, that was where his political inspiration came from – and for many, many others in the party it was the same.

One hugely significant figure was George Lansbury. He was an Anglican, but his politics sat uneasily with a Church in which many members still believed that the class system was ordained by God. He was leader of the party for only four years, from 1932 to 1935, but his political career spanned half a century – the period in which foundations were laid for post-war government.

Lansbury was a passionate campaigner for women's suffrage. The key principle for him was equality. All humans were created equal by God and were therefore equally valuable. This same God had created a world full of riches and abundance and had told us to love our neighbours. Therefore goods should be distributed according to need and society should be organized into systems of co-operation not conflict. Lansbury went so far as to say that all Christians ought to become Socialists: 'Socialism, which means love, co-operation, and brotherhood in every department of human affairs, is the only outward expression of a Christian faith.'[7]

For Hardie, Lansbury, or any other of the Christian Socialists who helped to influence the early direction of the Labour Party, there was no doubt that Socialism was essentially an ethical political system. Socialist principles and the policies that came from them were to be based on a moral understanding of the individual and society. Politics was value driven and value based, and these values were Christian values. Lansbury said that Socialism 'without religious enthusiasm ... will become as selfish and soulless as any other movement that has cursed the world'.[8]

Another figure of immense importance as a contributor to the party's ideology leading up to 1945 was R.H. Tawney. In his biography Tony Wright quotes Tawney's explanation of his commitment to equality: 'In order to believe in human equality, it is necessary to believe in God. It is only when one contemplates the infinitely great that human differences appear so infinitely small ... what is wrong with the modern world is that having ceased to believe in the greatness of God, it has to emphasize distinctions between men.'⁹

These foundational values, laid throughout the early years of the Labour Party, were to form the basis of the policies upon which the party would win power in 1945 and from which it would implement its programme to reform and transform British society. For our core values, the Labour Party owes a much bigger debt to Christian influences than we do to anything else.

I want to conclude by looking forward rather than back, and to argue – contrary to the views of many – that Christian Socialism will be just as big an influence on the Labour Party in the future as it was in the past. It is already the case that the last two party leaders, John Smith and Tony Blair, have asserted strong commitments to Christian Socialism. They have sparked a big increase in the size and profile of the Christian Socialist Movement, and have profoundly influenced the party's programme.

Outside the party, heavy-duty engagement with issues of social exclusion – employment, housing, rough sleeping, drug abuse, community health – is developing rapidly among many of the faster-growing churches. That is a new phenomenon and I believe it will feed into a profound influence on the party in the future. The potential is well illustrated by the remarkable success of the Jubilee 2000 campaign and its influence on the present Government. It was not just a church campaign, but 80 per cent of those who have been active participants were from the churches – and for many of them it was the first experience of engaging seriously with political issues of any kind. It will not be the last. I agree with Will Hutton's assessment of the significance of all this. 'Leviticus Chapter 25 is a passage that makes *Das Kapital* look tame,' he wrote in a piece in the *Observer* about Jubilee 2000. 'The Left of Centre should take note; it is no longer Morris, Keynes and Beveridge who inspire and change the world – it's Leviticus.'¹⁰

A little while ago, the Newham branch of the Christian Socialist Movement went on a walk along the Barking Road through Newham. We started at Rathbone Market in Canning Town and the organizer told us how many churches had been in the vicinity 60 years ago. Most had been bombed and nobody had ever bothered to rebuild them. Others had been sold and bulldozed after their congregations dwindled. Further along we knew there was a large Baptist chapel which had been converted in the 1940s into a warehouse with a shop on the front selling tea towels and pillowcases. It looked like a depressing picture of decline and for many years it was exactly that.

As we walked along, however, we saw that something new was happening. It was the shop names which showed it first – we came to the Amazing Grace Mini Mart, Signs and Wonders Hairstylists and Redeem Travels. Then we came to that disused Baptist chapel – and we saw that the tea towel shop had closed down and after more than 50 years the building had been converted back into a church again. It is the Glory Bible Church now, and it is bursting at the seams every Sunday. Two hundred yards away is another Baptist church – apparently one of the fastest growing in Europe.

What has happened? Many of the African people who have moved to Newham – in many cases having fled from their home countries – are committed Christians. For others, the trauma of the move has revived their faith or caused them seriously to consider the gospel afresh. Now they want to celebrate and they are injecting a huge new surge of worship into the area. It is not just the newly arrived either – the evidence is that the indigenous population is going to church much more than it was 10 years ago too. Older churches are providing night shelters for the homeless, Sunday meals for people living alone, English classes and counselling services, while many share their premises with other language congregations. In my constituency, the biggest congregation is Tamil-speaking, with people who came from Sri Lanka for asylum.

What we found was not a picture of decline, but of growth. I believe we are going to have much more exposure to Christian activism in the future than we have done in the recent past. These enthusiastic churches are full of people whose lives have been changed by believing in Christ, just as the hidden lives of those who built that chapel in the Fens were changed by the same experience 200 years ago. Like the Methodists, the more recent believers are having an impact on their communities, working to tackle the problems, wanting to bring some hope to people who are in the position they used to be in themselves. Their efforts are based on the Christian vision of a world where people are not valued for what they own or what they earn, but for being human, each one made in the image of God. We need to embrace that vision as Socialists and point out its political consequences to those who share the vision with us.

We can see here the contours of a new Christian Socialism – activist, local, committed to changed lives, rooted in worshipping communities and inspired by a biblical vision. This new Christian Socialism will, in my view, play just as big a role in inspiring the Labour Party in the future as Christian Socialism has played in the past. In 100 years' time, Ely Cathedral will still be there to be cherished by our descendants, but the hidden lives and vision of Christians in far meaner halls will have been the force that shaped our party.

CHAPTER 1

Conception

THE CHRISTIAN SOCIAL JUSTICE TRADITION

*H*arry Moncrieff, recently deceased, had a clear memory from when he
was small of his old grandfather coming to stay. His grandfather stood
beside his mother, old and weary of years but still proud, square shouldered
and upright. His mother was smaller, with sharp dark eyes. Her black hair
was piled up high and contrasted with his grandfather's silvery greyness.
They talked in an animated way, laughed and then suddenly burst into
song. It was an old marching song called 'With the ballot in our hand'.

> The land, the land,
> 'Twas God who made the land,
> The land, the land,
> 'Twas God who made us free,
> How can we be beggars
> With the ballot in our hand,
> God made the land for the people.[1]

*The song captured the enthusiasm of a generation of working people who
now had the chance to vote. Working people were being elected to Parliament
as well as city and borough councils. It was a peaceful political revolution
that would change Britain for ever. Moncrieff's family, like numerous others,
was captivated by this almost messianic vision, that through the ballot box
squalor, want, hunger and illness would be banished. It was a vision that
helped create a new political movement – the Labour Movement, and a new
political party – the Labour Party. The people who had lived in the darkness
of poverty and powerlessness had seen a great light and the future looked
brighter for their children and their children's children.*

The momentum for change

The twentieth century saw progress that revolutionized ordinary lives. In science, medicine and travel it was undeniably a revolutionary age. Revolutions of a different kind, however, marred the century through bloodshed and war. Across Europe, monarchs and tzars were losing what once belonged to them: their absolute control over people's lives. For Russia the revolution came in 1917, 130 years after the French had violently dispatched their aristocracy. The fact that Britain had no similar violence may have been due to the eighteenth-century evangelical revival, as argued by the historians Ross McKibbin and W.E.H. Lecky.[2] In Britain, religious organizations connected the working and middle classes in a way that simply did not happen in continental Europe. Nevertheless, while the expression of revolution varied across Europe, the inexorable momentum was the same. Ordinary people were taking control of their lives and were no longer subject to the whims and wishes of 'divinely appointed' rulers. Struggles were often bloody and even Britain's relative peace required the Army to sustain the Empire on which the sun never set. Yet the sun was setting and Britain's very own political revolution was about to arrive.

Embryonic democracy had come in the Parliamentary Reform Acts of 1884 and 1885. The number of voters increased from 2.5 to 4.5 million, with votes being provided for all male rural workers in addition to those already enjoyed by town and city dwellers. Combined with the Redistribution of Seats Act in 1885, it meant that Britain was being steadily democratized. Before this the workers had no voice, no power and only limited rights. More than any other factor, these Acts ensured the demise of the belief in the divine right of kings and the landed gentry to rule. At the height of the Empire the seeds of its demise were sown. Like a seedling germinating in the crack of a rock and growing to split that rock, so democracy would grow and change Britain for ever. This fledgling democracy provided a vision for ordinary people that things could be better. It was the working classes who lived the hardest, shortest and most precarious of lives. They would start work as children and work long hours, every day, with no welfare state or health service to protect them against illness or destitution. It was these people who dreamed of a better life and, in the absence of a violent revolution, it was democracy that was their bright, shining hope.

Progress and poverty

The funeral of Queen Victoria in February 1901 marked the end of an era in British life. As a constitutional monarch she had limited powers, but she had presided over 10 Prime Ministers in her 64-year reign. That reign spanned the careers of two great statesmen and political rivals, William Ewart Gladstone (1809–98) and Benjamin Disraeli (1804–81). Gladstone's career as four-times Liberal Prime Minister was dominated by his progressive attitude towards Irish self-rule. In contrast, the Conservative Disraeli was credited with rebuilding 'Toryism' around the aristocracy, the Queen and the Church.

Victoria's reign witnessed rapid industrial growth, and Britain's population had grown from 20 million in 1840 to nearly 40 million by 1901. It was Britain's golden age in the world and at home. It was an age of great buildings such as the Crystal Palace (1852), the Royal Albert Hall (1871) and Tower Bridge (1894). The railways mushroomed from only 500 miles of track in 1838 to 17,000 miles in 1875.[3] It was an age, too, of the great Victorian values of self-reliance, family discipline and enterprise, public health projects, urban planning and education.

Yet there was another side to this prosperous image, reflected in the arts and in the writings of the social activists. Charles Dickens (1812–70) drew attention to abuses in schools, orphanages and prisons and Charles Kingsley wrote about the plight of child chimney sweeps in *The Water-Babies* (1863). The Irish playwright Oscar Wilde and writer George Bernard Shaw revealed the hypocrisies and absurdities of Victorian life. This underside of Victoria's Britain contained levels of poverty, ill health and limited opportunity that would have every politician and cleric condemn it if discovered today. In Victoria's Britain, however, few politicians and clerics did condemn it. Most enjoyed the benefits of growth and lived cheek by jowl with the poverty that was its by-product.

Not all had benefited from the economic wealth that made so many Victorians synonymous with invention and leadership. Wealth was concentrated in the hands of the few and when they died it remained in their hands. As late as 1914, less than 4 per cent of deaths accounted for 90 per cent of the entire capital bequeathed. The upper classes remained the greatest beneficiaries of the rise in national wealth and some of the largest increases were secured through the unearned income of shares and dividends. Wages for the workers either remained constant or fell in real terms because of inflation. It was a case of the rich becoming richer and the poor becoming poorer.[4]

The Church and the urban poor

A direct consequence of the Industrial Revolution was the movement of people from the country into towns. By 1901 an estimated 78 per cent of the population lived in towns and over half of the towns comprising more than 50,000 people were on or near the coal fields.[5] Those previously employed in domestic and rural industries had moved in tens of thousands to the new factories and mines. The inadequate infrastructure of the new towns meant poor housing for families as well as poor factory conditions for workers.

In addition, these population movements paid no attention to the churches, and soon there were scores of industrial towns and villages without any church or priest. Previously the Church of England had played a role in social welfare through its parish system and charitable work, but the Industrial Revolution had left many rural churches redundant and many urban churches struggling to cope. An effective response would require a radical reshaping of Church structures, but the Church of England in particular needed complex and protracted Acts of Parliament in order to establish new parishes. The constitutional upheaval this would require meant that there was neither the will nor the means to change. Where there were churches, they were often overwhelmed by the sheer numbers of urban poor and were consequently unable to sustain any serious role in social relief. The fact that church absenteeism was now most pronounced in the new industrial towns merely added to the churches' inability to cope.

Some churches, however, did try to respond to the needs of the new urban populations. The Glasgow-based Church of Scotland minister Thomas Chalmers believed the parish structure could in fact cope with the challenges of the urban poor. As Chairman of the Church of Scotland's extension committee he authorized 200 new churches in the 1830s alone. Chalmers taught political economy at St Andrew's University and as an early sociologist was best placed to guide the churches' efforts. Yet even his expertise and authority ultimately failed to deal with the high levels of need. A report from a Doctor Russell illustrates the difficulties faced by the mid-1880s:

> *Of the inhabitants of Glasgow, 29% live in dwellings of one room. And no less than 14% of one-roomed dwellings and 27% of the two-roomed dwellings contain lodgers, strange men and women, mixed up with husbands and wives and children within the four walls of tiny rooms. Of all the children who die in Glasgow before they complete their fifth year, 32% die in houses of one room, and not 2% in dwellings of five rooms and upwards. From the beginning to rapid ending these children play short parts in a wretched tragedy.*[6]

Nonconformist churches, less constrained by ecclesiastical law and historic buildings, faired better in the new towns. These included Methodists, Baptists, Congregationalists and the Salvation Army, who had all rejected the authority of the Church of England. Their preachers established churches in all kinds of places and by the 1851 census Nonconformist attendance equalled that of the Church of England overall and far outnumbered it in urban areas. Yet despite this limited success it became increasingly clear that churches alone could not respond to the new widespread poverty. Steeped in centuries of tradition and overwhelmed with huge new social problems, they were swamped by the scale of the need.

Political complacency

If the Church of Scotland and the Nonconformists had failed to provide an adequate social response, then perhaps the Church of England could provide a political one. The privileged role of its bishops in the House of Lords saw them strategically placed to initiate political reforms on behalf of the urban poor. They did not take action, however. The bishops in their palaces had much to lose from any political revolution and were reluctant to disrupt a system that had served them so well for so long. The links between God, king and country meant that the Church of England could not or would not deliver the necessary revolution. For many this reinforced the view of the Church as 'the Establishment at prayer'.

The failure of the churches to respond to the crying needs of the day did not go unnoticed. Even the Tory Lord Shaftesbury declared the clergy frigid and hostile towards his proposed reforms in the Ten Hours Bill, designed to protect women and children in factories and mines. His tone was critical: 'They are timid, time serving and great worshippers of wealth and power. I can scarcely remember an instance in which a clergyman has been found to maintain the cause of labourers in the face of pew holders.'[7] In 1909 the Socialist Joseph Clayton was even more scathing about the failure of the Church to respond adequately to the needs of the poor. He accused the Church of England bishops of doing little to justify their salaries and palaces:

> *They have not agitated in Parliament for international peace, or for mercy to the poor and needy, or for the protection of the weak against the strong. They have voted time and time against reforms long demanded by common sense and neighbourly being. They have shown by their absence and silence their indifference to great questions of national well being. They refused to help in the work of saving children from the gallows and from a 14 hour day in the cotton factories. They opposed admission of Jews, Catholics and Nonconformists to the full rights of citizenship. The Bishops have not justified in the past their right to the large salaries they receive and they do not justify it today.*[8]

Later in the century R.H. Tawney, in his major work on the withdrawal of the Church from public life, wondered at the political ineptitude of the clergy in failing to support reform even when reform was inevitable: 'While in France when the crash came, many of the lower clergy threw in their lot with the reformers, in England it was rare that the officers of the Church did not echo the views which commended themselves to the rulers of the state.'[9]

An unchallenged hierarchy

One of the reasons for this chronic complacency towards chronic poverty was the pervasive belief in 'the rich man in his castle and the poor man at his gate'. The prevailing theological hierarchy believed that God had established the authorities of government and business under which ordinary people lived. If God had arranged things this way, then it must be the way he intended them to be. Individuals who were distressed about poverty were at liberty to do charitable work, but they would find it difficult to challenge the structures that fuelled the poverty.

While the Church may have prevented a violent revolution in the eighteenth century, therefore, its assumptions now rendered it incapable of fomenting a peaceful one. Three 'self-evident beliefs' conspired in an unholy alliance to dissuade activists from questioning the prevailing hierarchy. These beliefs led Mrs C.F. Alexander to pen her environmentally progressive but socially backward hymn 'All things bright and beautiful', which presented the social hierarchy as God-ordained:

> *All things bright and beautiful,*
> *All creatures great and small,*
> *All things wild and wonderful,*
> *The Lord God made them all.*
>
> *The rich man in his castle,*
> *The poor man at his gate,*
> *God made them high and lowly,*
> *And ordered their estate.*

The first of these self-evident beliefs was in a divorce between Christianity and economic practice. R.H. Tawney later argued that following the English Civil War, the claim of any Christian standard in economic life had finally vanished.[10] Commerce was regarded as one thing while religion was quite another and never, or at least only through charity, did they meet. The Church's moral judgements were thus relegated from a place in public life to the realm of the personal.

This collapse in confidence in the Christian worldview coincided with the second 'belief', that one's personal relationship with God was of primary importance. The Church therefore commanded authority in the personal and not the public realm and it was in the personal realm that holiness and good works should flourish. This emphasis on individual salvation and self-improvement, typified by the Puritan legacy, made Christians wary of political solutions for social problems. Personal holiness and charitable works had become a way to heaven. Politics had become a slippery slope to hell.

The third 'belief' that made it difficult for activists to challenge the economic structures was in the so-called 'natural laws' of economics. According to Adam Smith (1723–90) in his work *The Wealth of the Nations*, these laws were that competition, free trade and *laissez-faire* economics are good and unwarranted state control is bad. Smith's ideas dominated business practice and conviction throughout Europe and America in the nineteenth century. Private enterprise was seen as an expression of the way God had ordered things – Smith's 'invisible hand' – and it was just a short step from there to the belief that these economic structures were the will of God. A benevolent God had established them to secure the greatest happiness for the greatest number and therefore Dean Tucker could write, 'National commerce, good morals and good government are but part of one general scheme in the designs of Providence.'[11]

Seeking social justice

The impact of such beliefs led to the exploitation of people on a grand scale in both rural and urban communities. George Edwards was one such person. He was born the sixth child of a poor Norfolk family in 1850 and his mother Mary was so malnourished that she was confined to bed and unable to breastfeed. George survived by eating onion gruel – onions cooked with dripping and salt and pepper, thickened with flour. His father Thomas, an ex-soldier who was denied his war pension, worked hard as a casual labourer for wages too inadequate to feed his children. Distress turned to despair when George's father was caught stealing turnips for the children's food and was sentenced to two weeks' hard labour. Not knowing where their father was, the family went to bed hungry and the loss of the breadwinner meant that they ended up in the workhouse.

Young George tried to assist in these dire conditions and when he was almost six he started work as a crow-scarer, chasing birds from dawn to dusk. It was gruelling work for a young boy, and if he fell asleep he was thrashed by the farmer and his wages were docked by two pence. Nonetheless, when he got his first week's wage of one shilling he ran to his mother and proudly exclaimed, 'Mother this is my money. Now we shall not want for bread any more and you will not have to cry again. You shall always have my money, I will always look after you!'[12]

George Edwards' later life is typical of the many people in this book who challenged prevailing beliefs that the poor were the servants of the rich. His experience of poverty and his Christian commitment led him to question the exploitation of the poor and to do something about it. He learned to read by becoming a Methodist lay preacher and later founded and led his agricultural union. His commitment to people and social justice would eventually lead to his election as a Member of Parliament.

Another agricultural worker and Methodist lay preacher was Joseph Arch, the first agricultural labourer to become an MP and a man who inspired Edwards and countless others. Arch also started his life as a crow-scarer, but by the age of 46 he had become a leader of men. On a cold February night in 1872, on the green of his village home, Arch addressed a crowd of 600 people on the need for a union to fight for a living wage and a nine-hour day. He later recalled, 'These white slaves of England stood there with the darkness all about them, like the Children of Israel waiting for someone to lead them out of the land of Egypt.'[13] He then led his fellow workers to start the first agricultural union, and within weeks Joseph Arch had become a household name, revered and reviled in equal measure.

Two of his contemporaries welcomed the news of the union's formation. The great Baptist preacher C.H. Spurgeon is reported to have said it was 'the best news I have heard since the gospel'[14] and Karl Marx wrote that 'the great event here is the awakening of the agricultural labourers'.[15] The union's historian later recorded the role of the chapels in the formation of the men who started the union, overcoming any lack of formal education: 'Here labourers learnt self-respect, self-government, self-reliance and organization; here men learnt to speak, to read, to write, and to lead their fellows.'[16]

At a time when few could actually read and write, it was songs which expressed both the hope and the opposition these first union men faced. One favourite told the story of Arch and his enemies:

> *When Arch beneath the Wellesbourne tree*
> *His glorious work began*
> *A thrill of hope and energy*
> *Through all the country ran;*
> *But farmer, parson, lord and squire*

Looked on with evil eyes,
Some looked with scorn and some with ire
And some with dumb surprise.

Chorus:
The rich and great our cause may hate,
We care not for their frown;
The strongest are not strong enough
To keep the labourer down.[17]

Others in the towns also rejected the complacency towards poverty that sadly characterized the Church and those in authority. One such person was Alfred Salter, a brilliant young medical student at Guy's Hospital in London. Salter could have chosen a lucrative practice among the rich of Harley Street, but instead chose to follow his conscience and serve the poor in the slums of Bermondsey. He moved there in 1898 and through his work he met and married Ada Brown. Ada's life and influence reconnected Alfred with his childhood faith and Christ's principles led him to start a practice of like-minded doctors who served the poor of the community. Fenner Brockway later wrote about the practical compassion of Dr Salter:

> *Stories spread of his devotion to his cases and of his kindness: of the stable-boy too ill with pneumonia to be removed, with him he stayed up two nights until the danger had passed. Of a girl in the last stages of consumption whom he visited every day however busy he was, although she was beyond medical aid; of innumerable cases which he treated without charge, of many cases which he sent away to the country or the seaside at his own charge.*[18]

The Salters lost their only daughter Joyce to scarlet fever when she was eight. This tragedy appeared to give them extra determination to improve the lot of Bermondsey children. Alfred's favourite Bible text was Christ's words, 'I have come that they may have life, and have it to the full' (John 10:10). Alfred and Ada realized that improving social conditions needed not just good works but also good politics, so they got involved. Ada soon became the first woman on Bermondsey Council and later the first female Labour Mayor in the country. Alfred was elected as the MP for West Bermondsey in 1922.

By the end of the nineteenth century, Edwards, Arch and the Salters represented a new movement of people who were turning to politics to improve social conditions. Many were doing this *because of* their faith not despite it, and often against the complacency of the wider Church. Yet people such as George Edwards, Joseph Arch and Alfred and Ada Salter were not entirely unique as Christian activists seeking social change.

Whitefield and Wesley

In his book *Streams of Living Water*, Richard Foster identifies six interwoven themes of Christianity throughout the history of the Church. One of these he calls the 'social justice tradition', which expresses how first the Jews, then the Christians expressed God's love in society.[19] From the law and the prophets in the Old Testament came God's call to social justice and in the New Testament this law was summed up in Christ's commandment 'to love God and one's neighbour as oneself'. This care for others in wider society forms a tradition that still continues, and many Christians whose names are respected today have stood and served in it.

While the Church as a whole failed to respond adequately to the challenges of the Industrial Revolution, there were nevertheless some notable individuals who did – men and women who stood in the social justice tradition and refused to stay silent in the face of human need. These people caused mini-revolutions that changed both the Church and the social circumstances in which they lived. Two such individuals were George Whitefield (1714–70) and John Wesley (1703–91). These men became role models for a new type of Christian activist and were behind the evangelical revival that saved Britain from the revolutionary fate of its European neighbours. Whitefield pioneered a new open-air style of preaching and Wesley founded the organization that reached the urban masses with the Christian message.

Since the people were increasingly outside the churches, Whitefield and Wesley went straight into the fields and streets. In the eighteenth century such open-air preaching was shockingly radical and scandalized the religious Establishment. In 1739 Whitefield preached to 20,000 miners in Kingswood, Bristol. He introduced Wesley to 'this strange way of preaching in the fields' and both began delivering numerous sermons and travelling gruelling distances to do so. Before his death in 1770 Whitefield had preached in almost every corner of England and Wales, had visited Scotland 15 times and travelled to America seven times. Together he and Wesley created a new kind of clergyman for a new kind of society and central to their preaching was a concern for personal and social reform. They had a biblical vision for social justice.

Wesley took the newly formed Holy Club and moulded it with the 'methods' that became the foundations of Methodism. He aimed for intensive spiritual improvement, expressed in serving the neediest in society, visiting prisons and workhouses and assisting the sick and poor. Loving God and loving one's neighbour was the essence of Methodism, at once a message of spiritual hope and a practical response to the needy. Wesley set up dispensaries for the sick and mutual benefit societies to help workers save and make the most of their meagre earnings. His labour co-operatives helped those least able to secure employment and his schools provided for their children. He set up orphanages to care for children whose parents were victims of industrial accidents and he was particularly concerned about the dangerous conditions of the miners. Wesley's whole life personified the Christian tradition of social justice and after his death in 1791 he was called 'the St Francis of the eighteenth century'.[20]

Wilberforce

Another important figure in the social justice tradition was William Wilberforce (1759–1833). His was a different response to a different need and opportunity. Like Wesley, Wilberforce was committed to Christ and saw his life's work as an expression of that commitment. Already a successful politician, he was persuaded by friends to focus his career on the quest to abolish slavery. In this he was joined by people of all faiths and none and through a combination of argument, parliamentary manoeuvring and mass protest they saw the abolition of the British trade in 1807, and the complete emancipation of slaves by 1833.

One of Wilberforce's unique legacies was the development of a new way to achieve change. He pioneered pressure groups and single-issue campaigning in a way that had not been done before. For this task he gathered around him the 'Clapham Sect', a group of men who shared his goals and enthusiasm. A Slavery Abolition Committee was established in 1787 to change public opinion on slavery from apathy to anger. The Committee provided information, organized mass petitions and arranged meetings where prayers and preaching were combined with education and persuasion. Public opinion duly began to shift and MPs continually heard from concerned constituents. This pressure and argument was maintained for over 20 years before success was finally achieved. In Britain Wilberforce also supported his friend Richard Oastler in his campaign against 'Yorkshire Slavery' and the conditions in which people were forced to work. He was one of the most vocal critics of the ineffective Factory Acts of 1802 and 1818 and his efforts led to their eventual strengthening in 1833 and 1842.

His motivation in his work for the most marginalized in society was a commitment to the social justice tradition of Christianity. In one speech he said, 'Christianity assumes her true character when she takes under her protection those poor degraded beings on whom philosophy looks with disdain. On the very first announcement of Christianity, it was declared by its great Author as "good news to the poor", and ever faithful to character, Christianity still delights to instruct the ignorant, to succour the needy, to comfort the sorrowful, to visit the forsaken.'[21] Wilberforce came from a privileged background and was undeniably a child of his time. Alongside his progressive legislation, he also supported repressive measures to protect the Establishment that had served him so well. Despite these failings, however, Wilberforce had done much to teach a new kind of politics by the time he retired in 1825.

Shaftesbury

Like Wilberforce, Anthony Ashley Shaftesbury (1801–85) was a beneficiary of a good education and other privileges. A student at Harrow and Oxford, he became a Tory MP in 1828. However, he became more politically independent as his concern for the conditions of working people grew. He picked up where Wilberforce had left off and was able to exploit an outraged public following the publication of the 1842 Commission on Mining, which reported that children as young as six were being made to pull trucks through underground passages too narrow for grown men.

Shaftesbury was behind the Ten Hours Act of 1847, which limited the amount of time children could be forced to work. The employers found a loophole, however, and began to work the children in relays, broken by useless intervals. This meant that, while they were not at the looms for more than the legal six and a half hours for children or 10 hours for teenagers under 18, they were on call for 11 or 12 hours at a time. In 1850 a test case judged that employers were acting within the law. In response Shaftesbury brought in a Bill to restrict the legal working day for all young people and women to the hours between six in the morning and six in the evening, with one and a half hours for meals. The Bill received royal assent on 26 July 1850. In 1875 he secured legislation against the use of children as chimney sweeps, having obtained further rights for workers in the Factory Act of 1874. His concern for the most disadvantaged also led him to support the world's first animal welfare charity, the RSPCA, which was established by his friend the Revd Arthur Broome.

His concern for the weakest in society was in contrast to what he regarded as the prevailing complacency of the Church. He was scathing in his attacks on the Church Establishment: 'Talk of the dangerous classes, the dangerous classes in England are not the people! The dangerous classes are the lazy ecclesiastics, of whom there are thousands, and the rich who do no good with their money.'[22]

Like all those who responded to the physical needs of the poor, Shaftesbury was accused of abandoning the priority of the Christian gospel. His response to such attacks was blunt: 'When people say we should think more of the soul and less of the body, my answer is that the same God who made the soul, made the body also … I maintain that God is worshipped not only by the spiritual but by the material creation. Our bodies, the temple of the Holy Spirit, ought not to be corrupted by preventable disease, degraded by avoidable filth, and disabled for his service by unnecessary suffering.'[23]

Booth and the Salvation Army

William Booth (1829–1912), the founder of the Salvation Army, was another influential agitator and follower of the social justice tradition. As a fiery evangelist Booth was initially suspicious of what he regarded as the distractions of social justice. His 1865 move to London's East End was out of concern for the spiritual and not the material needs of the Mile End residents. However, his friendship with J.B. Paton, a Congregational minister, and W.T. Stead, the editor of the *Pall Mall Gazette*, led to a wider concern than simply saving souls. In 1872 his Christian Mission began selling cheap food and thereafter he started a plethora of social initiatives that were often the first of their kind. He started a bank for those who could get no credit, organized farm work for the unemployed, established a missing person's bureau and provided legal aid for the poor. One characteristic of all these projects was equality of service, meaning that working-class people would serve alongside university graduates, and women as well as men could be leaders. Booth declared that women who were gifted could preach and fill any office in the Salvation Army.

By the late nineteenth century Booth's Army of 16,000 male and female officers were responding to social ills both in Britain and overseas. This was made possible by his rigid, military-like discipline, which he saw as an essential element in 'winning the war'. Booth's use of military language jars in modern ears, but it reflects his willingness to plagiarize in what was a militaristic society. (He also borrowed musical hall tunes for his hymns, started a match factory to highlight contrasting conditions at Bryant & May and used slavery images to highlight the plight of a submerged tenth of English society.) His authoritarian style and seizure of the mission in 1877 was even a model military coup.

While the Salvation Army may appear anachronistic today, in the late nineteenth century it was very progressive in both communication and activism. One of Booth's defining acts was to publish the bestseller *In Darkest England and the Way Out* (1890). While it did not provide a manifesto for a future Socialist government, it did begin to map out the needs of the working classes. In many ways this book reflected the second conversion of a man whom the *Methodist Recorder* described as the 'General turned Socialist'.

The need for co-ordinated action

Wesley, Wilberforce, Shaftesbury and Booth all represented the Christian social justice tradition. They refused to stay silent in the face of suffering and spoke what they believed to be on God's mind about human need. They all declared the wider Church guilty in its complacency towards the poor. They were from different backgrounds and ages and had different strategies, styles and strengths. Wilberforce and Shaftesbury remained firmly within the Establishment and the national Church. They tackled social need through their privileged positions in Parliament by using all the resources available to them – money, education and political connections. In contrast, Wesley and Booth were part of the Nonconformist tradition that rejected the established Church and its constraining culture. They relied on mass movements and populist communication to deliver a range of charitable works.

Despite all their efforts, however, by the end of the nineteenth century none of these initiatives had provided the comprehensive plan and political revolution that was necessary to combat widespread social injustice. Even the parliamentary reforms of the harshest social conditions only tinkered at the edges of a huge need. What was required was not more Christian charity but a political programme to tackle the structural economic injustices at the root of nineteenth-century society. Charity, no matter how effective, was always going to be dependent on the whims and abilities of individual leaders at various times. Genuine social justice, genuine economic redistribution, would never be achieved through charity alone. A new political Christian activism was needed – and already, as the century closed, there were a few tentative steps towards that goal.

The first Christian Socialists

In 1890 when the *Methodist Recorder* described William Booth as a 'Socialist', it was using a word first seen in English in 1827.[24] The adjective 'Christian' was attached 21 years later when two Anglican priests and a lawyer declared their intention to 'Christianize socialism and socialize Christianity'.[25] They wanted to show that Christians as well as political reformers were on the side of the poor. These men regarded the new political philosophy of Socialism as a vehicle that could deliver the political revolution so many desired. So F.D. Maurice (1805–72), Charles Kingsley (1819–75) and J.M. Ludlow (1821–1911) became Britain's early Christian Socialists and began a creative relationship between Christianity and Socialism that has lasted for 150 years.

The 1850s were revolutionary times and the three men talked about how the Church could help avert the growing threat from the workers whose reasonable grievances were being ignored. Maurice wanted to socialize Christianity by teaching the social dimensions of what was for many too individualistic a faith. Ludlow, in contrast, sought to Christianize Socialism as he believed structural change was needed and charity was not enough. He had been a social worker in London and had commented, 'It seemed to me that no serious effort was made to help a person out of his or her misery, but only to help him or her in it.'[26] These twin goals remain the goals of Christian Socialists. The group published two journals, *Politics of the People* (1848–9) and *The Christian Socialist, a Journal of Association* (1850–51) to inform and influence others. There were also pamphlets called *Tracts of Christian Socialism* and other initiatives including night classes for workers which would develop into working men's colleges.

While the group did not flourish, it did set in train a series of ideas that were to influence deeply a new political force in Britain. A study by Peter Jones of the Christian Socialism of the period between 1877 and 1914 concludes that it was an enigma. The various groups never agreed on a way to relate Socialism to Christianity so that justice could be done to both sets of beliefs. Nevertheless, the attempted union would influence a new generation of Christian political activists.

In 1877 the Anglican priest Stewart Headlam gave Christian Socialism its first real organizational structure in the Guild of St Matthew. From 1877 until its demise in 1909 this small group of mainly Anglican priests studied political questions in the light of the incarnation. They argued for a political revolution in their *Priests' Political Programme* and declared that to deny workers their wealth was contrary to the doctrines of brotherhood and justice.[27] Nevertheless, the Guild remained on the fringes of society, adopting the stance of a prophet crying in the wilderness rather than offering a serious start to a new political movement. Headlam remained suspicious of politicians and the compromises he believed were inherent in politics. 'The ideal commonwealth,' he said, 'cannot be realized through the immoral and mechanical processes of any one party outwitting, outbribing, outvoting, confounding and crushing any other party.'[28]

The Guild's prophetic idealism was in contrast to the more pragmatic and political Church Socialist League, formed in 1906. Its first President (up to 1909) was Algernon West, who declared, 'The League stands for economic socialism. It exists to further the socialism of the Independent Labour Party and the Social Democratic Forum among Churchmen.'[29] Other key clergy figures included Bishops Charles Gore (1853–1932) and B.F. Westcott (1825–1901). Bishop Gore of Birmingham preached on the social doctrine of the Sermon on the Mount, saying, 'Bad dwellings, inadequate wages, inadequate education, inability to use leisure – these are stones which lie upon the graves of men spiritually dead. We must take away these stones.'[30]

In an address to the Co-operative Congress at Hull, Bishop Westcott of Durham described Socialism as co-operation: 'The method of socialism is co-operation; the method of individualism is competition. The one regards man as working with man for a common end; the other regards man as working against man for private gain. The aim of socialism is the fulfilment of service; the aim of individualism is the attainment of some personal advantage – riches, or place, or fame. Socialism seeks such an organization of life as shall secure for everyone the most complete development of his powers; individualism seeks primarily the satisfaction of the particular wants of each one in the hope that the pursuit of private interest will in the end secure public welfare.'[31]

Socialism and the Nonconformists

While Socialist values made some progress within Anglicanism, the working-class nature, democratic governance and lay participation of Nonconformism proved even more fertile ground. Some Congregation-alists such as R.J. Campbell enthused that Socialism was 'the practical end which alone could justify the existence of the churches in the real-ization of the Kingdom of God'.[32] Like Socialism, Nonconformism taught the equality of all and stressed a social responsibility to all. Lay participation provided a unique training ground for those without formal education and it was a simple step from leadership in the Church to leadership in the community. The Primitive Methodists, like other Nonconformist churches, nurtured a new breed of political activists. J.H.Y. Briggs comments, 'Involvement in chapel affairs made them into natural community leaders. They learnt organization, how to speak in public and how to deal with men. The local preacher could step readily from the pulpit to the strike platform.'[33]

The willingness of Nonconformists to begin new structures and movements resulted in the formation of the Labour Church and Socialist Sunday Schools. These began in the 1890s and existed in some cases through to the 1960s. The Labour Church became a Church in its own right more by accident than design. Its founder, the Revd John Trevor, was the minister of Upper Brook Street Free Church in Manchester. In 1891 he decided that he wanted to encourage the spiritual life of people in the Labour Movement and planned to become an independent preacher. His preaching received immediate interest and, instead of being a lone voice, he soon became the leader of the Labour Church. His message was that obedience to God's law would bring real liberty and that God was behind the Labour Movement.

By 1907 there were 30 Labour churches throughout the country, some with Socialist Sunday Schools. They had strong links with other churches, especially the Congregationalists, but they also ran into controversy. In his Congregational Union address in 1894, the Revd G.S. Barrett challenged Christians to take a prominent role in the struggle for economic welfare, but he criticized the Labour Church for its lack of theology and its social divisiveness.[34] The Labour Church had no creed and this inherent weakness meant that by 1912 the Church's Statement of Principles had dropped all reference to God. Instead it described the Church as expressing the religious and general principles of Socialism – and said that it was definitely not theological.[35] Nonetheless, the initial enthusiasm for the Labour Church was evidence that the mainstream churches, with their pew rents and dense sermons, remained unattractive to many working people.

While the Labour Church became mostly defunct by the end of World War I, the Socialist Sunday Schools continued. By 1898 up to 17 Labour churches were running Socialist Sunday Schools, often in conjunction with the activities of the Independent Labour Party. However, as one member called Helen Cameron noted, 'Most of the people that were in the Socialist Sunday Schools never joined the Labour Party.'[36] Strongest in Glasgow and London, the Socialist Sunday Schools provided national and local history lessons as well as a range of recreations, singing, dancing and libraries. In 1912 a council was established to oversee the 15 affiliated schools in Glasgow as well as 18 in London, and there were many more unaffiliated schools. They continued between the wars and by 1964, 17 still operated throughout the country. Jim Mortimer of London remembers the 'Socialist Ten Commandments' which taught moral principles and concern for other people – 'teaching internationalism, that all people have equal rights. Brotherly feeling towards other people, these were the sort of things.'[37] *The Socialist Sunday School Hymn Book* of 1911 included them all:

1 Love your school fellows who will be your fellow-workmen in life.
2 Love learning, which is the food of the mind. Be as grateful to your teachers as to your parents.
3 Make every day holy by good and useful deeds and kindly actions.
4 Honour the good. Be courteous to all. Bow down to none.
5 Do not hate or speak evil of anyone. Do not be revengeful, but stand up for your rights and resist oppression.
6 Do not be cowardly. Be a friend to the weak and love Justice.
7 Remember that all the good things of the earth are produced by labour. Whoever enjoys them without working for them is stealing the bread of the workers.
8 Observe and think in order to discover the Truth. Do not believe what is contrary to reason and never deceive yourself or others.
9 Do not think that those who love their own country must hate and despise other nations, or wish for war, which is a remnant of barbarism.
10 Look forward to the day when all men and women will be free citizens of one Fatherland and live together as brothers and sisters in peace and righteousness.

The role of the Roman Catholics

The Roman Catholic Church as represented by Henry Edward Manning (1808–92) also played an important part in the reception of Christian Socialism in Britain. Manning's roots were in the Church of England, but he later became a Roman Catholic Cardinal. His life had spanned the growing inequality of the Victorian era and he became an unstinting advocate of the poor and the working class. Manning played a crucial role in settling the London Dock Strike of 1889 and influenced Pope Leo

XIII's encyclical *Rerum Novarum* (1891), which defined Catholic social principles.

On the centenary of his death, Ron Todd of the Transport and General Workers' Union paid tribute to a man who was 'one of the architects and champions of the dignity and rights of labour'.[38] 'The dignity and rights of labour' was in fact the title of an 1874 speech outlining Manning's 'third way' between *laissez-faire* economics and class war. He argued that industry was made for man and not man for industry and that concern for people should come first. He advocated rights for all industrial workers – 'the right to own property, the right to freedom, to work or not to work, to choose where he will work and for whom and to say whether he can subsist on a certain wage'.[39]

Co-operation between workers and capital, Christian self-sacrifice and support for trade unionism were all teachings expounded by Manning and later the papal encyclical. *Rerum Novarum*, however, opposed Socialism as a movement, arguing that it contained all kinds of revolutionary and anti-Christian thinking. It accused Socialism of being based on the envy of the poor and of erring in advocating common ownership over the divine right of personal property. The fear of Socialist revolution led Pope Leo to write a further encyclical in 1901 in which he gave encouragement to the growth of Christian Democrat parties in Europe. This tension in Catholic social teaching between advocacy of the values of Socialism and rejection of it as a movement was later expressed in the criticism of initiatives like the Catholic Socialist Societies[40] or in the strike-breaking role of Father James O'Reilly in Massachusetts in 1912. O'Reilly feared that the striking workers would bring an end to the social order and believed like many that the maintenance of order was a higher priority than the risks associated with a new way of ordering society.[41]

Secular social forces

Socialism in Britain was also developing in the context of other social forces outside the Church. Three in particular were to have an impact on the development of the Labour Party. The first force was the trade unions, which had their roots in the collective bargaining pioneered by the Tolpuddle Martyrs, a group of mainly Methodist farm workers who were sentenced to seven years' transportation in 1834. The Trades Union Congress (TUC) was established in 1868 to co-ordinate the growing number of workers' councils co-operating and negotiating with employers for better working conditions and pay. Historic victories like the Great London Dock Strike in 1889 brought a new confidence and professionalism to the unions. With success came new members and industries such as the mines and docks claimed to have tens of thousands in their unions. By 1886 the unions affiliated to the TUC represented 500,000 members and by 1900 this had grown to over 2 million.[42]

The second social force was the Co-operative Movement and its new kind of business practice. It grew from the activities of the Rochdale pioneers, ordinary workers who pooled their resources to buy and sell produce. The first Co-operative store opened in 1844, with workers and consumers as shareholders who all received a share of the profits. The economic co-operation, business skills and self-reliance that grew from the Co-operative Movement led many to ask whether national economic structures could be constructed in the light of these local solutions.

The third force was the Temperance Movement, which promoted abstinence from alcohol and campaigned against the brewers. It was closely associated with the Nonconformist Churches and shared many speakers, leaders and events. The Temperance Movement was mainly a response to the damaging impact that alcohol had on the fragile health and incomes of the working poor. Seebohm Rowntree's study of poverty in York in 1899 showed how precarious the lives of the working classes were. The only way to escape such precarious poverty was to avoid wasteful expenditure on drink and gambling. Such 'luxuries' could literally take the food from children's mouths.

The trade unions, the Co-operative Movement and the Temperance societies all practised member participation and it was through organizations like these that people learned democracy and became skilled in listening, organizing and leading. The 1884 and 1885 Parliamentary Reform Acts gave people the chance to vote for the first time and their experience in organizations like these led them to argue for more rights and to win them. As Moncrieff concludes, 'It was this ability to discuss and come to agreement, to take a vote and pass a resolution, and to campaign to make that resolution a reality that provided the escape route from the violent revolutions that engulfed other nations.'[43]

Overview

In the centuries before democracy the social justice tradition of Christianity was expressed through the Church. The advent of the industrial society rendered the Church's charitable structure impossible to sustain. Since then Christians have explored different ways of bringing gospel values to bear – and much of this is recent and ongoing as modern society changes and becomes increasingly global. We have seen how great individuals whose names still inspire today began movements and secured change, but the conservative nature of the Church meant that while individuals acted, the Church as a whole did not. Neither great charity nor great individuals were enough to deliver the radical revolution that Britain's poor desperately needed.

In the last half of the nineteenth century new ideas for constructing society appeared in the context of political reforms which made the application of these ideas possible. Christian Socialism was one such idea. Those who had the learning to speak, lead and organize within the Church were now well placed to be the leaders in the coming political revolution – so while the revolution would happen outside the Church, many from within it would take part. The teachings of Christ still compelled men and women to change society and those who embraced the social justice tradition were now convinced that only a political revolution would satisfy.

This revolution had been brewing for decades, but it was only when all the strands were brought together in a new political party, the Labour Party, that it would finally take place. It would be as profound a revolution as any in the past and would be driven by the ideals of equality and community. It found its voice and power not through violence but through faith in politics and faith in the Labour Party. This is a book about those Christians who served in the Labour Movement and the Labour Party and finally delivered the political revolution for which Britain had yearned for so long.

CHAPTER 2

Birth

KEIR HARDIE, THE MCMILLAN SISTERS AND WILL CROOKS: UP TO 1906

The people who created the Labour Party were working people at a time when work was hard, dangerous and insecure. Even at the age of 10, Keir Hardie was already the family's breadwinner. His alcoholic father was workless and his pregnant mother cared for his terminally ill brother. Hardie worked 12 hours a day for a Glasgow baker, a man of great religious zeal and harsh discipline. One day the young boy arrived 15 minutes late. He was wet from the rain and had no food in his stomach or shoes on his feet. Instructed to wait outside the master's dining room, he heard prayers as God was thanked for breakfast. Hardie entered the room, to find a veritable paradise of food and comforts unimaginable to his young mind. None of this was for him, however. Instead he received a lecture on the sin of sloth and was offered forgiveness only on the condition that it did not happen again. Two days later it did happen again. This time his punishment was the loss of work and the docking of two weeks' wages.

This incident seared the mind of the young Hardie. It helped to form the passion for justice that would drive him on for 50 years. It helped to inspire his leadership of many movements and of a new political party. This party would stand up for 10-year-olds against bad employers. It would deliver change to protect vulnerable families. Yet for Hardie the Glasgow baker was more than just a bad employer – he was also a bad Christian. His bad religion revealed hypocrisy and Hardie later wrote, 'The memory of those days abides with me and makes me doubt the sincerity of those who pray.'[1] This was enough to put a boy off religion for life, but Hardie discovered faith for himself. That faith would strengthen rather than weaken his resolve for justice and his struggle for those who had no voice.

A new political force

The Labour Party's first and biggest achievement was its own birth. The official history declares that, 'unlike its rivals the Labour Party was created in direct response to the social conditions of grinding poverty in which millions were living in the early 1900s'.[2] At the end of a century of unchecked inequality, it was a party that would act where politicians and clergy had so far failed to act. This new political force would secure the economic and social justice that had been denied for so long. For Christians following in the social justice tradition, it was an answer to their prayers.

The key reason why Labour was born in 1900 was support from the trade unions. In 1871, at the third TUC, the workers had got political. They sought amendments to the 1871 Trade Union Act and then began to challenge the candidates for the 1874 General Election. This growing militancy stirred employers into action and in 1898 the Employers' Parliamentary Council began to promote their interests in Parliament. The TUC now recognized its own need for political power and in 1899 the railwayman Thomas R. Steels put forward a resolution calling for workers' representation in Parliament. The vote was won by 546,000 to 434,000.

This decision coincided with the growing political activities of three Socialist societies. The largest of these was the Independent Labour Party (ILP), formed in Bradford in 1893 with the goal of securing workers' representation in Parliament. The ILP may have been the largest Socialist society with around 6,000 members, but its organization and finances were precarious, involving more ideals than infrastructure. It was a pragmatic, working-class organization with its roots in the Nonconformist chapels and Temperance associations of the north of England and Scotland. It shared its membership, speakers and style of meetings with those of the Labour churches and its inaugural meeting took place in Bradford's Labour church. Keith Laybourn, Professor of History at the University of Huddersfield and author of many books on Labour history, describes the main leaders of the ILP as the 'big four' of Labour's early leaders – Keir Hardie, Ramsay MacDonald, Bruce Glaiser and Philip Snowden. Their background is one reason why the early Labour Party had such a crusading and revivalist tone.

The second society was the Social Democratic Federation (SDF), formed in 1881 to promote Marxist thinking in the British context. Karl

Marx (1818–83) had provided a critique of economic structures in his *Communist Manifesto* of 1848. Putting forward his theory of 'dialectical materialism', he had talked of the inevitable revolution of the workers against the owners. Yet while Marxism fuelled revolutions elsewhere, it would remain only one strand of Britain's Socialist revolution. The SDF was active in elections, but its appeal was limited as many working-class people failed to connect with its ideology. The SDF regarded the ILP with suspicion, believing that it was not Socialist enough. It was largely controlled by the self-declared atheist H.M. Hyndman, and reflected much of his antagonism towards religion and the Nonconformist conscience.

The third influential group was the Fabian Society, established by London intellectuals in 1884. It supported electoral action but was initially lukewarm at the prospect of a new political party. Leading Fabians included Beatrice and Sidney Webb and the two famous writers H.G. Wells and George Bernard Shaw. The Fabians, like Marx, believed in 'the irresistible momentum of socialist ideas'.[3] Instead of violent revolution, however, they argued for redistribution and public ownership via a gradualist approach of education and parliamentary reform.

This mix of Socialist ideals and trade union membership had great electoral potential, but up to 1900 no one had managed the change from diverse protest to political party. The decision in 1899 to explore the possibility of creating a new political party was a step that would have massive ramifications. On 27 February 1900, 129 delegates from the trade unions, Socialist societies and co-operatives met in London's Memorial Hall. They agreed the formation of the Labour Representation Committee (LRC) and in doing so became active in the party political system. No one present could have imagined the impact this new political force was to have on Britain and the world.

The early years

Almost immediately, in October 1900, the LRC fielded its first 15 candidates at a General Election. It won two parliamentary seats. The first years for the LRC were both exciting and traumatic. In 1901 the SDF withdrew, citing its reluctance to participate in an organization not fully committed to Marxism. The LRC remained small and there was no guarantee that it would ever grow, let alone challenge the Liberals or Tories. However, in 1901 a decision by the House of Lords on the Taff

Vale railway dispute saw the traditional union support for the Liberals begin to shift.

The Lords declared that no employer should be disadvantaged by a strike and that unions would be financially liable. This struck at the heart of the trade unions and was a wake-up call to their need for parliamentary muscle. One by one the unions switched allegiance from the Liberals to the fledgling LRC, providing it with much needed money and momentum. The LRC grew steadily and as a result of a deal with the Liberals at the General Election of 1906, 30 of its 50 candidates became MPs. Shortly after the election the LRC changed its name to the Labour Party.

For Christians the advent of this new political party offered an opportunity for service. It brought together Christian service and political action to deliver the justice and equality that many believed was God's will. While Christians did not play the same formal role as the trade unions or Socialist societies, their informal role was widely recognized. Philip Gould identifies three creative forces at Labour's beginning: the first was Fabianism, the second religion and the third unionism. As Gould comments, 'Religious language and metaphor abounded in the Party's early years.'[4] For many early activists there was a genuine blurring between their work for God and their work for Socialism. They saw the Labour Party as a practical expression of God's purposes on earth. One Labour MP has commented:

> For very many working people the Methodist Church was their moral and practical university where they learnt what would now be termed 'life skills' as well as faith ... My own grandfather, who left school at a tender age and sought work at coal-mines throughout the region and became ... county councillor and a highly respected community leader, is a prime example. So ordinary people learnt skills, and they learnt them in the context of improving themselves whilst helping others and building communities. This was the basis on which the Labour Party could build.[5]

Keir Hardie – the father of Labour

Among those early activists who looked to God for their inspiration and who were central to the creation of Labour were Keir Hardie, the McMillan sisters and Will Crooks. A.J. Davies describes Keir Hardie as the person most associated with the birth of Labour – 'the undisputed father of the modern British Labour Movement, a pioneer who worked unceasingly for "the cause"'.[6] Hardie's credentials as a Labour leader are impressive. Before the party was born, he was the first Socialist to be elected an MP in 1892. He performed a strategic role in the party's formation in 1900 and became its leader in the Commons from 1906 to 1910. A self-confessed 'young man in a hurry', he was an early advocate of parliamentary representation for working people. Kenneth Morgan says, 'Hardie's contribution to the British Labour movement was a unique one … he was its supreme strategist … he created not a narrow sect but an outward-looking alliance of the dispossessed.'[7]

Harold Laski, Labour's 1945 Party Chairman, said that Hardie had provided two keys to the party's success. He had stressed the belief in the solidarity of the working class and he had urged that its programmes must be based on ethical foundations. While many have been tempted to idolize Hardie, he did have his weaknesses. Nevertheless, his ability to judge the public mood yet stick to his principles gave him leadership skills that few could match. Undoubtedly his tough upbringing formed the leader that he became.

Early life

Hardie was born in 1856, the illegitimate son of a farm worker, in a one-roomed cottage in Lanarkshire. His biological father's identity remains unclear, but it is rumoured that the local doctor persuaded a miner to put his name on the birth certificate. His mother, Mary Keir, later married David Hardie, so the young boy came to be called James Keir Hardie. Mary taught her son to read and encouraged in him a passion for books that proved crucial to his future life.

Hardie did reveal some bitterness about his childhood. His father David's drunkenness led to him taunting Mary about her son's illegitimacy. At 10 years old Hardie became the family breadwinner, then lost the job on which the family depended. This resulted in an even more demanding job as a miner's assistant. The family moved from Glasgow to Hamilton and Hardie was sent to work long hours on his own underground. Here he experienced at first hand the hazards and ill health associated with mining and became aware of the carelessness of mine owners and the daily struggle for survival by the workers. This was before the 1880 Employers' Liability Act, when employers first became liable for accidents caused by their neglect in the workplace. Even this Act did not cover accidents caused by other workers, however. One day the pulling equipment broke down, trapping Hardie underground. He spent hours waiting for rescue and, although he eventually escaped, the incident focused his mind on the vulnerability of workers and the carelessness of many managers.

He later wrote that the mines, with their long hours underground and no sight of the sun, did nothing to develop the sunny side of his nature. Hardie was never the life and soul of the party and even in later life, when invited to dine with the rich and famous, he rarely went. He believed that companionship was good but solitude was best and not even friendships would deflect him from the cause of his life's struggle. It was underground in the cold and dark that his character was moulded and his dreams of a better world were formed. These dreams spurred on his desire for personal development and he started attending Fraser's Night School in Holytown. Back underground the next day, he would practise his shorthand and grammar by scratching figures on slabs of stone.

Conversion

In 1877, aged 21, Hardie wrote in his diary, 'Today I have given my life to Jesus Christ.' It was an event that had as profound an effect on him as the poverty of childhood or the danger of the mines. Hardie appears to have attended the campaigns associated with the American evangelist Dwight Moody, who had been to Glasgow and Edinburgh during the mid-1870s. Hardie does not describe the details or emotions associated with this event, but is content with the simple fact of his conversion. He later described his faith as sacrifice and service:

Christianity represents sacrifice, having its origins in love. And the Christian who professes faith is thereby under obligation to make whatever sacrifice may be necessary in order to remove sin, suffering and injustice from the lives of those around him. It is not enough to pray to God; it is a mere mockery to sing hymns unless our lives are consecrated to the service of God through humanity. Make no mistake about this. The only way you can serve God is by serving mankind.[8]

As an outward expression of his faith, Hardie joined the Evangelical Union. Throughout the nineteenth century the Churches in Scotland experienced many divisions, with independently minded ministers rejecting Church authorities and appealing instead to the authority of the Bible. The Evangelical Union's founder, James Morison, had been excommunicated from the United Secession Church. He had argued that salvation was available to all people, in contrast to the strict Calvinism of the day. The Evangelical Union adopted a democratic ethos and stated that, as salvation was a gift to all, all could be active in the business of the Church. This Nonconformism was attractive to working people who felt excluded from the hierarchies of the established Churches. When Hardie later moved to Cumnock, he attended a Congregational church, where he would sometimes preach on the importance of personal discipleship over the details of theology.

Hardie's conversion had also reinforced his zeal for the Temperance cause. He had joined the Good Templars at the age of 17, possibly as a reaction to his father's drinking. This had provided him with experience in campaigning and public speaking, as well as in analysing social ills. Alcohol was not only a personal weakness but a social evil supported by the brewers. Both Temperance and Christianity helped Hardie to see that social problems were as much structural as personal.

Political action

As the 1880s progressed, Hardie became increasingly convinced that political solutions were needed to tackle social problems. At the age of 22 he became an agent for the Lanarkshire miners and led strikes in protest at conditions in the mines. He often saw the strikes broken by the mine owners. As a result of his agitation Hardie was expelled from the Hamilton pits and forced to move to Ayrshire. Unemployed and only recently married to his Temperance friend Lillie Wilson, Hardie found some meagre paying work as a journalist in 1881. So began his long career in promoting the workers' cause through the written word. He would later develop his ideas and campaigns through his own journals, *The Miner* from 1887 and the *Labour Leader* from 1889.

One campaign by the *Labour Leader* was on behalf of the men of Rutherglen. The men worked for Lord Overtoun, a prominent Liberal and generous benefactor of Christian mission. Overtoun's employees worked 12 hours a day, seven days a week without a meal break and all for the sum of four pence an hour. The work also involved chemicals and many of the men suffered respiratory and skin diseases. Hardie took up a clever and effective campaign that accused Overtoun of hypocrisy and, while Overtoun never responded publicly, conditions at his factory did improve. Hardie's tactics included reminding Overtoun of the words of Christ, 'So in everything, do to others what you would have them do to you, for this sums up the Law and the Prophets' (Matthew 7:12).

Hardie's political development was as pragmatic as his approach to Christianity. As long as the job of meeting working-class concerns got done, he was not so concerned about ideology. He wrote to Friedrich Engels in 1889, 'We are not opposed to ideals and recognize to the full the need for them and their power in inspiring men. But we are more concerned in the realization of the ideal than in dreaming of it.'[9] One result of this approach was Hardie's initial support for an alliance with the Liberals, really the only progressive party to choose. However, he soon realized that his efforts to build unions were, in fact, often frustrated by Liberals. While the Liberals had support from working people and the Nonconformist Churches, Hardie began to ask what exactly that support was securing for the workers.

When he was adopted as a miners' parliamentary candidate in North Ayrshire in 1887, he took the opportunity to ask these questions publicly. In a speech in Irvine he said, 'The Liberals and Conservatives have, through their organizations, selected candidates. They are both, as far as I know, good men. The point is these men have been selected without the mass of people being consulted. We are told that Sir William Wedderburn is a good Radical and that he is sound on the Liberal programme. It may all be true, but we do not know whether it is or not. Will he, for example, support an Eight Hour Bill? Nobody has asked him, and nobody cares except ourselves. Is he prepared to establish a wage court that would secure to the workman a just reward for his labour? Nobody knows whether he is or not. Is he prepared to support the extension of the Employers' Liability Act, which presently limits compensation for loss of life, however culpable the employer may be, to three years' wages? Nobody knows.'[10]

Although Hardie lost that election, he had begun to lay down challenges which the Liberals would have to answer if they were to retain the support of the workers. The 1888 by-election in Mid-Lanark proved to be the final straw that broke the relationship between Hardie and the Liberals. Hardie had been put forward as the miners' candidate in a predominantly mining community, but the Liberals rejected him. Undaunted, he declared his intention to stand anyway and the Liberals realized that he would split their vote and could lose them the seat. Hardie was wooed to stand down in return for a large salary and a safe seat at the next election. It must have seemed a temptation akin to that of Christ in the wilderness – 'all this can be yours' – but, like Christ, Hardie rejected the offer and set himself on a collision course with the Liberals. Hardie lost that election too, but it strengthened his resolve to find better ways of securing worker representation in Parliament than having to rely on the Liberal Party.

Hardie and the ILP

Hardie began to work towards creating a distinct political party to fight elections for Parliament. In May 1888 he called a meeting with 27 other activists to agree the formation of the Scottish Labour Party. Hardie was its secretary and R.B. Cunningham, the son of a Scottish laird, became its president. Cunningham's involvement showed that the group was not exclusively working class and revealed Hardie's pragmatism in working with anyone in order to secure his goal. The Scottish Labour Party made little electoral impact, however, and within a few short years it merged with the Independent Labour Party.

Hardie was chair of the ILP from its start in 1893 and he managed its merger with the Scottish Labour Party. As chair he held together the coalition that was the ILP and resisted pressure from the SDF and SLP to make it more Marxist or exclusively working class. Nevertheless, the ILP did have a radical programme. Its members were committed to deny any electoral support to Liberals or Conservatives and instead to work for workers' priorities and policies. These included an eight-hour working day; the abolition of unpaid overtime and child labour; state provision for the sick, disabled, widows and orphans; nonsectarian education; tax on unearned income and the extension of democratic rights.

Hardie was the key strategist in the ILP's birth and its subsequent merger with the SLP. In this A.J. Davies sees his long-term strategy developing: 'Hardie was shrewd enough to realize that creating a new party in Britain would be no overnight job – which is why he cautiously started in Scotland.'[11] Yet Hardie's broad alliance would be stretched to the limit in his relationship with the Marxist SDF. He believed that change for working people could only be done through peaceful means and not through violence. He often repeated that the Socialism he believed in had nothing to do with class conflict. Hardie travelled to the second Workers' International in Paris in 1889 to argue that there was no sympathy for anything other than democratic Socialism in Britain.

Through his friendships with other union leaders as well as Friedrich Engels and Eleanor Marx, Hardie began to develop his understanding of Socialism and started to talk of labour as the sole creator of wealth. The idealistic language of labour was one thing, however; securing the workers' support for a political party was quite another. Hardie knew that without the electoral strength and money of the trade unions, no embryonic party would succeed.

The first Labour MP

In 1892 Hardie's career had taken a surprising upturn when he was selected as the parliamentary candidate for West Ham South in London. He stood as an Independent Labour candidate and developed a broad-based radical platform to secure the votes of both workers and Liberals. It was a winning strategy and Hardie was duly elected as the first Independent Labour MP in July 1892. His election was a catalyst both to him and to others to pursue the formation of the ILP the following year.

Hardie's strategy up until now had involved building coalitions, but in the Commons it would involve confrontation. This in a sense was his genius – an ability to build up and tear down, to gather stones as well as scatter them. On his first day in the Commons he provocatively wore his working man's tweed and cloth cap. Such dress was an affront to the protocols and ceremony of the ancient Parliament, but instead of kowtowing to these traditions, Hardie compounded the scandal by hiring a marching band to play some revolutionary tunes. Hardie's passion for justice generated his disdain for the self-importance of the place. However, the press disdained Hardie in equal measure and took great delight in parodying the new member.

In Parliament Hardie focused on unemployment and became known as the 'Member for the Unemployed'. His first request was for an extra session of Parliament to consider measures to improve the lives of ordinary people. He was ruled 'out of order' by the Speaker. When Parliament returned in 1893 he moved another amendment to correct an omission in the Queen's speech, which was void of any reference to the unemployed. The amendment was defeated, but over 100 MPs had voted with him, demonstrating some success at least for his confrontational tactics. He campaigned for higher income tax for those earning over £1,000 a year, and for the money to go towards old-age pensions and schooling for the working class. His biggest storm, however, came in June 1894. Hardie was enraged to discover that Parliament had found the time to congratulate the Duchess of York on the birth of her new baby but was sending no message to South Wales where 260 people had been killed in a mining accident. His protests were fobbed off, so he spoke against the motion to send congratulations to the Duchess. In doing so Hardie uncovered a core sympathy of the House, as its members howled, yelled and screamed at him for displaying such insolence.

The creation of the Labour Representation Committee

At the election of 1895, Hardie lost West Ham South. He continued undaunted with his twin tactics of confrontation and coalition-building. An early advocate of women's suffrage, Hardie was arrested in 1896 at a meeting in support of Emmeline Pankhurst, but the subsequent public outcry persuaded the Home Secretary to order his release. As well as pursuing such confrontational activities, Hardie also returned to his goal of securing trade union support for a new and effective political party. One way to influence the British TUC was through its Scottish counterpart and Hardie argued for a special conference of the Scottish TUC at which the issue could be discussed. This took place in March 1899 and a motion was carried in support of united working-class action at elections.

The British TUC met later that year in Plymouth and, strength-ened by the decision of the Scottish TUC, the railwayman and ILP member Thomas R. Steels presented a motion to 'devise ways and means for securing the return of an increased number of labour members to the next Parliament'. While there is no direct evidence of Hardie's involvement in this motion, his language is reflected in it and Philip Snowden confidently claimed that both Hardie and Ramsay MacDonald drafted it. The motion was passed by 546,000 to 434,000, despite its rejection by the major unions of cotton and coal. Hardie was jubilant at having secured the TUC's support for a new political party.

He was also a key player at the meeting on 27 February 1900 which agreed the formation of the Labour Representation Committee. This meeting of trade unions, Socialist societies and co-operatives was a practical expression of his broad labour alliance. At the meeting Hardie successfully steered a path between the Marxism of the SDF and the more Liberal-inclined trade unions. An SDF amendment to restrict can-didates to working men or those endorsing a class war was voted down. The Lib-Lab advocates proposed working arrangements with the Liberals, but this was also voted down. Hardie's proposals for a distinct Labour group in Parliament with its own whips and independent policies was carried, however. It was also agreed that the new group would co-operate with other parties promoting legislation in the inter-ests of labour. Hardie had secured a remarkable consensus and his broad labour alliance was formed at last.

Re-election to Parliament

Within a year Hardie was elected as the LRC MP for Merthyr Tydfil, alongside a second LRC MP, Richard Bell, in Derby. At Westminster he resumed his campaign on unemployment. He argued for land reform to allow the unemployed to become self-sufficient. 'The chief wealth of the nation consists in the product of the soil,' he said. 'What I seek is the development of 16 million acres of land that it might be put to good advantage and by which the unemployed might be absorbed and turned to good account.' He also called for a new obligation on local authorities to provide work: 'Parliament compels local authorities to live up to certain sanitary regulations. They are compelled to educate children.

Compulsion is applied in various directions for the health and wellbeing of the community. This principle should be developed so as not to deny employment to the able, willing unemployed man, who requires as much State protection as the health and welfare of the community at large.'[12] These arguments later formed the basis of Labour's Unemployed Workman's (Right to Work) Bill in 1907. It sought to establish local and central employment schemes and to guarantee basic maintenance pay for the unemployed.

A short-lived leadership

After the 1906 General Election Hardie was elected as the newly named Labour Party's first leader. This proved to be short-lived. Many in Labour regarded him as too involved in the controversial issue of women's suffrage. Many suffragettes were prominent in the ILP, including Margaret Bondfield, Sylvia Pankhurst and Margaret McMillan, and Hardie submitted an ILP-drafted suffrage Bill to Parliament. This issue, and Hardie's limited ability for people management, led to an early dissatisfaction with his leadership of the party. His great strengths were that he could inspire a vision and build coalitions for a cause. He was less skilled in managing the competing demands of his MPs in the development of party policy and in complex legislative procedures. It was therefore welcomed when he stood down as party leader through ill health in 1908, although he remained the leader in the Commons until 1910.

From 1908 until the outbreak of World War I, Hardie did what he did best, preaching the gospel of Socialism among the rank and file of the party and potential converts. He also developed his internationalist views during this time, which included self-rule for India and equality for non-whites in South Africa. World War I was a devastating blow to Hardie's ideals of international Socialism. Despite being ill, he took part in various anti-war demonstrations, but found himself at odds with mainstream opinion in the country. He never recovered from the shock of the onset of war and returned to his native Scotland, where he died on 25 February 1915.

Hardie's contribution to the cause

Hardie's political life and values were informed by his faith. In 1910 he wrote, 'The impetus which drove me first of all into the Labour movement and the inspiration which carried me on in it, has been derived more from the teachings of Jesus of Nazareth than all other sources combined.'[13] He was no saint, however, and if he had not been a political leader it is unlikely that he would ever have been a Church leader (although married, he kept up a six-year relationship with Sylvia Pankhurst). Hardie was also critical of Establishment politicians and Establishment clergy who failed to take injustice and poverty seriously. He was uncompromising in his criticism of complacent churches:

> When I think of the thousands of white-livered poltroons who will take Christ's name in vain, and yet not see his image being crucified in every hungry child, I cannot think of peace ... A holocaust of every church building in Christendom tonight would be an act of sweet savour in the sight of him whose name is supposed to be worshipped within their walls.[14]

Nonetheless, throughout his life he maintained a relationship with the Church and with clergy friends who gave their advice and prayers.

No autobiography exists to describe at first hand Hardie's life as miner, journalist, trade unionist and MP, but photographs and other people's accounts reveal an uncompromising man, standing alone in a crowd or in the House of Commons. Hardie admitted that he was not a good party man, enjoying instead the role of 'stirring up divine discontent'.[15] With his white beard he resembled an Old Testament prophet, an image that was enhanced when many clergy refused to share a platform with him – he was not afraid of speaking unpalatable truths. He also had an image of being a man who did not do deals, yet this was not the whole truth. Politics demands compromise and Hardie's success was in knowing when to stick and when to twist, and this was the recipe that led to the beginning of the fledgling Labour Party in 1900. Bealey's and Pelling's assessment is typical: 'Credit must be given to Keir Hardie for his skill and discretion. Hardie had built up a popular reputation of being an outspoken agitator but in negotiations of this character he knew the value of give and take.'[16]

Hardie is the archetypal example of those who saw their service to 'the cause' as indivisible from their service to God. He presented Socialism as an ethical and moral gospel. Kenneth Morgan describes his campaign in 1906 as that of an 'evangelist, not an organizer. Crowds flocked to hear him proclaim the gospel of Labour.'[17] Hardie was no theologian, but he had a deep sense of social justice. Speaking in the Commons in 1901, he said, 'Only by moral power can the necessary zeal and sacrifice be developed to carry our work through. I know of no movement for the good of the human race that has not been inspired by moral purpose. The best in life cannot be gained by looking after Number One. Socialism is a religious movement akin to the Reformation and it is the only force able to inspire men with the boundless devotion and utter disregard for personal interest or even personal safety. We are called upon to decide the questions propounded in the Sermon on the Mount as to whether we worship God or Mammon.'[18]

Strategist, agitator, idealist and evangelist – all of these designations apply to James Keir Hardie, the father of the Labour Party. Keir Hardie as youth worker is not, however, a description which will be familiar to many. Yet in 1893 Hardie called on a generation of young people to be 'Crusaders for Socialism' and over the next two years over 1,000 children joined classes for education and recreation. Most religious movements try to educate children with their values, but Hardie also wanted to teach Socialism as history in a way that was never done at school. One of the children who attended these classes, Jean White, recalled, 'In school there was always a big blank in the history they taught you. They seemed to teach you up to the time of King Harold who got an arrow in his eye, and then there was nothing until the time you were living in.'[19] In 1896 Margaret McMillan took these gatherings and built them into the Socialist Sunday School Movement. McMillan worked with Archie McArthur, a former member of the Glasgow Christian Socialist League. McArthur edited the regular 'Crusader' column in Hardie's *Labour Leader* newspaper. By 1900 there were seven Socialist Sunday Schools in Glasgow and one each in Paisley and Edinburgh. Others existed in London and northern towns such as Bradford.

The McMillan sisters

Margaret McMillan and her sister Rachel were early activists in the Labour Movement. The sisters were born in New York, of Scottish parents from Inverness. Following the death of their father, their mother brought them home to Scotland, where they attended Inverness High School. After their mother's death in 1877, Rachel cared for her grandmother while Margaret went to London to train as a governess. Rachel was visiting a cousin in Edinburgh when she heard a sermon by John Glasse and met a group of Christian Socialists. She wrote to a friend, 'I think that very soon when these teachings and ideas are better known, people generally will declare themselves socialists. They are bound to do, if they think at all. I instinctively felt they were good people, and now I believe they are the true disciples and followers of Christ.'

Following her grandmother's death, Rachel joined Margaret in London. There they became active in Christian Socialist education and wrote for the *Christian Socialist* magazine. In 1889 they helped the workers in the London Dock Strike, but later moved to Bradford. They attended the Labour church there and were founding members of the Independent Labour Party. In 1892 Margaret worked with Dr James Kerr on Britain's first medical report on primary school children. It highlighted the conditions children were living in and argued that local authorities should install bathrooms in homes and provide free meals in schools. When Margaret was elected as the ILP candidate to the School Board she influenced the conditions of children throughout Bradford, but it was her writings that would have a much more widespread effect. She wrote books and pamphlets on child development and welfare and lectured widely throughout the north of England, as well as undertaking her pioneering work with the Socialist Sunday Schools in Glasgow.

Campaigning for women and children

The sisters returned to London in 1902. There they helped to develop policy with Keir Hardie and George Lansbury on issues ranging from child welfare to women's suffrage. Margaret continued to write, including the influential *Education through the Imagination* (1904) and *The*

Economic Aspects of Child Labour and Education (1905). They campaigned with Elizabeth Glaiser for free school meals and were eventually rewarded in the Provision of School Meals Act (1906). The logic of their argument that hungry children do not learn had won through. In 1908 the sisters opened the first ever health clinic in Bow and later another clinic in Deptford to serve the schools in the area.

In her book *The Child and the State* (1911), Margaret criticized schools in working-class areas for reinforcing low expectations among the children. She saw education as a liberator and believed that through it all children should have their horizons raised and become skilled and equipped for life. In a lecture in the same year on the work of Socialist Sunday Schools she said, 'On the free development of the child depends the future of the race. You must teach consciously and continually or you will be blighting the young minds under your charge.'[20] In 1914 the sisters opened a nursery and training centre in Peckham. When Rachel died in 1917, Margaret continued her work in Peckham and wrote other books including *Nursery Schools: A Practical Handbook* (1920). Ten years later Margaret opened the Rachel McMillan College in Deptford for the training of nurses and teachers.

Before her death in 1931, Margaret wrote her memoirs and described the work she and Rachel had carried out. They had been tireless and determined campaigners, particularly in the interests of children and women. One story she told vividly demonstrates the forces they were up against in their agitation for women's rights. The sisters were demonstrating at the House of Commons over the Cat and Mouse Act, which was being used to reimprison suffragettes on the same day as their release. Margaret wrote:

It was a beautiful day in August 1913 when we set off, all full of zeal, across the paved lawns about St Margaret's, till we reached the House and mounted the steps leading to the foyer in front of the ante-room, whose swinging doors were closed to us. There we stood a long time. An old lady was on the step above us – she was dressed very daintily in amethyst silk, her hair swathed in lace, among whose folds gleamed a thin gold chain. I was looking admiringly at her when suddenly a force of policemen swung down on us like a Highland regiment. We were tossed like dust down the steps. A moment later I was on the floor, the crowd behind flung over me in their wild descent. There was a big meeting that night at which I was to speak, but, of course I did not speak at that meeting, nor at any other – for weeks.[21]

Will Crooks

There were others in these early years who also regarded their faith as central to their politics. One such person was Will Crooks, who described Labour as 'the new force by which God is going to help forward the regeneration of the world'.[22] Crooks was one of the first LRC MPs, elected in 1903. Born in Poplar in 1852, he was one of seven children in a family that worshipped at Trinity Congregational Church in Poplar. The family was very poor. Will's father had lost an arm in an industrial accident and as this was before the advent of industrial compensation, it left his mother as the sole breadwinner, single-handedly trying to keep the family together. As a child Will experienced the trauma of poverty that would motivate his life's work. One night he woke to hear his mother crying. He asked why she was crying and persisted with his questions, although she urged him to sleep. She eventually confessed that she was crying because she did not know where the next meal would come from. There was plenty of bread in the shops, she told him, but the family had no money to buy it.

When Will was eight, his mother's struggle to keep the family together failed. Will, his father and brother were sent to the Millwall Workhouse while his mother and the other children fended for themselves. Will recalled, 'Every day I spent in that school is burnt into my soul.'[23] The workhouses were established by Parliament to deal with the destitute poor – not as a compassionate act but as a warning, as demonstrated by one Commissioner's views: 'I wish to see the poorhouse regarded with dread by our labouring classes and the reproach for being an inmate of it extending downward from father to son. Let the poor see and feel that their parish, although it will not allow them to perish through absolute want, is yet the hardest taskmaster, the closest paymaster and the most harsh and unkind friend they can apply to.'[24]

While in the workhouse, Will Crooks vowed that he would one day help people like his mother who were too poor to feed their children. It was a vow he was able to realize partly thanks to his mother's encouragement to her children to read. Later he became an avid reader and devoured Dickens, Scott, *The Pilgrim's Progress* and *Hamlet*. Crooks argued in later life, 'Surely it is far cheaper to be generous in training Poor Law children to take their place in life as useful citizens than it is to give the children niggardly training and a branded career.'[25]

Activist and teacher

As a young man Crooks found work as a message boy and blacksmith's labourer. He also began to read radical newspapers and learned of campaigns to improve people's lives. Because of his knowledge and confidence, his workmates asked him to speak to the boss about excessive overtime and lack of pay. As a result Crooks was branded an agitator and banned from every shop and yard in London. In 1876, just recently married and with a young child, he was forced to walk to Liverpool to find work. It was a journey of many days without any food, his very own 'pilgrim's progress'. His wife later joined him, but within a month their child had died and they soon ventured a return to London.

Crooks managed to find an employer who appreciated his hard work and he stayed there for 10 years. During this time he began what was to become his life's work. He strongly believed that books and education had transformed his life, so he started classes for the workers outside the gates of the East India Dock. He lectured on trade unionism, temperance and the co-operative societies and his meetings soon became known as Crooks' College. He urged working men to become active in politics, to agree on what needed to be done and to argue their case. Crooks regarded adult education as a powerful religious force that would help the men strive for the ideals of Christ. He developed links with local clergy, including the rector of Poplar, and one of his greatest supporters was the Revd John Wilson, founder of the Woolwich Labour Party and a president of the Baptist Union.

The London Dock Strike

One of the most significant events in the life of many early Labour leaders was the London Dock Strike of 1889. The strike started after demands from workers at the South West India Docks for a minimum wage of sixpence an hour and an end to contract work were refused by the management. Crooks emerged as a key leader in the strike that was to change the face of British industry. On 13 August 1889 Ben Tillet, a 28-year-old union leader, called for a strike across the whole 50 miles of London's wharves. By 14 August the normally bustling docks were at a standstill. By 15 August other established unions had joined the strike and swelled the number of strikers to 100,000 men.

Ben Tillet was the main inspiration and strategist for the nonviolent strikers. He had become a Christian Socialist after moving with his new wife from Bristol to Bethnal Green. There he attended the local Congregational church and Temperance Society. His ambition was to be a barrister and he devised his strategy for the strike during a lecture from a young law student called Cosmo Lang, who was later to become Archbishop of Canterbury. It was the 82-year-old Cardinal Manning who had the most decisive impact on Tillet, however, acting as his friend and mentor. After five weeks of the strike, Manning helped to secure a compromise that was in fact a dramatic victory for the workers. Tillet later said that Manning had supported 'with a sense of responsibility' the dockers' central claims, i.e. the minimum hourly wage and recognition of their union. However, it was largely the dockers' dignity, the justice of their cause, their discipline and responsibility that had led to their landmark victory.

Tom Mann was also a decisive player in the leadership of the strike. Tillet asked Mann to take on the huge logistical task of providing relief to the strikers as the employers tried to starve them back to work. Mann organized the distribution of relief that came from outside organizations including the Salvation Army and the Labour churches. The most significant expression of solidarity came from Australian dockers, who sent £30,000 to feed the strikers and their families. External support also came from Socialist leaders such as Keir Hardie, and public opinion was in favour of the strikers. One reason for this was the effectiveness of Henry Champion, a Fabian and former editor of the *Christian Socialist* magazine, who had become the strikers' press officer.

After the strike the dockers formed a new union with Tom Mann as its president and Ben Tillet as general secretary. Mann became one of the country's leading trade unionists and was particularly associated with the campaign for an eight-hour day. Mann had been an Anglican Sunday School teacher and Christian Socialist, but had also held Communist ideals ever since reading *The Communist Manifesto*. Yet his was not an atheistic Communism but a Christian one and in 1893

Mann, by then a union leader, considered becoming an Anglican minister. He was a close friend of Hardie and fought as an ILP candidate three times, only narrowly missing being elected for North Aberdeen in 1896. However, Mann's radicalism led him in later years to try to establish a confederation of unions, with the intention of calling a general strike to bring down capitalism.

Political progress

During the Dock Strike Will Crooks had used his communication skills and network of relationships to raise support for the workers' cause. Following the strike Crooks was elected as a Progressive Party candidate to the London County Council. There he campaigned alongside union leaders to secure better conditions for workers. One of their first tasks was to insert a Fair Wages Clause in council contracts and to establish parks and recreation spaces for people to enjoy. Crooks gained respect from political friends and foes alike. Fellow council member Lord Welby said, 'Mr Crooks' knowledge, his experience, his courage, his readiness for humour, his good temper and above all his devotion to the work he has undertaken, have made him one of the most popular members of the London County Council.'[26]

For Crooks, one of the most poignant aspects of his political career was his election with George Lansbury to the Poplar Board of Guardians. This was the body of people responsible for administering the workhouse in which he had been placed 30 years before. Crooks soon developed a strategy to get all children out of the workhouses and to begin to support old people and families in the community. He also wanted to establish the workhouses as places of support and provision rather than punishment. Crooks was attacked for these revolutionary views, but eventually his reforms in the Poplar workhouses became a model for the rest of the country.

Crooks had initially joined the Social Democratic Federation, but became disillusioned with its leader Hyndman because of his atheism and views on class conflict. Edward Aveling, another leading figure in the SDF and the son of a Congregationalist minister, expressed Hyndman's views in pamphlets with titles such as *The Wickedness of God* and *A Godless Life the Happiest and Most Useful*. Crooks was more sympathetic to the approach of the Fabians and joined the society in 1891.

His parliamentary career began in Woolwich in 1903. Standing as the LRC candidate, he received support from a cross section of workers, clergy and businessmen. The union leader John Burns told a crowd of 5,000 that Will Crooks was someone who pursued his ideal of brotherly love and Christian charity. Crooks was elected and spoke of his victory in prophetic terms: 'What the workman has done in Woolwich you will find he will do in other towns.'[27] His prophecy was to prove true, since three years later in 1906, 30 LRC candidates were elected as MPs.

In Parliament Crooks worked with Hardie to raise the issue of unemployment and appealed to the practical projects in Poplar as models of how to get men into work. Crooks successfully combined his grass-roots activism with his parliamentary skills to secure change. An unemployment conference in 1904 saw many of his 'Poplar proposals' later included in the Balfour Government's Unemployment Bill (1905). This Bill controversially included compulsory work for the able-bodied unemployed. The *Daily News* reported that the member chiefly responsible for the success of the Bill was Mr Crooks, who had shown undoubted subtleness as a parliamentary tactician.

Crooks returned to the Commons in 1906, in 1910 and in 1918, but was forced to retire due to ill health in 1921. He died on 5 June 1921, in the Poplar home where he had always lived. The leader of the Labour Party, Joseph R. Clynes, said of him, 'No man of his time did more to awaken the conscience of the nation upon social conditions.'[28] In his *Memoirs* (1937) Clynes later described something of the humanity of Crooks that lay behind his social conscience: 'Will Crooks combined the inspiration of a great evangelist with such a stock of comic stories, generally related as personal experiences, that his audience alternated between tears of sympathy and tears of laughter. I know of no stage comedian who can move his audience today to such roars of merriment as could Will Crooks.'[29]

Building a new society

Keir Hardie, Margaret and Rachel McMillan and Will Crooks were typical of a new breed of Christian – they were Christians who chose social activism and politics as a vehicle for their beliefs and actions. Not only were they politically active, but they helped to create a new political party that would transform Britain. They had a deep sense that their work was consistent with the new society God was building and that injustice and poverty should have no part in this Socialist vision.

These early Labour leaders were on a mission from God and, as the nineteenth century ended and the twentieth century began, they shared in the social justice tradition that had inspired the Old Testament prophets, Jesus Christ and the reformers of the eighteenth and nineteenth centuries. Crooks' prophetic challenge to the Free Church Council shortly after the 1906 election reflects the heart of this mission. He said, 'You Free Churchmen have to come out of yourselves, you cannot live for Sundays alone and you must take your share in the work of social reorganization.'[30]

CHAPTER 3

First Steps

ARTHUR HENDERSON AND RAMSAY MacDONALD: 1906–18

If Keir Hardie was the father of Labour, Arthur Henderson was its uncle. 'Uncle Arthur' would influence the party more than any other single person. Not only did he draft and deliver its constitution, but he also managed and manipulated the party into an efficient electoral machine. If there was ever a spirit in the Labour Party machine, that spirit was Uncle Arthur's. Yet the Labour historian Kenneth Morgan called him a bully and one-time Labour Chancellor Hugh Dalton referred to him as a silly old ass. Beatrice Webb said of him, 'I have never known a man of undoubted power with so little personal charm or magnetism.'[1]

Arthur Henderson was party leader during World War I when Labour had its first taste of power, and he was party secretary for over 20 years. In 1918 he gave the party its two most controversial legacies – Clause 4 and union domination. Clause 4 aimed to 'secure for producers by hand or by brain the full fruits of their industry … upon the basis of the common ownership of the means of production'. The clause was always a fudge, meaning exactly what you wanted it to mean, and secured maximum co-operation with minimum obligation. Yet Labour's ideals could not be so easily packaged for posterity and Clause 4 became the totem around which the left and right of the party fought for decades. Ironically it was Henderson's second legacy of union domination that protected the party against the more fanciful ideas of full-blown nationalization and other radical Socialist policies. While the dominance of the unions meant efficiency and financial strength, it also meant caution.

⟫●⟪

Teething problems

After the General Election in 1906 Labour found itself with 30 MPs. It was a remarkable achievement for such a young party, but it had only been secured because of a deal with the Liberals. Ramsay MacDonald, Hardie's ILP colleague and LRC secretary since 1900, had struck the deal. Judging electoral success to be elusive, he had brokered an agreement in which there would be 50 constituencies where Liberal candidates would not stand, in return for no Labour candidates standing elsewhere. This targeting of seats likely to return workers' candidates paid dividends and now the party had 30 MPs arguing for policies favourable to working men. Within two years this number was swelled by 12 Miners Federation MPs, who took the Labour whip.

Money

Hardie's original goal for a distinct party in Parliament with its own whips and agreed policy had been secured. Maintaining Labour's presence in Parliament, however, meant repeatedly fighting and winning elections and money to fund such efforts was dangerously low. While affiliated membership had grown since the Taff Vale ruling, the original fee had only been 10 shillings per 1,000 union members. Labour's financial problems were further compounded by the 1909 Osborne Ruling, when a Conservative Party union member complained that his subscription was being used to fund Labour. The ruling effectively cut the party's main source of income and it had to wait until the 1913 Trade Union Act before unions were free to make donations from clearly identified funds.

The funding crisis and the fact that MPs were not paid at that time meant that the party struggled to meet the costs of elections. It resulted in the irony of a political party hoping that elections would not be called. Yet they continued to be called, two in 1910 alone, as the Liberals battled with the House of Lords on constitutional amendments. One result of Labour's difficulties in this respect was a drop from 45 MPs at the beginning of 1910 to 42 MPs by the end of that year.

The Liberals

In the Commons there was also continuing debate about Labour's relationship with the Liberals. MacDonald was an advocate of more openness and stronger alliances, but in contrast Hardie could think of nothing worse, denouncing 'the slobbering talk about the friendly understanding between the Liberals and the Labour Party'.[2] Hardie was especially critical of Labour's reluctance to fight the Liberals at by-elections and called the party 'Asquith's poodle'. Hardie also mobilized the ILP to reject Lloyd George's proposal that Labour join with a coalition of moderate Liberals and Conservatives. Nonetheless, Labour did co-operate with the Liberals to secure some mutual goals. These included the Trades Disputes Act (1906), the Old Age Pension Act (1909) and the third Irish Home Rule Bill (1912–14). In 1911 MacDonald became Labour's leader and promised support for Lloyd George's Insurance Bill in return for legislation to provide MPs with a salary. The precarious nature of party finances and the circumstances of most Labour MPs meant that the £400 salary was a great benefit.

Despite these small victories, however, Labour's influence in the Commons remained only at the Liberals' bidding. The necessity to co-operate with the Liberals and talk of mergers underlined Labour's insecurity as a party. Following its impressive start, the years immediately before World War I became more of a slog than a sprint. With the loss of momentum, Labour lost six by-elections between 1911 and 1914, and internal policy disputes were common. Independent characters such as Keir Hardie and George Lansbury often bucked the party line in these difficult days. Hardie had resigned the leadership of the party in 1908 and returned to rallying the workers up and down the country.

Strikes and suffragettes

The general climate of industrial disputes between 1910 and 1914 placed Labour MPs in many dilemmas, raising the fear that their association with such disputes was doing damage to the party. Hardie, by contrast, had no such fears and in 1913 he supported the workers in the Dublin Transport Workers' dispute against the violent strike-breaking tactics of the police.

A further area of controversy was the question of women's suffrage. Suffrage protests were often violent and reached their peak when Emily Davison threw herself under the King's horse on Derby Day in 1913. Davison's funeral provided an insight into the Christian inspiration that motivated many of the suffragettes. Her cortege banners read, 'Greater love hath no man than this, that he lay down his life for his friends' and, 'He that loseth his life shall find it.' Lavinia Byrne argues that many who gave money, energy and their lives in the suffrage struggle were indeed motivated by Christian faith.[3] In the Commons, Hardie and Lansbury criticized Labour's failure unanimously to support the women's cause or condemn the force-feeding of prisoners. The focus of the struggle was the 1912 Franchise Reform Bill that still denied women the vote. In protest Lansbury resigned his East London seat and Hardie resigned from Labour's executive. The executive responded by rejecting Lansbury as a future candidate, but other party figures continued to support him.

Lansbury failed to win his seat back, however, and Labour lost an important electoral foothold in East London. Such episodes plainly indicate the party's failing momentum in the pre-war years. Labour was becoming unmanageable and many yearned for a more co-ordinated and financially stronger party that would articulate clearly what it stood for and campaign effectively on its Socialist policies. Labour seemed to be in its erratic adolescent years – beyond its exciting birth but before its development to full adulthood.

Nevertheless, there were changes taking place that would soon propel the party to both maturity and dominance. The pre-war industrial unrest had placed the Liberal Party in even greater dilemmas than Labour as they tried to hold together a growing class-consciousness between workers and capital. Liberal vacillation in repealing the Osborne Ruling also backfired and the unions moved decisively to Labour. Yet it was the 1914 war that would seal the fate of the Liberal Party and bring about the Labour Party's rise. The war would change things for many people, of course, but it also provided a catalyst for Labour's coming of age.

Wartime changes

The outbreak of war was a watershed for the party and the country at large. The underlying causes of World War I were the same power games that rulers had played for centuries, yet this time it was different. Humans always had the capacity to kill, but industrialization and alliances between nations meant that any war in modern times was going to be big. Britain had avoided revolution at home, but the territorial ambitions of others were about to engulf it. The assassination of Archduke Ferdinand in Sarajevo in 1914 was the spark that lit the tinderbox. With German encouragement, Austria declared war on Serbia and, by proxy, Russia. Martin Gilbert describes the thinking in Berlin: 'In the perspective of the German diplomats, politicians and court, it was Russia that was the great danger to their future dominance in Europe. Any chance to challenge Russia before she became even stronger was to be welcomed.'[4] Germany declared war on Russia on 1 August 1914 and then invaded Luxembourg and Belgium. With Belgian neutrality violated, Britain was unavoidably sucked in.

The campaign included tank attacks and air bombardments, and trench warfare saw the lines of battle almost stationary for three of the four years the war lasted. There were massive casualties, often due to inadequate leadership, but all efforts failed to break the deadlock. In the second battle for Ypres in April 1915, the Germans introduced an innovation: poison gas. Its use led one soldier to write this couplet:

> *After two thousand years of Mass;*
> *We've got as far as poison gas.*[5]

Yet despite the very real and widespread suffering, there were great ironies about this war. Before the war, emigration from Britain was running at a figure of 300,000 people each year. This exodus was halted while the war was on, of course, which meant that Britain's post-war population was effectively greater as a direct result of war. A second irony was the way in which the war benefited the poor, especially women, who worked and earned for the first time. Charles Masterman noted, 'The women and children of the poor were better fed and clothed at the end of the war than at its beginning.'[6]

Hardie and MacDonald against the war

At the outbreak of World War I, nationalism was spreading like wildfire across Europe. Not all were excited at the prospect of war, however. Keir Hardie and Labour's leader Ramsay MacDonald were horrified, and Hardie gave the last of his life's energy in campaigning against it. Hardie hated the leaders who started wars and then called working men to fight in them. His vision was of a day when wars would be declared but men would refuse to fight. It was a vision whose day had not yet come, however, and Hardie had to watch as both the nation and the still fledgling Labour Party rallied to the call to arms.

In the early days of the war, Hardie and MacDonald campaigned to gain worker support for a strike against it. Although Hardie was a pacifist, he also recognized the need for political leaders to resist rebellious forces, and the need to support the frontline troops once the situation had gone too far to pull back. In the journals *Pioneer* and *Forward* he defended himself against accusations of irresponsibility. He wrote, 'A nation at war must be united especially when its existence is at stake. With the boom of the enemy's guns within earshot, the lads who have gone forth by sea and land to fight their country's battles must not be disheartened by any discordant note at home.' However, he also urged that the lessons of war should be learned and peace grasped at the first opportunity. The fact was that this war, coming at the end of a career in which many of his ideals had been secured, was devastating for Hardie. He hated the very thought of it.

Even the ILP was initially uncertain of its views, but eventually strengthened its support for Hardie's and MacDonald's anti-war stance. The Labour Party was also sympathetic to the idea of a strike, but increasingly such calls were submerged in the massive public support for the war effort. Indeed, it was Labour MP Will Crooks who led an emotional rendering of the national anthem during the House of Commons debate on the war.

Hardie's Christianity and his emphasis on living according to the Sermon on the Mount undoubtedly influenced his views. He made clear his goal to live as Christ taught, including the teaching on retaliation: 'You have heard that it was said, "Eye for eye, and tooth for tooth." But I tell you, Do not resist an evil person. If someone strikes you on the right cheek, turn to him the other also' (Matthew 5:38–9). Loving one's enemies and doing good to those who hate you was not a popular philosophy, however, and Hardie received little solace from the Church. The Bishop of London, preaching on what the Church should do, urged it to 'mobilize the nation for a holy war'. His Advent Sermon of 1915 included the injunction 'to kill the good as well as the bad, to kill the young as well as the old'.[7] Despite such exhortations, most of the 16,500 conscientious objectors in World War I were Christians, a large majority of them Free Churchmen.

Ramsay MacDonald was the only other Labour MP who spoke against the declaration of war by Foreign Secretary Edward Grey. MacDonald's attitude cost him the party leadership and damaged his political career as a whole. His speech in response to the declaration of war was thoughtful, and he persuaded four other Labour MPs to join him in voting against the use of war credits to finance the conflict. In October 1914 MacDonald shared an anti-war platform with Hardie in Merthyr Tydfil. They argued that Russian militarism and the abuses of the Tsar were more to be feared than Germany's militarism. Perhaps in an effort to get onto more familiar ground, they also argued that the low pay and dismal living conditions for the troops at the front were a disgrace. So too was the meagre six months' allowance granted to women widowed by the war. They also warned that compulsory conscription would be an inevitable consequence of the war and on this they were right. In January 1916 conscription was imposed on all single males between the ages of 18 and 41.

Hardie and MacDonald continued to receive great criticism for their stance on the war, but Hardie died in 1915 and MacDonald was left to carry on alone for the duration. His 'pro-German' stance resulted in him being thrown out of his Scottish golf club and then from his Leicester constituency when the first opportunity arose in 1918. A.J. Davies sees this period as reflecting MacDonald's inherent strength of character: 'The abuse and hostility which MacDonald endured stoically over the next four years contradict the argument that he was essentially an opportunistic and unprincipled man.'[8]

Peacetime chances

On 11 November 1918 the armistice was signed at Compiègne. An estimated 8,700,000 people had perished – but one young soldier called Adolf Hitler had survived. He would be back, thanks to the failure to make a lasting peace at the Treaty of Versailles in June 1919. The 'war to end all wars' would not see the end of conflict after all, but it did herald huge change right across Europe. One of the most significant changes was in the way that ordinary people viewed their lives and liberty. Working-class soldiers who had lived in the trenches with their middle-class 'betters' were no longer willing to be quite so socially subservient. Women who had worked and earned in the factories were no longer willing to return to silent domesticity.[9] They had kept the country going through the war and they could no longer be denied the vote.

The legislation that provoked many more changes was the Representation of the People Act (1918), which doubled the electorate to include all men over 21 and most women over 30. This Act was to benefit the Labour Party disproportionately, because enough workers voted Labour to secure large successes in the first-past-the-post system. There was more to Labour's post-war successes than this legislation alone, however. Before the war the party had been internally fractious and had lacked momentum, but during the difficult years of the war Labour had grown up and got itself organized. It had moved from a party of disparate voices to a coherent force able and willing to take on the political Establishment.

Arthur Henderson

One of the people who helped in this task was Arthur Henderson. Henderson drafted the party's first constitution, formalized its rules and secured the financial support needed to fight elections throughout the country. His was a crucial role in taking the young, unruly, pre-war party from organizational chaos to a condition in which it was fit to fight and win. While war raged in Europe, Henderson engaged in a different kind of struggle for the structural future of the Labour Party.

In 1912 Bruce Glaiser, a leading British Socialist and Labour Party leader, addressed the party conference and questioned the very nature and structure of the party. He used the spiritual imagery of the day to declare, 'We have no confession of faith, no means of giving testimony to a whole-hearted support of the principles of the party. It is a federation of national organizations, a loose and ill-defined alliance rather than a coherent party with specific policies.'[10] Glaiser acknowledged publicly what many had been arguing privately: the party had to develop its organization if it was to become a serious political force.

Arthur Henderson accepted these electoral truths and used similar images from the parables of Christ to describe 'the unwisdom of contesting by-elections, unless the soil has been well prepared and every part of the constituency is sufficiently organized to ensure the gathering in of the fruit'.[11] Henderson acknowledged the devotion of activists, but claimed that the future of the party would depend on professionalism not simply passion. The party needed 'capable permanent constituency agents, ward committees and canvassing of voters, to counteract the shameful misrepresentation to which our candidates are subjected'.[12]

For Henderson, these sentiments expressed before the war were to be translated into action during it. It was Henderson who gave the party its famous Clause 4 and Leventhal notes, 'Labour emerged from the war with a new image, a new structure and a new organizational apparatus. Credit for all these belongs chiefly to Henderson. Although these changes may well have been inevitable, a reaction to the experience of war and the enlarged electorate, it was Henderson who acted as the necessary catalyst.'[13]

Early life and faith

Who, then, was this Henderson and what values lay behind the man who so transformed the party? Arthur Henderson was a Christian whose faith infused all that he did. His brother said of him, 'For Arthur, life began with conversion. Before that, he was just an ordinary boy.'[14] Leventhal comments, 'His closest friendships were made in the chapel, with those he shared his faith with, rather than in political circles.'[15] Henderson also saw the Church as a force for good in the world. Speaking in Bradford in 1908, he said, 'The great organized forces of Christianity recognize, as they never recognized before, that there is some positive relationship between the affairs of everyday life and the principles of their great Master. No longer are they satisfied to lead the individual to patient resignation with the things he possesses or does not possess. The doctrine of contentment has given way to one of divine discontent.'

Arthur Henderson was born in Glasgow on 13 September 1863. His father was David Henderson, a manual labourer whose early death pushed the family onto the breadline. As a result young Arthur stopped attending school and went to work in a photography shop. Later his new stepfather Robert Heath took the family to Newcastle. In Newcastle Arthur went back to school, but at the age of 12 he was apprenticed to an ironmoulder where he worked for 11 hours a day, six days a week. Despite these long hours, he attended night class and later formed a reading and debating society at the Stephenson locomotive works where he was employed. After his apprenticeship Henderson became an active trade unionist, although he also found time to play football and helped start the club that eventually became Newcastle United. At 21 he was made redundant – at a time when his widowed mother was dependent on him.

Unlike Hardie, Henderson was born into a family of faith. The children were taught the Bible by their mother and taken along to the local Congregational chapel. However, when Henderson was 16 he experienced the conversion that his brother claimed transformed his life. He encountered Gypsy Smith, a travelling evangelist working with William Booth's Christian Mission. The kind of itinerant evangelism pioneered by Wesley a century earlier was still alive and well. It was to Wesley's Methodism that Henderson now committed himself, attending and soon teaching at the Sunday School in the Elswick Road Wesleyan Chapel. Here the principles of Methodism formed his own values of personal discipline and social conscience. The chapel provided a focus for his energies and an opportunity for new experiences – he first tried public speaking there, initially as a Sunday School teacher and then as a licensed lay preacher.

Methodism derives its name from the 'methods' adopted by Wesley's followers. Wesley had first preached in Newcastle in 1742 and had commented on the 'drunkenness, cursing and swearing, especially among the children'.[16] He preached to crowds of over 20,000 shipyard workers and it was in the churches that grew from these events that Henderson was reared. Methodism moulded Henderson's views on democracy and social action and exposed him to the Temperance Movement, whose principle of teetotalism he maintained all his life. In Methodism personal holiness was inseparable from the corporate life of the chapel. It was personal and social religion that preached an obligation of responsibility to the community at large. Henderson would eventually translate the solidarity taught in the chapel into solidarity with his union and, in due course, with the Labour Party.

Political development

Throughout his teenage years Henderson made progress as an ironworker, eventually becoming a manager. He joined the Friendly Society of Ironfounders and also made progress within his union. In 1891, at the age of 28, he was encouraged to become involved in politics by Robert Spence Watson, the National Liberal Foundation's president. He became an active supporter of the Liberals and in 1892 was elected to Newcastle City Council. In the same year he was appointed district organizer for the Ironfounders Union in the north of England and secured an agreement to continue both his union and political activities. As a result of these twin roles, Henderson became a strong advocate of arbitration and industrial co-operation. His early opposition to the creation of the General Federation of Trade Unions was due to his belief that it would increase industrial disputes.

As an able and committed Liberal, Henderson was asked to put his talents to use as agent to Sir Joseph Pease, the Liberal MP for Barnard Castle. His family relocated to Darlington, where Henderson's political career took off. He was elected to Durham County Council in 1897 and to Darlington Town Council in 1898. In 1903 he became the first working man to be Mayor of Darlington. Despite his obvious Liberal credentials, Henderson was one of the delegates at the inaugural meeting of the Labour Representation Committee in 1900, and he voted with Hardie in support of a distinct political grouping for workers in Parliament. His Ironfounders Union immediately affiliated to the LRC and in 1902 they asked Henderson to stand as their parliamentary candidate under an LRC banner. Henderson agreed to this, despite continuing his role as a Liberal agent.

By 1903 he realized that he had to decide where his future lay and when a by-election was announced in Barnard Castle he decided to act.

The LRC quickly adopted him as their candidate, catching the Liberals off guard. Although they approached him to stand as a Lib-Lab candidate, Henderson said that his union and LRC connections meant he could no longer do so. His conversion to Labour was therefore not so much a blinding light as a simple acceptance of his union's decision to promote the LRC. As a Methodist and trade unionist, Henderson found it difficult to break allegiance with the Liberals, but there was little doubt that his sympathies now lay with the LRC. The transfer of his allegiance was to have a dramatic effect on the future of Labour.

Allegiance to Labour

Henderson is a prime example of the many working-class Nonconformists who started in the Liberal Party but switched to Labour. At the beginning of the twentieth century, Nonconformists had been strong supporters of the Liberal Party. Kenneth Brown comments, 'It was their votes which helped to return an estimated 200 Free Churchmen to the House of Commons in 1906.'[17] Historically, Nonconformists had been banned from public office by the seventeenth-century Test and Corporation Act. Following its repeal in 1828, Nonconformists elected to Parliament were invariably Liberals. Yet many Nonconformists were now following the same path to Labour taken by Arthur Henderson. Of Labour's 30 MPs after the 1906 election, 18 described themselves as Nonconformists and 17 were members of the Fellowship of Followers, a group whose purpose was to encourage each other in faith and promote the teaching of Jesus. Their motto was, 'If any man would come after me, let him deny himself, and take up his cross and follow me.'

In 1906, the writer and researcher W.T. Stead embarked on an assessment of the influences that had formed and shaped the members of the Labour Party. He concluded that what was notable was 'not their love for Marx, or … their love for the "classics", but … the frank manner in which many of the members express their indebtedness to the Bible as their most helpful book'.[18] This Christian presence in the early Labour Party led one enterprising evangelist to arrange a series of meetings in Browning Hall at which 10 prominent Labour figures, including Keir Hardie, Will Crooks and John Hodge, testified to their faith. The purpose of these meetings was not to propound the gospel of Labour but to win souls for Christ. This belief that change was needed person-ally *and* socially was a recurring theme of ethical Socialism. At the Browning Hall event Henderson said, 'If reformation and reform could save the world, the world would have been perfect long ago. What we want along with our reforms is the spirit of regeneration.'[19]

When Henderson became the Labour MP for Barnard Castle in 1903, his rise in the party was swift. He became its treasurer in 1904 and its chair in 1905. In this position he immediately saw the need to build up the party machinery in preparation for the General Election of 1906. His commitment to structures and methods, whether in the chapel, union or party, was total and his zeal for the party, its independence and its distinct agenda was now wholehearted. It was said of Henderson that 'he was there for the Party, not the Party there for him'.[20] Like many before him, Henderson saw the party as God's instrument to do good in the world, and because of this he believed it deserved his unceasing effort. After the 1906 election he became the chief whip and it was in this role that he was guilty of demanding from others the same total allegiance that he maintained himself. Leventhal says, 'He was prone to bully Labour MPs whose attendance, once the initial excitement wore off, was intermittent.'[21] His ability to manage people but also to gain their respect became increasingly evident, however, and earned him the defer-ential but affectionate title 'Uncle Arthur'.

Henderson v. MacDonald

Arthur Henderson was chief whip and Ramsay MacDonald was the party secretary when in 1910 the Liberals called two elections. MacDonald and Henderson knew that more work needed to be done on the party's infrastructure before it could risk challenging the Liberals in more constituencies. At a time when the party was still financially chal-lenged, they succeeded in restricting the list to 78 candidates in January 1910 and to 56 in December 1910. While continued co-operation with the Liberals was controversial, they believed that Labour was still not strong enough to go it alone.

This unanimity of thinking between two of Labour's leading figures was in stark contrast to their bitter personal relationship. Henderson and MacDonald shared the same goal of moulding the party into a fit state for growth but, as McKibbin says, 'as types they could not have been more different, and they disliked each other personally. Yet for the most part they worked together precisely because their differences were personal and only marginally political.'[22] In 1908 MacDonald had called Henderson a 'bloody liar' and later Henderson resigned from the party's executive in protest at another remark made by MacDonald.

One source of this contentious relationship was religion, since MacDonald was a Unitarian. Unitarianism sought to unite all the Nonconformist groups in one single religious movement, but despite having no set dogma it had so far failed to do this. For Unitarians religion was a personal journey inspired by the example of Jesus, while social injustice was a human creation and humans therefore had the capacity to fight it. Human progress was therefore possible through a combination of personal endeavour and divine inspiration. Their belief in human progress motivated many Unitarians to involve themselves in political action and despite their small numbers they were often at the forefront of reform. MacDonald regularly propounded Unitarian views in the journal of the Ethical Movement. 'Doctrines and creeds, indeed anything "purely intellectual", should be abandoned as a test of religious feeling,' he wrote. 'For the religious spirit is an indwelling impulse and if any attempt were made to put it into words it would slip away. Thus dogma is the enemy of the aspirations it presumed to formalize.'[23] MacDonald's theology, free from prescriptions and doctrine, was in stark contrast to Henderson's Methodism with its emphasis on doctrine, obligation and personal discipleship.

The different theologies of the two men informed their different approaches to political alliances and later also to World War I. While both of them recognized the need to work with the Liberals, MacDonald was willing to go further and consider a new party altogether. He was not bound by any creed that made the Labour Party inviolable as an entity. Such a thought was beyond the pale for Henderson, however, who was not only a faithful party man but one for whom allegiance was a central tenet of his faith. Moreover, Henderson's methodical and pragmatic approach was in contrast to MacDonald's journalistic and intellectual flair, and it was personality as well as theology that exacerbated their stormy relationship.

It was Labour's response to World War I that eventually produced the political split between the two leaders. MacDonald's rejection of war was based on his deep convictions about human progress and international solidarity. Henderson did not share these notions of social progress and instead embraced a theology of the evil within humanity. Henderson was no warmonger, but he believed in the obligation to fight for liberty, justice and democracy. He did have concerns about the war and addressed an anti-war rally in Trafalgar Square on 2 August 1914, but his pragmatism led him to vote with the Government the following day, in support of entering the war. Henderson accepted that in a civilized world Britain was duty-bound to defend the neutrality of Belgium, and he believed 'that Britain entered the war with clean hands in support of high ideals and great principles'.[24] His pacifist ideals would be seen in later life when as British Foreign Secretary he travelled to Berlin in 1931 to persuade Germany to pursue disarmament.

Party leader

The onset of war was the catalyst for MacDonald's resignation as Labour leader – following his defeat within the party over Labour's position on war – and Henderson took his place. Henderson's first agreement as party leader was an electoral truce for the duration of the war, and in contrast to Hardie and MacDonald he accepted the use of credits to finance the conflict. The Liberal Government needed the whole nation behind them and Henderson's connections in the trade unions made him invaluable in this respect. Thus Henderson and George Barnes (deputy leader of the Labour party 1908–9 and leader 1910–11) took places in Asquith's Coalition Government in 1915 and Lloyd George's War Cabinet in 1916. In doing so they became Labour's first Cabinet ministers. Henderson's roles included President of the Board of Education from May 1915 to October 1916 and Paymaster General from October 1916 to April 1917.

Some in the Labour Party opposed these moves, but they had the support of the wider membership. It meant that for the first time a Labour leader was in a real position of power and immediately Henderson helped to draft the 1915 Treasury Agreement. This established a new relationship between the Government and the trade unions and included a 'no strike' clause. In return it provided a significant level of material benefits and recognition for unions at a national level. Some felt Henderson had gone too far by sacrificing the right of workers to strike, but Henderson had little sympathy for such ideological anti-business sentiments and believed that workers and employers had to pull together for the good of the nation. In fact these developments enhanced the trade unions, who saw their membership grow from 4,189,000 in 1913 to 8,081,000 by 1919. However, there was further criticism of Henderson when in January 1916 conscription was introduced. He stood his ground in support of the measure and challenged his detractors to join him in resigning their seats 'to see how the public felt'.

Despite winning the arguments, these were difficult days for Henderson. He was under attack from the anti-war and anti-Liberal elements in the Labour Party and his dual role as party leader and Cabinet member was difficult to sustain. His difficulties were compounded by the death of his eldest son David, who was killed on the Somme. In April 1917 Henderson dealt with the tension of his twin roles by resigning from both. He had wanted to travel to an international Socialist conference on the chaos in Russia, but Lloyd George had refused to let him go. This snub was enough to push Henderson over the edge. Now outside the Government, but having gained much valuable experience within it, Henderson devoted himself to building up the Labour Party in preparation for its future role in power.

Creator of Labour's first constitution

He did not do this alone, but benefited from the support of Beatrice and Sidney Webb. Henderson had first met the Webbs when he joined the Fabians in 1912 and now he worked with them on the development of Labour's constitution. Within a month of leaving the War Cabinet he tabled a motion to Labour's national executive. He sought 'the reorganization of the Party with a view to a wider extension of membership, the strengthening and development of local parties in the constituencies, together with the promotion of a larger number of candidates, and the suggestion that a Party programme be adopted'.[25] A subcommittee was established to develop and propose reforms, and provisional plans were quickly agreed. Henderson set about convincing the rest of the party by campaigning throughout the country.

The new constitution would formalize the constituency parties and individual membership would be included for the first time. It would also increase the role of the unions at every level, from constituency and party conference to national executive. Thirteen of the 23 members of the national executive would automatically be trade unionists and the unions would also influence the remaining 10, who represented women, Socialist societies and other elements. In some respects, the dominance of the unions was understandable given their financial and electoral might. Henderson was merely providing a role for the organizations he knew best, just as Hardie had secured a disproportionate role for his ILP at Labour's birth. Henderson's constitution now inextricably bound Labour to the unions, and the clear losers were the Socialist societies.

Henderson's legacy, however, was not just a constitution but a 'vision statement' around which the different strands of Socialist Labour could gather in distinction to the Liberals. This, at least, is one explanation as to the original purpose of Clause 4. Ross McKibbin describes it as an 'uncharacteristic adornment' to the new constitution.[26] David Howell describes its purpose as the 'maximization of support', ensuring that as many as possible would see the words of the clause as an expression of their own political commitment.[27] In meaning different things to different people, however, Clause 4 would not provide a clear way forward and was in fact destined to become a focus of controversy until it was rewritten in 1995. Henderson himself, writing in a paper entitled 'The Outlook for Labour' (1918), believed it meant a balance between capitalism and Socialism – what he called 'industrial democracy'. In his view it would mean increased nationalization through control of the railways, ships and mines.[28] How it would work out in practice would become clear later, but in theory the clause was acceptable to the party and in February 1918 the party conference voted for the new constitution.

A coherent force

By the end of the war Labour, like the country at large, had changed dramatically. No longer was it an erratic and unstructured party dominated by pioneers and evangelists. Its new constitution was a collective declaration of what it was, where it was going and how it proposed to get there. By 1918, its eighteenth year, the party had grown up. Future victory was not yet secure, but the structures were in place to ensure a coherent and well-financed electoral campaign.

More than any other individual, Arthur Henderson had been responsible for this transformation. He had been the bridge between the unions, the Socialist societies, the grass roots and the Government. Henderson also remained a bridge between Christianity and Labour, even as the religious idealism of the ILP radicals became increasingly marginalized. Henderson continued his involvement in religious affairs and joined George Lansbury and the retired Bishop Charles Gore at a 1919 conference on 'The Religion of Labour'. At the conference Bishop Gore described the spirit of Labour as 'justice not charity', a description of which even Keir Hardie would have been proud.

In contrast to Labour's consolidation, the Liberals had been badly split by the war. Asquith had fallen out with Lloyd George, and Lloyd George's Coalition Government was heavily dependent on the Conservatives. This led many Liberal radicals to abandon their party for Labour. In the General Election of 1918 Labour's organization was not yet able to crush the Liberal Party, but signs of its demise were clear. Labour fielded 388 candidates but won only 57 seats out of its target of 100. Significantly, however, Labour candidates came second in another 79 seats. The domination of the Liberals and Conservatives as the two main British parties was about to be broken. Ironically Labour's leaders, including Henderson, MacDonald and Philip Snowden, all lost their seats in 1918. All of them would be back to fight another day, however.

CHAPTER 4

Early Learning

JOHN WHEATLEY AND PHILIP SNOWDEN:
1919–26

Sidney Webb described the coming of a Labour Government as the 'inevitability of gradualness'. For a time he seemed to be right. In 1922 Labour won 142 seats to become Britain's second-largest party, and by 1924 it was the party of government. J.R. Clynes said of this time:

> As we stood waiting for His Majesty, amid the gold and crimson magnificence of the Palace. I could not help marvelling at the strange turn of Fortune's wheel which had brought MacDonald the starveling clerk, Thomas the engine driver, Henderson the foundry labourer and Clynes the mill-hand to the pinnacle, beside the man whose forebears had been Kings for so many splendid generations. We were making history! We were, perhaps, somewhat embarrassed, but the little, quiet man whom we addressed as 'Your Majesty' swiftly put us at our ease.[1]

On the heads of this first Labour Cabinet lay a great responsibility. Arthur Henderson was Labour's first Home Secretary and Sidney Webb its first President of the Board of Trade. The disabled Yorkshireman Philip Snowden became Chancellor and the red Clydesider John Wheatley became Minister for Health. Ramsay MacDonald, who had so recently been ejected both from his golf club and the Commons, became Prime Minister and Foreign Secretary.

Labour's ascendancy had been rapid and had come at the expense of the Liberals, who collapsed from over 400 MPs in 1906 to just 62 in 1922. This was due to the wartime split between Asquith and Lloyd George and the dramatic growth of the unions, who now favoured Labour. Many

Christians had also swung decisively to Labour. Nonconformists felt betrayed by Lloyd George, who 'had flattered their vanity and ignored their views'.[2] The Church of England, in the form of 510 Anglican vicars, welcomed Labour as the new official opposition in 1923 (they presented Ramsay MacDonald with a plaque in March of that year) and even Cardinal Bourne, the Catholic Primate of England, reluctantly declared that the Labour Party had nothing in its programme that threatened religion.

Labour's rise to government supported by endorsements from royalty and the Church seemed absurd in the light of its anti-Establishment roots. All was not quite as it seemed, however. The British Establishment would not so readily roll over and allow Labour to govern at will. After only 10 months in government, Labour was once again languishing in opposition, and 18 months later it found itself impotent in the face of the biggest confrontation between workers and capital Britain has ever seen. The inevitability of gradualness appeared less inevitable after all.

———————

The results of war

In 1918, at 11 o'clock on the eleventh day of the eleventh month, World War I came to an end. In the House of Commons Prime Minister Lloyd George outlined the conditions of the armistice and declared, 'I hope we may say that thus, this fateful morning, came to an end all wars.' World War I dramatically affected the future of Britain. Despite its victory, Britain's war debts were greater than those of any other victor nation and it would still be paying off those debts when World War II arrived. Added to this, its Empire was disintegrating, with rioting in Cairo, massacres in India and turmoil in Ireland. The General Election of 1918 produced an unstoppable momentum for Irish independence as 76 Sinn Féin MPs rejected Westminster for a Dublin Parliament.

World War I represented the failure of the past and few people wanted to return to the old ways. They looked to the future, therefore, but new ideas and optimism were mixed with uncertainty and the need to face new challenges. The early 1920s saw the growth of Fascism, in a reaction to the perceived failures of parliamentary democracy, especially Socialist democracy. Its leaders were frontline troops returning from war and looking for strong leadership at home. In Milan on 23 March 1919 a new Fascist movement was formed under the leadership of former soldier Benito Mussolini.

One positive legacy from the war was the creation of the League of Nations. The League formed part of the Treaty of Versailles, designed to manage and enforce international treaties. Its 26 articles included commitments on arbitration, the curbing of arms and basic human rights. It was a sign, many hoped, that the world had learned from war and wanted a new kind of internationalism no longer based on militarism and might.

Further afield, the Bolsheviks under Lenin were fighting for survival. Their victory was secured when the Allies, including the USA and Britain, stopped supporting the forces ranged against them. The Labour Party said that Soviet Russia should now be given a chance and it was a view that received widespread support. Labour had established a 'hands off Russia' committee, although a delegation in 1920 returned to describe the Bolsheviks as dictators.

Labour's first taste of power

For Labour, the 1918 General Election brought mixed blessings. By fielding 388 candidates it had shown itself a viable electoral machine, but it only secured a modest 57 MPs. Despite this, a mood of change was sweeping across Britain and the electoral tide was clearly turning in Labour's favour. Labour continued to build on its pre-war presence in parish councils, rural and urban councils and boards of guardians. By the General Election of 1922 Labour had become the official opposition and shortly after the 1923 election it would enter government. No wonder Sidney Webb, speaking at the party conference in 1923, believed that the party would have a clear majority somewhere around 1926. By 1922 industrial areas of Scotland, South Wales, Yorkshire and London had swung Labour's way. The election returned new MPs such as Sidney Webb, but also readmitted Ramsay MacDonald and Philip Snowden to Parliament. MacDonald and Snowden had both lost their seats in 1918 for their anti-war views. On his return MacDonald was soon re-elected party leader, his pacifist views not only forgiven but even admired in the aftermath of war.

Despite these successes for Labour, the Conservatives were the ones in power. They were struggling with post-war unemployment, however, and their new leader Stanley Baldwin wanted to reverse an established policy by introducing tariffs on imports. To secure a mandate for this he called another General Election in December 1923, but instead of winning the Conservatives actually lost many seats, leaving no party with overall control. Labour had campaigned on a programme of national work but had not expected to have the chance to implement it so soon. The Labour Party secured 191 seats, and when the Conservatives lost a vote of no confidence, Ramsay MacDonald was invited to form a minority Labour Government on 22 January 1924.

New challenges

For the first time Labour moved from being a party of protest to a party of government. It was a culture shock that was hard for many to take in, especially those who travelled to Buckingham Palace to receive their seals of office. Within three short decades, the party that had been established to secure representation for workers in Parliament had now secured power in the country. It is worth reflecting on what Keir Hardie would have made of those Labour MPs dressed in their finest at Buckingham Palace. The era of Hardie and old-style Socialism was coming to an end. The vigour and vision of the Socialist societies was being replaced by the stability of the unions. Henderson's legacy of a clear constitution and rules to follow heralded a new age of efficiency in winning elections, and Labour had indeed won through.

The challenge for the party now that it had secured power was what it would do with it. It needed to develop workable ideas and parliamentary skills in order to translate principles into legislation. The responsibilities of government would present Labour with its greatest challenge yet, both for the party and for the individuals who now made up the Government. They would need tact and perseverance, especially in the light of comments made by the popular press, who talked up the likely excesses of a Socialist government.

Although Labour would be in power for only a short time, it was nonetheless an opportunity to prove its responsibility and learn lessons for the future. As Davies notes, 'The quest for a new Jerusalem undoubtedly remained but now it was a far-off and probably unattainable hope, secondary to the administrative detail of running a practical, down to earth organization.'³ Yet the 'revivalist' era was not completely over. When Ramsay MacDonald went to South Wales as Labour's first Prime Minister in 1924, a vast crowd sang a messianic hymn in a scene straight out of an earlier evangelical revival. MacDonald's address was in tune with the hymn – he preached peace and prosperity, if only the people had courage to grasp it.

Early achievements

The first Labour Government was in power from January to November 1924. Given its lack of experience and the fact that it had no working majority, it is remarkable that it achieved anything at all. Yet despite some accusations of failure it did make some progress. One major achievement was in public housing. Minister for Health John Wheatley's 1924 Housing Act aimed to secure subsidies for local authorities to build 2.5 million homes for rent. This was the first large-scale council house development the country had ever seen. In addition to this, Chancellor Philip Snowden provided £28 million for roads and public works as a response to the Cabinet's special unemployment committee. In his capacity as Foreign Secretary, Ramsay MacDonald persuaded the French to accept the Dawes Plan on war reparations that would help ease the tension between France and Germany.

One significant factor in this first Labour Cabinet was that many shared a Christian faith. It was their faith that had brought them this far in politics, and it would now sustain them as they faced the pressures of government for the first time. Christianity had fired their ideals and now it helped them apply these ideals to the practical demands of governing the country. Two notable characters in the Cabinet were John Wheatley and Philip Snowden. Both were Christians and it was this as much as anything else that had shaped their politics.

John Wheatley

John Wheatley has been credited with the greatest success of Labour's first Government. He was born in Bonmahon, County Waterford, on 19 May 1869, but when he was seven years old the family moved to

Ballieston in Glasgow. Ballieston was a mining community and the pits provided work for the men, whose families lived in primitive, one-roomed houses, often shared with a lodger. Wheatley shared his room with his mother, father and seven brothers and sisters. Growing up in these conditions helped develop his convictions about the need for good housing. All that was in the future, however, and at the age of 14 Wheatley followed his father, brothers and all the young men of the community into the mines.

He knew even then that the mines were not for him and, as with many other future Labour politicians, it was education that helped him escape from the Ballieston pits. After a full day underground he would complete the 10-mile round trip to evening classes in the Athenaeum College in Glasgow. It was a place whose philosophy was one of self-help and enterprise and, as Ian Wood comments, 'the miners from the Lanarkshire coalfield did not predominate among its enrolled students'.[4] The lessons in enterprise led Wheatley to become first a publican in 1893 and then a grocer in a small business started with his brother. When that business failed, he became an advertising salesman on the local Catholic newspaper, the *Glasgow Observer*.

Political convictions

At this stage in his life Wheatley's politics were confined to his membership of the Irish National League. The League provided a network of social centres, mirroring the Protestant Orange Lodges. However, the League's executive would also direct the Catholic population on how to vote in elections – and this would invariably be for the Liberals, given their support for Irish Home Rule. Nonetheless, the monolithic Catholic support for Liberalism was changing and in the 1906 General Election two Labour MPs were surprisingly elected in Scotland. The local Catholic vote appeared to be a factor in this, since Scotland had not been included in MacDonald's noncompetition pact with the Liberals. Labour's success focused concern in the Catholic hierarchy about the growth of Socialism among its flock. As a result it stepped up its anti-Socialist propaganda and organized a conference at which an eminent representative from the Catholic Truth Society spoke of the dangers of Socialism, especially the radical, anti-Church variety trumpeted by Robert Blatchford.

Blatchford was a Manchester journalist who had been traumatized by the poverty he had witnessed during his research into slums in 1890. His passionate writings had a profound effect on the cause of Socialism, although he never accepted any ideology or political party. In fact, Blatchford later abandoned his left-wing views and once described the Conservative Baldwin as Britain's finest politician. In 1891, however, Blatchford was driven by what he called 'the moral evil of poverty' to found the *Clarion* newspaper which was based on a policy of humanity, 'not of party, sect or creed but of justice, reason and mercy'. The *Clarion* sold 30,000 copies a week and in 1893 Blatchford's articles were published in a book entitled *Merrie England* which sold over 2 million copies in many languages. Blatchford's tirades were often directed towards the Church, which he saw as presiding over poverty and not living the message of Christ.

When Blatchford was attacked by the Catholic Truth Society at the conference in 1906, John Wheatley felt compelled to defend him. Like Blatchford, Wheatley also felt that poverty was a moral evil which needed an urgent response from the Church. The conference provoked Wheatley into a direct response and he wrote in the *Glasgow Observer* under the pseudonym of a Catholic Socialist (at this stage he was reluctant to be identified, or to start any movement):

> *It is obvious that a vigorous attempt is being made to set the organization of the Church against the Socialist movement of Great Britain. I hope such a policy will fail because I believe such a course would be contrary to the traditional teaching of the Church, unjustifiable and bad policy ... Surely it is the duty of a Catholic to attack a system which makes the practice of religion practically impossible. Why should the work of bettering the poor be left to the people who are non-Catholic or anti-Catholic? Catholics know that the reformation required must be moral as well as material. Their place is in the struggle that they may temper the new economic and political doctrines with a religious spirit.*[5]

Wheatley also argued that Catholic Christianity was collectivist and concerned to root out inequality and social injustice. 'The Catholic Church has always leaned more to socialism or collectivism and equality, than to individualism and inequality. It has always been the church of the poor and all the historical attacks on it from the rich. Its

Divine Founder on every occasion condemned the accumulation of wealth.'[6] Wheatley was influenced in these thoughts by the writings of the Italian political economist Francesco Nitti. Nitti had argued that Christians should hold everything in common and, if need be, this could be through the moral agency of a collectivist state. In Wheatley's mind this was consistent with the practice of the Early Church, where 'all the believers were together and had everything in common. Selling their possessions and goods, they gave to anyone as he had need' (Acts 2:44–5).

The Catholic Socialist Society

The newspaper correspondence that arose from these exchanges would eventually lead to the start of the Catholic Socialist Society (CSS) in November 1906. George Hardie, the brother of Keir, spoke at its launch on 'Some Misconceptions of Socialism' and from the start the CSS set itself the task of persuading Catholics that their faith compelled them to be Socialists. By 1907 Wheatley had started a printing business which helped get the views of the CSS published and spread more widely. An American priest called Father Hagerty wrote its first pamphlet, *Economic Discontent*, and a massive 50,000 copies were sold. Wheatley's own pamphlets included *How the Miners are Robbed* (1907), *The Catholic Workingman* (1909), *Mines, Miners and Misery* (1909) and *Eight Pound Cottages for Glasgow Citizens* (1913).

From these beginnings, the CSS was established for 'the propagation of socialism among Catholics by means of meetings, lectures and distribution of literature'.[7] The CSS was strengthened by the fact that it required all its members to be practising Catholics, and Wheatley's own parish priest, Peter Terken, supported him. Wheatley developed arguments from Church history, the writings of Cardinal Manning and even the Archbishop of Glasgow to present Catholic Socialism as consistent with the Church's teaching. In the pamphlet *Mines, Miners and Misery* he convincingly argued that British Socialism was different from the continental versions which involved violent and illegal seizure of property: 'Our socialism is not confiscation or robbery nor the destruction of family life, nor anything like what you have heard our opponents describe it. It differs from the Socialism condemned by the Pope in that it retains the right to own private property. It is simply a scheme to abolish poverty.'[8]

Antagonism

Nevertheless, many in the Church remained deeply angry at Wheatley's claims for Catholic Socialism. They were fearful of the Socialism prevalent in Europe, which was anti-clerical and atheistic and in some places was causing the closure of Catholic schools. Father Louis Puissant, a Belgian missionary to Muirkirk, became a self-appointed critic of Wheatley. In 1908 he wrote a eulogy to the Holy Mother and concluded, 'Socialism hath the devil; thou hast the word of truth.'[9] Equally melodramatic was his argument that Socialism was a slippery slope from faith into 'a world with human stud-farms and nursery-pens, a world of vice and filth, without religion and without grace'.[10]

One eventual result of this ongoing controversy was the arrival of a Catholic mob outside Wheatley's home. As his family looked on from inside, the crowd burned his effigy while singing the hymn 'Faith of our Fathers'. Wheatley wrote a measured response in the ILP's newspaper *Forward*:

> On Monday night, you gathered in your hundreds and in thousands to demonstrate that you hate me. If I am your enemy, am I your only enemy? Don't you know that God who gave you life has created for you green fields and sunny skies? That he has given you the material and the power to have in abundance beautiful homes, healthy food, education, leisure, travel and all that aids in the development of cultured men and women? These gifts of God have been stolen from you.[11]

Despite such attacks, Wheatley continued to observe Mass and in time, perhaps as a result of his faithfulness to the Church, the Glasgow archdiocese became more moderate in its criticism. Nonetheless, it did label him a malcontent willing to listen to unbelievers and rationalists.

Wheatley was not alone in his advocacy of Catholic Socialism. Frank McCabe was arguably Scotland's first Catholic Socialist and had a regular column in the ILP's *Forward*. Like Wheatley, McCabe remained faithful to the Church but challenged its views on Socialism. He wrote, 'Christianity wants to raise up beautiful souls; socialism wants to raise up pure wholesome bodies so that these souls will have a healthy and suitable habitation. Both should work together for their mutual good.'[12] McCabe and Wheatley never saw eye to eye on a strategy for starting the

CSS, however, and they parted on bad terms when McCabe emigrated to Australia in 1912.

Building bridges

The Glasgow CSS became successful despite such internal wranglings, and provoked the start of three others in Scotland, two in England and one in Belfast. The Leeds society was stillborn, however, because the bishop condemned it in his pastoral letter and support dwindled as a consequence. It was men like McCabe and Wheatley who battled on and in time successfully built bridges between the fledgling Labour Movement and the Catholic Church. As Purdie notes, 'One of the most important achievements of the labour movement in Scotland was to win over the Irish workers. This came about only after bitter resistance from the religious and political leaders of the Irish community.'[13]

Partly provoked by the CSS, the Catholic Social Guild later provided a wider network of Catholic social study groups. In his 1908 *Plea for Catholic Social Action*, Father Charles Dominic Plater had called on clergy and laity to discuss social problems and train as labour leaders in the workplace. The Catholic Social Guild flourished after World War I and its secretary from 1919 was Henry Somerville, the young man who as a 19-year-old had earlier led the failed attempt to establish the Leeds CSS. Now in the Guild, Somerville reassured many Catholics by arguing that, despite the 'common ownership' theme of Clause 4, the Labour Party did not advocate the kind of Socialism which was being condemned by the Church. The fact that the Communist Party of Great Britain was operational from 1920 also meant that by contrast Labour could be identified with less extreme forms of Socialism. Somerville and the Guild's newspaper *Christian Democrat* remained influential throughout the 1920s and '30s, and continued to be critical of both Communism and Fascism.

A politician with a cause

John Wheatley first stood for election in Shettleston in 1907, the same year in which he joined the Independent Labour Party. He was eventually elected in 1912 as an ILP candidate for Shettleston Council, which later became the Glasgow Corporation. Wheatley's attention was immediately taken up with the question of slum housing, one of Glasgow's most pressing problems. He published a detailed plan to replace the tenement slums with municipal cottages, believing this was one way to tackle the high tuberculosis rates in the city. His reputation as the people's representative on housing issues developed, and during the war he led a successful strike against rent rises. Like many in the ILP, he opposed Britain's involvement in the war and the imposition of conscription, and he did not endorse some of the wilder calls for Socialist insurrection common in Glasgow before World War I. His rejection of violence also tempered his support for the anti-British riots in Ireland, although he believed it was violence against the Irish that was the root cause of the whole problem.

In 1918 Wheatley stood unsuccessfully in the General Election and it was perhaps the recognition that more electoral work needed to be done which led to the ending of the CSS in 1919. Its reason for existence had largely been achieved, for Catholic voters had now moved decisively to Labour, despite the reservations of the Church. Labour's support for Irish Home Rule and the tackling of social injustice secured the support of rank-and-file Catholics, even if the Church leadership remained lukewarm.

After the war the Labour Party swept to power in many municipal and town councils. By 1920 Wheatley was one of 44 Labour representatives on the Glasgow Corporation and in 1922 he was elected MP for Shettleston and travelled to Westminster with nine other Labour MPs for the City of Glasgow. Wheatley and his colleagues transferred the urgency of their cause to Westminster, soon developing a reputation as the unruly 'Red Clydesiders'. Impatient for change and frustrated by a Government complacent to the needs of Glasgow, their methods were deemed 'unparliamentary', and within six months Wheatley and his colleague James Maxton had been suspended from the House.

On 23 June 1923 many MPs had gone to the races, because the main business of the day was Scottish health estimates and they were simply not enthused. The Government appeared to have no intention of tackling the desperate plight of Scotland's ailing city populations and put forward proposals to reduce funding for child health centres. The Clydesiders erupted in a tirade of abuse. Maxton accused Government ministers of negligence in failing to tackle tuberculosis in Scotland, running at rates 25 per cent higher than those in England. He then called one minister a murderer. This was too much for other honourable members, and they called for Maxton to withdraw his accusation. He refused, and continued to do so despite pleas from his own front bench. Gunnin describes the conclusion: 'After forty minutes of tense debate, the exhausted Maxton asked Wheatley to stand in his place and Wheatley repeated the epithet, "Murderer" and also refused to withdraw. A Tory Member then moved that the House suspend both men, and by a Division of 258 to 70, Wheatley and Maxton were suspended.'[14]

Minister for Health

Despite this incident, it was John Wheatley who one year later became Minister for Health in the first Labour Government. Ramsay MacDonald disapproved of Wheatley's behaviour but respected his ability as a tactician. For Wheatley this was the ideal job and provided him with the opportunity he had so passionately wanted, to secure decent health through decent housing. Almost immediately, he introduced the 1924 Housing Bill. It was a complex Bill involving 15-year subsidies for local authorities who co-operated with building committees of employees and employers. The proposal was that 190,000 new council houses would be built in 1925 and this figure would gradually increase until it reached 450,000 in 1934. While the intended goal of 2.5 million homes would not be fully realized due to future underfunding, it was nonetheless the first major housing programme of its kind. Wheatley eventually secured Liberal support for his proposals by some clever debating at committee stage – he must surely have kept in mind the tenements of Glasgow or the single room in which he had lived as a boy as motivation for his perseverance when the going got tough. He watched delighted as the Bill was passed into law.

Wheatley demonstrated all the skills that were needed for good government. These included a boldness to aim high and the political shrewdness to secure a result. His contribution to the Labour Government of 1924 was secure and his example of a new kind of political passion was timely. Fellow MP C.F.G. Masterman commented:

The house has found a new favourite in Mr. Wheatley, the former revolutionary member for Glasgow, now Minister of Health. He has been the one conspicuous success in the new Parliament. A short, squat, middle-aged man, with a chubby face beaming behind large spectacles. He possesses a perfect Parliamentary manner; a pleasant voice, confidence without arrogance, a quick power of repartee, a capacity of convincing statement, and above all a saving grace of humour. [15]

Philip Snowden

Philip Snowden, Labour's first Chancellor, was the man who provided the money for Wheatley's Housing Act. In 1907 Snowden had written *The Socialist's Budget*, an outline of his goals for redistribution and economic equality. In 1924, however, he was roundly criticized for failing to introduce a truly Socialist budget. His defence was simple: as a minority Government, it had not been possible to do so. Snowden exemplified the tension between opposition ideals and government reality. His first budget in April 1924 was as much an attempt to reassure people of Labour's fiscal competence as it was to introduce a radical Socialist agenda. He described it as 'vindictive against no class or interest'.

The budget was based on an estimated £38 million surplus and included tax cuts across a range of basic and luxury goods. Yet if tax cuts were not what Labour Chancellors were to become known for, the budget also gave notice of Labour's other spending priorities. In education Snowden allowed local authorities to increase free secondary school places and reintroduce scholarships to universities. He found money for increased unemployment benefit and pensions and secured wage increases in agriculture through his Agricultural Wages (Regulation) Act. Later, during his time as Chancellor in 1929–31, he did shift the tax burden from the poor onto the rich. Snowden's legacy was a twin commitment to balancing the books and tackling social injustice. Nevertheless, in difficult times his commitment to fiscal orthodoxy would limit his ability to deliver social justice.

Formative influences

It was Snowden's background in the ILP and Methodism that had influenced his political development. He was brought up in a church that preached strongly for conversion among its flock. Unlike Keir Hardie and Arthur Henderson, however, Snowden never experienced a distinct moment of conversion. One day, when his father saw the young Philip about to go forward at an evangelical meeting, he grabbed his son's arm and pulled him back. Although Snowden's father was a Sunday School superintendent in the church, he was also suspicious about this method of 'recruitment' and simply wanted to help his son resist the pressure to conform. Such pressure does not appear to have been brought to bear again, and Snowden reflected later that if he had gone forward that day he would probably have ended up as a Methodist minister.[16] Instead he became a politician and Labour's first Chancellor, but he remained a Methodist and a teetotaller throughout his life.

Snowden was born in West Riding, Yorkshire, on 18 July 1864. He was successful at school and by the age of 15 was doing well in an insurance firm. However, physical disability was to have a most profound effect on his life. During the 1890s he became progressively paralysed from the waist down. He had contracted a form of spinal tuberculosis that was both painful and disabling. Despite the pain, he made every effort to keep walking, but was eventually discharged from his work. While being cared for by his mother, he soon became the best-read person in his village as most of his days were spent reading. He also gave regular lectures to the Wesleyan Mutual Improvement Society and in 1893, as chairman of the Liberal Club, he was asked to give a lecture on the dangers of Socialism.

If Snowden had been denied a religious conversion, he now experienced a political one. As a result of his research, he found the arguments for Socialism entirely convincing and the lecture on the dangers of Socialism turned into an appeal for it instead. Snowden became one of the first Nonconformists to abandon the Liberals for the ILP, and he was to become its national chairman in 1903.

The ILP immediately recognized Snowden's skills as a speaker and it was said that only Hardie was his equal as a captivating orator. Snowden was not merely polished and political, however. He connected with the religious aspects of Socialism and working-class culture in a way that few others could. One experienced manager of working men's meetings gave advice to a would-be political speaker in the following terms: 'We want no Karl Marx and surplus values and that sort of stuff. Make it plain and simple. Tha' can put in a long word now and then so as to make them think tha' knows a lot, but keep it simple, and then when tha'rt coming t' finishing up, tha' mun put a bit of Come to Jesus in like Philip does.'[17] The Philip referred to was Snowden, and his Socialism was more connected than most to the message of Jesus.

Snowden was also a gifted writer and became the editor of a local Socialist newspaper. He wrote regularly about faith and politics and regarded Socialism as a practical expression of Christianity. He argued that 'personal salvation and social salvation are like two palm trees which bear no fruit unless they grow side by side'.[18] In *The Christ that is to be* (1903), Snowden argued that the religion of the future would be a political one, seeking to realize its ideals in society through political means. Snowden believed that salvation in social and political problems would be achieved through personal sacrifice, just as Christ's salvation was achieved through his sacrifice.

Political rise and fall

Snowden's electoral career began in 1899 when he was elected as a local councillor. He was later one of the 30 Labour MPs to enter the Commons following the 1906 General Election. In 1905 he married Ethel Annakin, a teacher he had met at the Leeds Fabian Society. Ethel was a Christian Socialist and helped Snowden engage with the cause of women's suffrage. She was a leading speaker in the National Union of Women's Suffrage Societies (NUWSS) and a member of the Women's Peace Crusade. As a prominent activist in the Labour Party, she could have been elected as an MP herself, had it not been for her primary commitment to her husband's career. She was, however, elected to Labour's national executive, and to the board of governors at the BBC.

As a result of his wife's influence, Snowden became a leading advocate for women's suffrage. The women's leader Millicent Fawcett wrote to him after the Franchise Bill of 1918, expressing her gratitude and acknowledging that it was largely Snowden's influence that had finally brought the Labour Party to support women's suffrage. In the Commons from 1906, Snowden's status as an economist also grew steadily and he became Labour's expert on economics. He advised the Liberal Chancellor Lloyd George on the 1909 budget, which was to provoke a constitutional conflict with the Lords and eventually lead to the Parliament Act of 1911.

Meanwhile, he continued his lay preaching and was one of 10 Labour evangelists who preached in Browning Hall in 1910. Snowden also continued to write about Christian Socialism, economics and alcohol, and his works included *The Socialist's Budget* (1907), *Socialism and the Drink Question* (1908) and *The Living Wage* (1909). In his 1934 autobiography he repeated his lifelong argument that drink lowered the standard of living for the poor, sometimes to the point of destitution. His Christian and ILP ideals also meant that, like Hardie and MacDonald, Snowden opposed World War I, and this cost him his seat in the 1918 election. In 1922, however, he returned to the Commons as MP for Colne Valley – and locally it was Snowden's brand of ethical Socialism that would influence the one-time Liberal Herbert Wilson, father of the future premier, to become a Labour supporter.

Snowden's rise through Labour to become its first Chancellor provided him with both the peak and crash of his career. It was his failure to deal effectively with the economic crisis of 1929–31 that led directly to the collapse of Labour's second Government. Snowden's economic orthodoxy – or his adherence to the Treasury's economic orthodoxy of balancing the books – meant that he refused to borrow at a time when borrowing was legitimate. Instead he insisted on cutting expenditure, and his proposals to cut unemployment benefit were simply unacceptable to other Labour ministers and the Cabinet was split.

To add insult to injury, Snowden then followed Ramsay MacDonald into the National Government of 1931.[19] As a result both Snowden and MacDonald continue to be condemned as betrayers of Labour. Keith Laybourn, however, argues that 'it should not be forgotten that Snowden was one of the Labour Party's great leaders in its formative years'.[20] Following the collapse of Labour in 1931, Snowden did not stand again for Parliament but instead accepted a seat in the House of Lords. He died on 15 May 1937.

Wheatley in opposition

When Labour's 1924 Government came to an end, ex-Minister for Health John Wheatley returned to the back benches and the company of the uncompromising Clydesiders. One of the areas in which Wheatley was most critical of MacDonald's leadership in the following years was Labour's vacillation over the General Strike of 1926. As a result of this criticism, MacDonald refused to appoint Wheatley to Labour's second Government in 1929. It was Wheatley who led the opposition from Labour's own benches to the Government's attempts to limit payments to the unemployed in the National Insurance Bill.

There is little doubt that Wheatley would also have rejected Snowden's efforts to balance the budget if he had remained alive to witness them. Since 1924, however, Wheatley had suffered from high blood pressure and on 12 May 1930 he suffered a cerebral haemorrhage which proved fatal. Despite his success in government, Wheatley had become disillusioned over Labour's inability to achieve radical change. It was a disillusionment that many felt as the constraints of government became evident. Labour's 10 months in office in 1924 had demonstrated its responsibility but also its impotence, as many saw it, radically to transform the system.

Labour's loss of power

Ramsay MacDonald resigned his Government towards the end of 1924 following a Commons vote to investigate Labour's links with Communism. Public anxiety about Communism, exacerbated by a forged letter, was to have a devastating impact on Labour's vote in the November election.

While in government, Labour had restored diplomatic relations with Russia, granting it 'most favoured nation' trading status. In addition, although the party continued to deny any affiliation to the Communists, there were many sympathizers within Labour's ranks. Four days before the election the Conservatives released the Zinoviev Letter, which provided 'evidence' of a Communist plot for a workers' uprising in Britain. The public's uneasiness about Labour and Communism was expressed in a Conservative landslide of 410 MPs. The Zinoviev Letter was later proved to be a forgery, but public fear about a workers' revolution still remained. It was a fear the Conservatives would ruthlessly exploit 18 months later in the General Strike.

The General Strike

The General Strike of 1926 revolved around Britain's miners, the largest and most needy group of workers who were more concerned about fair wages than class war. By 1925 the miners were under threat of longer hours for less pay because of the availability of cheap foreign coal. Prime Minister Baldwin delayed the crisis with a temporary subsidy and a Royal Commission review. However, the Commission's report in March 1926 rejected nationalization and proposed no further subsidies. The miners held to their position – 'not a penny off the pay, not a second on the day' – and went on strike on 1 May. The TUC supported the miners by calling a general strike on 3 May and within days over 2 million workers were out on strike and large tracts of British industry fell silent.

The strike was the closest Britain ever came to class warfare. It demonstrated the unions' power, but also their lack of strategic planning. In contrast Baldwin had prepared well, maintaining control of the radio stations and organizing volunteers to run essential services. Armoured vehicles were deployed on the streets, not because of worker violence but in order to reinforce the message about who was in control. Meanwhile, the TUC became anxious about the undemocratic forces it might have unleashed and Ramsay MacDonald, J.R. Clynes and Arthur Henderson rushed around denying that the strike had any revolutionary intent. Nevertheless, some union leaders were presenting it as the last great battle against capitalism. In their urgency to resolve the dispute, the TUC failed to secure any concessions and after only nine days the strike was over. The miners continued to fight on, but were forced back to work before Christmas – to pre-1921 levels of pay and conditions.

Conflicting Church attitudes

The General Strike was a watershed event not only for the unions but also for the various Churches. It polarized the forces of labour against the forces of capital, and the Churches were caught in the middle. Many ordinary churchgoers were sympathetic to the plight of the miners, but many feared the strike could destabilize the nation. In contrast to Cardinal Manning's support for the dockers in 1889, Cardinal Bourne condemned the workers in his Sunday sermon from Westminster

Cathedral during the strike. He said there was no moral justification for a strike of this nature and it was a sin against God. The Government used his words extensively and many Catholic trade unionists felt betrayed.

Archbishop Keating of Liverpool was more in touch with the needs of miners when he said, 'The poor must live and if private enterprise cannot provide the worker with a living it must clear out for another system which can.'[21] A Congregationalist minister in Southport, D.R. Davies, was even more effusive in his support of the strikers and preached that 'the miners are altogether right and the owners are altogether wrong'.[22] There were other local expressions of church support too. In Poplar Father John Groser addressed large crowds of strikers and Rowland Jones, the curate of St Mary's, Somers Town, was 'up to his eyes in the strike'. He addressed the strikers alongside Herbert Romeril, ex-president of the Railway Clerks' Association and Labour MP for St Pancras South East.[23] Yet despite these notable exceptions, the Churches seemed paralysed by the strike.

The Free Churches looked to Archbishop Randall Davidson who, after some uncertainty, issued a conciliatory statement – 'The Crisis: an appeal from the Churches'. Davidson called for a return to pre-strike conditions, from which point negotiations could proceed. Ramsay MacDonald described Davidson's intervention as inspiring and future Archbishop William Temple said that it provided hope. In the heat of the battle, however, the statement was seen by many as an attempt to undermine the Government and the BBC refused to broadcast it. The Archbishop regarded this as the 'adoption by Government censors of the methods for which they blamed the strikers'.[24] John Reith, the director general of the BBC, feared that if he put the Archbishop's appeal on air it would provoke Winston Churchill to take control of the Corporation.

Churchill's influence

As Chancellor of the Exchequer, Winston Churchill's role throughout the General Strike was insidious and effective. H.G. Wells once wrote, 'The real definition of the class-war is the old habit of the governing classes.' Churchill was the editor of the *British Gazette*, a Government newspaper that demanded the total surrender of the workers. The

Gazette trumpeted about the threat to the constitution, a scare story designed to fuel the propaganda that the largely peaceful miners were intent on violence. What was at stake, however, was not the constitution but the ability of mine owners to cut wages at will. This was a danger the Establishment could not countenance – it seemed even more threatening to them than a minority Labour government.

Churchill's part in the events surrounding the strike had begun with his decision in 1925 to return Britain to the Gold Standard and restore the pound's parity to the dollar. This had made British coal uncompetitive and had created the demands to cut wages and increase hours. Churchill was then involved in the breakdown of last-minute negotiations between the Cabinet and the TUC,[25] and his subsequent willingness to bully the BBC into banning the Archbishop's appeal is staggering in view of his claim to be defending the constitution.

In 1926, therefore, the Church was effectively and symbolically shut out at a time of national crisis. Yet the Archbishop's appeal did make it to one newspaper, and the Wesleyan evangelist Ensor Walters said the report 'had saved the situation as regards the attitude of labour to the Churches'.[26] By this time it was too late, however, and the strike had been broken.

Stephen Fitzpatrick

In sharp contrast to Churchill's role was the part played by one Stephen Fitzpatrick, a Glasgow railway clerk. When the strike was called, the 22-year-old Fitzpatrick 'took out' the railway clerks and they marched around George Square in central Glasgow in support of the miners. Fitzpatrick was a determined and idealistic Christian and was absolutely sure that the labourer was worthy of his hire.

These were the very ideals into which the TUC had tapped when it called its ill-thought-through General Strike. While the TUC could take time afterwards to reflect on its failed strategy, however, the young Fitzpatrick paid the price of a lifetime's work without promotion for his role in mobilizing the workers. He spent 28 years as a competent clerk on the London and North Eastern Railway, yet received no rewards in terms of career development or salary rises, simply because of his leadership during one week in May 1926. Nevertheless, his service in the community with the St Vincent de Paul Society and his commitment to educate his children in a way he had never been himself would make up for his disappointments at work.

His daughter Janine has described how he suffered from a stomach ulcer and died early from cancer at the age of 51. 'Perhaps he had swallowed too much injustice and had too much anxiety for his fellow humans to be treated fairly,' she commented. Despite the failure of the General Strike for the miners and for workers everywhere, Fitzpatrick's daughter – now an activist for women within the Church and an educator in spirituality – continues the struggle today, believing 'the new Jerusalem' is nothing if not an image of a transformed world.

CHAPTER 5

Making New Friends

R.H. TAWNEY AND MARGARET BONDFIELD: 1927–31

*L*abour's experience in government begged one question: once power is
secured, what is to be done with it? Labour was no longer just a party of
protest or a party of opposition alone. It had become a party of power, a
truly political party. Nevertheless, although it now had an organizational
structure, a constitution and even Clause 4, it still did not have a developed
policy structure that would allow it to act and not simply react. This was a
different age and Labour needed different skills to deal with it. More worry-
ingly, Labour was still a party of the working class and not yet the party of
the whole nation; it was not yet 'the people's party', nor was it the natural
party of government.

What was needed at this stage were thinkers and strategists, and in the
mid- to late 1920s one such person to emerge was R.H. Tawney. Tawney
would assist Labour to break from its class confines and define a values-
based approach to policy development. It was Tawney who helped define
Socialism for the whole population, not just the working class, thus guiding
Labour forward to become truly the people's party. Tawney's policy framework would be as timely as Hardie's pioneering zeal or Henderson's organizational skills. He asked the basic questions about what kind of society
Labour wanted to build and then helped the party to define its answers. He
once said:

> The fundamental question is, who is to be master? Is the reality behind
> the decorous drapery of political democracy to continue to be the
> economic power wielded by a few thousand, or if preferred, a few
> hundred thousand bankers, industrialists and landowners? Or shall a

serious effort be made, as serious for example as was made for other purposes during the war – to create organs through which the nation can control, in cooperation with other nations, its economic destinies ... Capitalist parties presumably accept the first alternative. A Socialist party chooses the second.[1]

In the late 1920s, therefore, the Labour Party embarked on what was to be its most difficult challenge of all: working out its values in real and practical policy. In this task Tawney's contribution to Labour was timely and invaluable.

Labour in a changing world

The General Strike of 1926 had proved disastrous for the unions. While it had proved their undoubted power, the lack of strategic goals had resulted in glorious defeat. Baldwin's Conservatives exploited their victory in the strike by introducing the Trades Disputes Act (1927) which made general strikes illegal. This Act also cut into Labour's finances, requiring unions to donate only money specifically authorized by members. The aftermath of the strike heralded a bleak period for the unions, characterized by constant defensiveness over wages and conditions. Membership also began to fall, with a loss of 300,000 in the 12 months after the strike. Moreover, the defeat reinforced the view that politics was the only viable route to securing social justice, and union leaders like Ernest Bevin of the Transport and General Workers' Union redirected their efforts within the Labour Party.

As the Liberals continued their electoral decline, it seemed that only Labour could offer fulfilment of working people's hopes and an alternative to Conservatism. Despite the dominance of the unions, the party's challenge now was to appeal to the whole nation and not just those parts that had supported the General Strike. Society was shifting from the old certainties of class and tradition, and it was no longer adequate for Labour to appeal to the working class alone. Britain after World War I and the General Strike was a much more complex place in terms of politics and each new generation aspired for something better, a better life for their children. Labour had to keep up. The Conservative

Government had embraced the changes and made no attempt to roll back the social revolutions of women in the workplace or universal suffrage. The post-war Conservatives had successfully transformed themselves, leaving behind the reactionary pre-war Tories who had fought tooth and nail against progressive Liberal reforms.

R.H. Tawney

Meanwhile, Labour's brief experience of government had demonstrated that securing power was one thing, but delivering change was quite another. To prepare for a return to government it needed to develop its priorities and future programme in opposition. Following the General Strike, one of Labour's greatest challenges was to break free from its identity as a party of the working class alone. As Laybourn notes, 'By 1923, the message was clear: Labour was the party of the working class.'[2] Labour needed to construct a programme that was no longer based on class identity but on liberty and opportunity for all. In this quest, the party would benefit disproportionately from one man's thinking. His political philosophy was not only applicable to Labour in the 1920s but would inspire successive Labour leaders in the future. His name was Richard Henry Tawney and his framework for policy development would help Labour achieve its goal of becoming a party for the whole nation.

For Tawney such a goal was not a betrayal of Labour's roots but an extension of his basic Socialist belief that all people deserve equality and liberty. He would help Labour think through policy from first principles, not merely in response to specific issues. Tawney was at the heart of the struggle that was going on for the direction of the party. The ILP had put forward its own more radical programme, 'Socialism in Our Time', during its campaign of 1926–7, but it was Tawney who helped steer a more moderate step-by-step approach to achieving Socialist aims.

Equality and liberty for all

Tawney saw Socialism in terms of individual liberty and equality, not simply economics and nationalization. He recognized a conflict of interests in this, but argued not for a Marxist-inspired class struggle but for a

Christian-inspired revolution for equality and liberty. He wrote that these two principles were not contradictions but were in fact mutually enhancing, 'that every man should have this liberty and no more, to do unto others as he would that they should do unto him'.[3] This was liberty for capitalists as well as workers, but it was of necessity a constraining liberty, for the liberty of the weak depends on the constraint of the strong – or, in Tawney's famous expression, 'Freedom for the pike is death for the minnows.'[4] It would require basic civil and political rights as well as economic securities, which were to be subject to the will of all. Such equality, Tawney argued, is not incompatible with liberty but essential to it.

In talking of Socialism as equality and liberty, Tawney challenged the belief that *laissez-faire* capitalism was liberating and instead spoke for the workers, who were self-evidently not liberated by it. He described this thinking as 'ethical Socialism' and it provided both an analysis of what was wrong with society and a basis for action to tackle those wrongs. Tawney believed that the impulse behind British Socialism – and he believed in many kinds of Socialism – had always been 'obstinately and unashamedly ethical'.[5] The achievement of equality and liberty would lead to better factory conditions for workers and better education for their children.

These political reference points first laid down by R.H. Tawney would provide a template for Labour policy and enable it to become a party relevant for the whole of Britain. Labour's 1928 policy document *Labour and the Nation* reflected this new national consciousness. It was a landmark in Labour's self-understanding and furnished the first proof that it was no longer merely a class-based or narrow-interest party. This step was consistent with Tawney's vision of moving the party beyond its identity as working class or union dominated to appeal to all Socialists – including 'the teacher, the doctor, the scientist who had no love for capitalism'.[6]

Influence in politics and the Church

As the main architect of *Labour and the Nation*, Tawney played a crucial role in Labour's internal development and the long haul of challenging the Conservative claim to be the natural party of government. By January 1927 Tawney had already stood as a Labour parliamentary candidate three times, but in 1935 he refused a safe seat, realizing that his greatest contribution to the party could be achieved in ways other than as an MP. Tawney had a distinguished career as an educationalist, apologist and writer of memorable and eloquent prose, but it was through his work with the Labour Party that he would truly impact the nation. Parsons comments, 'His name will long be remembered among the founders of twentieth century social thought. Politically, he has proved the most catholic of all the British Labour Party's prophets of Socialism. All wings of the party have saluted him: the right, e.g. Gaitskell, the centre, e.g. Crossman, the left, e.g. *Tribune Weekly*.'[7]

If Tawney's impact on Labour was huge, so too was his impact on the Church. Adrian Hastings argues that in the move from the individualism and imperialism of the nineteenth century to the Socialism and collectivism of the twentieth, Tawney influenced Christians 'not only to welcome this change but to require it'.[8] Tawney's classic book on economic history, *Religion and the Rise of Capitalism* (1926), mapped the withdrawal of the Church from wider society but also issued a challenge to return to it. Tawney believed there was no area outside the sphere of Christian morality and called the Church to engage again with the economy it had abandoned. His influence was enormous and following his eightieth birthday party at the House of Commons in 1960, *The Times* concluded, 'No man alive has put more people into his spiritual and intellectual debt than Richard Henry Tawney.'[9]

Background and development

Despite his huge impact on Labour, Tawney was unlike many previous Labour leaders. In contrast to those who educated themselves at night after long hours of work, Tawney had a privileged education at Rugby and Oxford. It was while he was at Balliol College in 1901 that he was first exposed to a mix of academic study and social concern. The Master, Edward Caird, encouraged his students to think about the wider social realities and inspired the young Tawney to visit the university settlements of London's East End (ex-university students would go to live and work in a poor area, and were joined temporarily by visiting undergraduates). There he was challenged to ask why the poor were poor and why some people had so much while others had so little.

Such academic and practical experience provoked Tawney to question what his Christian faith had to say about social injustice. In this he was influenced by his friendship with Bishop Charles Gore (1853–1932), a radical bishop in the Church of England. Gore had pioneered the so-called second wave of British Christian Socialism from the 1880s onwards and it was to Gore that Tawney's *Religion and the Rise of Capitalism* was dedicated.[10]

Following his graduation in 1903, Tawney went with his friend and future brother-in-law William Beveridge to live and work in Toynbee Hall, a university settlement in the East End of London. It was Beveridge's experiences here that would mould the economic theories which so influenced the post-war welfare state. At Toynbee Tawney worked in a day job and then taught economics and politics to the workers in the evenings. He also started to research and campaign on issues such as juvenile labour, unemployment benefit and university reform. Tawney realized early on that charity was not enough, and he increasingly felt that the paternalism and evangelism of Toynbee Hall was not an adequate basis for the structural reform that was needed.

Educational work

Education was the most obvious avenue through which Tawney could express his social commitment. In 1905 he joined the executive of the Workers' Educational Association (WEA), set up to establish adult education classes in all industrial areas. He was to serve the Association for 42 years and acted as its president from 1928 to 1945. In 1906 he accepted an economics post at Glasgow University, happy at least that it was in an industrial city. It was in Glasgow that his career as a leader-writer on educational matters developed, mainly for the *Manchester Guardian*. Teaching working people was his ultimate goal, however, and in 1909 he moved to Manchester with his new wife Jeanette Beveridge to teach in the potteries of Longton, Littleborough and Rochdale. These classes were sponsored by the Oxford University Tutorial Classes Committee and were later to become a model for adult education in England.

In his lectures Tawney's politics were clear. He had been active in the Fabian Society from 1906, the ILP from 1909 and had eventually joined the Labour Party in 1918. While he was happy to be called a Socialist, he seemed less happy with the description 'Christian Socialist', believing that Christian values should influence all things but could not be defined by particular policy or exclusively claimed by any one party.

Tawney's teaching career soon brought him back to London as Director of the Ratan Tata Foundation, an offshoot of the London School of Economics. The Foundation's mandate was to promote the study and further the knowledge of methods of preventing and relieving poverty and destitution. It provided Tawney with the opportunity to research poverty in his distinctive manner, which he deliberately contrasted with the current fashion for gathering odd statistics and anecdotes. In his words, he would 'focus on the causes not symptoms, structures not individuals, remedies not palliatives, the normal not the abnormal'.[11] Tawney thus pioneered a much more methodical and systematic approach to research on social problems.

A moral framework

By 1914, Tawney had developed a unified framework for his work, whether educational, social or industrial. This framework was a moral one, a belief that in the final analysis morals underpin human society. He wrote in his diary:

> The industrial problem is a moral problem ... a problem of learning as a community to reprobate certain courses of conduct and to approve others. It ought to be possible to place certain principles of social and economic conduct outside the sphere of party politics as agreed upon the conscience of the nation. Could not one find some formula expressing the attitude of all good men to social questions, which should be so entrenched in public conviction to be drawn into dispute by no party?[12]

Anthony Wright argues that the basis of Tawney's thinking on social issues was the well of moral knowledge that is 'the common property of Christian nations'.[13] 'Tawney believed without apology or embarrassment that it is quite possible to distinguish "right" from "wrong", in economic affairs no less than in private conduct. And that the failure to act upon this distinction is the source of the contemporary social and industrial unrest.'[14]

In applying this to the pre-war years of industrial strife, Tawney argued that the source of social conflict was not just a struggle for higher wages but a demand for a new moral order in industry. He believed that the legitimate human demand for liberty was now being met to a degree in the Church and in politics but had yet to come to the workplace. For Tawney the supreme evil was not poverty but the absence of liberty and opportunity for self-direction and control over the material conditions of one's own life. The denial of liberty was therefore the most frustrating and dehumanizing element in modern industrial society. Tawney would maintain this principle throughout his life and wrote in 1926 that the chief end of man is not the making of wealth but the freedom of the spirit: 'No increase in wealth will compensate them for arrangements which insult their self-respect and impair their freedom.'[15]

World War I

Tawney fought in World War I and almost died while lying wounded and unrescued for 24 hours with dead colleagues all around him. The war heightened his sense of urgency about the need to secure the democracy for which it was fought. 'We need to close the gap between the ideals in whose name millions were fighting and dying and the social reality of home,' he said.[16]

Nonetheless, his view of a humanity created to be free did not extend to an idealistic view of mankind. The war reinforced his belief that while humans were only 'a little lower than the angels' (Hebrews 2:7), they were also subject to the frailty and failure of human nature. Tawney grappled with the nature of original sin, torturously defining it in the following terms: 'The goodness we have reached is a house built on piles driven into black slime and always slipping down into it unless we are building night and day.'[17]

Later in life he acknowledged that, despite the Labour Movement's ideals of community and co-operation, it seemed to have done very little to change people's basic motivation and character. He believed that Christianity was for 'bad' people like himself, and in this he shared the theology of the Puritans – those very zealots of individualism and social withdrawal for whom he reserved his greatest criticism.[18]

Involvement with industry

This idea of a new moral order based on liberty and legitimately demanded by the workers informed Tawney's increasingly public critique of industry. He exerted a considerable influence on the Church of England's Archbishop's Fifth Report, *Christianity and Industrial Problems* (1918). This was one of the Church's first efforts to develop a Christian response to industrial problems and called for mutual respect and harmonious co-operation between worker and employer. Individual freedom was emphasized as a priority, to be pursued through the provision of a living wage and adequate leisure: 'We hold that the payment of such a wage in return for such hours of work ought to be the first charge upon every industry.'[19] It condemned an excessive self-interest that degraded workers to mere 'hands' and challenged the extremes of wealth and poverty that made workers so insecure. The Report's detractors included Bishop Henson of Durham, who described it – fairly accurately – as a Socialist tract and a dangerous pamphlet.

Tawney's influence concerning industry was not confined to the Church and in 1919 both he and Sidney Webb represented the trade union side in the first Royal Commission on the mining industry, under Justice Sankey. Unlike its 1925/6 counterpart, it narrowly recommended nationalization as a means by which the industry could be reformed. If Lloyd George had agreed to this recommendation, then the General Strike of 1926 might have been avoided. Tawney believed – perhaps naïvely – that the workers in the newly nationalized mines would simply desist from trying to extract more concessions from their government owners through a sense of unity with the public at large.

Shortly afterwards Tawney's first major book, *The Sickness of an Aquisitive Society* (1921), described a nation suffering from the disease of inequality. This disease, he said, could only be cured through mutual respect and fellowship, through no longer treating people as a means to an end but as unique individuals. Like St Paul, Tawney believed in essential human dignity: 'There is neither Jew nor Greek, slave nor free, male nor female, for you are all one in Christ Jesus' (Galatians 3:28). *Religion and the Rise of Capitalism* (1926) was Tawney's second major work and was followed by his third, *Equality*, in 1931. Here he built on the work of the nineteenth-century political theorist Matthew Arnold, who believed that any system founded on inequality was 'against nature' and would ultimately break down. The task of individuals, governments and any civilized society, Tawney wrote, 'is to aim at eliminating inequalities as have their source, not in individual differences, but in its own organization'.[20]

Tawney and Temple

Tawney's relationship with the Church was reinforced through his lifelong friendship with William Temple, who later became Archbishop of Canterbury. They had arrived together as schoolboys at Rugby and both went on to Balliol. Temple wrote extensively on Christianity and social ethics and like Tawney he embraced the Labour Party as a means of securing social justice. Temple compared Labour's ideal of brotherhood with the Pauline image of believers as the body of Christ. In his contribution to the Pan-Anglican Congress in 1908 he spoke of the justice and essential Christianity of the Labour Movement, and he believed that the Church needed the Labour Movement and the Labour Movement needed the Church. For Temple the choice was clear, 'between Socialism and heresy, between Christ and selfish individualism'.[21]

With Temple in the Church and Tawney in the world, the two men provided each other with mutual support in their respective spheres of influence. This was especially true when dealing with critics such as Bishop Henson of Durham, who denounced Tawney's attempts to see economic matters as an area where morality or the Church had something to offer. Tawney's faith remained personal, however, and he rarely spoke about the basis of his beliefs. Yet his relationship with Temple kept him close to the Church and he remained a frequent churchgoer and one-time lay Reader. In later life his wife Jeanette also became a Christian, something Tawney had always hoped for. Whatever his outward expression of faith, there is little doubt that Christianity remained the core of his philosophy. His *Commonplace Book*, published posthumously in 1972, provides the clearest expression of his religious and political faith.

Education for all

Tawney's interest was not merely to analyse society but to change it. This was why he also set out to write Labour Party policy, including 'Secondary Education for All' (1922) and, two years later, 'Education: The Socialist Policy' (1924). These remain two of the major statements on education in Labour's history and Tawney's involvement in 'The Education of the Adolescent', with its proposals for universal education, formed the basis of the 1944 Education Act. In her diaries, Beatrice Webb comments that C.P. Trevelyan, Labour's first President of the Board of Education, got his ideas from Tawney,[22] and Terrill adds, 'Forty-five years and the Wilson governments later, these ideas had been little surpassed and still not entirely implemented.'[23]

Labour's 1928 manifesto commitment to secondary education for all was a direct result of the Hadow Report, set up when Labour was in government in 1924. The Education Act of 1918 had instructed local authorities to set up a universal education system for children up to the age of 14, but these aspirations were frustrated by government cutbacks. In the 1920s three-quarters of the country's children received an elementary education from the age of five, but only 7.5 per cent received secondary education. Most secondary schools charged fees, although some free places were available for those successful in exams at the age of 11. This led the Labour Party to adopt its 1928 manifesto pledge: 'That all normal children, irrespective of their income, class or occupation of their parents, may be transferred at the age of 11+ from the primary or preparatory school to one type or another of secondary school and remain in the latter till sixteen.'

For Tawney education was a great liberator from the limited opportunities that many working people experienced. Education would fan the flame of social change that he yearned would burn ever brighter. His own lecturing provided a small means to this end. The revolutionary nature of educating working people was appreciated by both Tawney and his enemies, including Dean Inge, Professor of Divinity at Cambridge, who commented, 'In the past the public schoolman has been exposed only to the natural competition of his own class, recruited very sparingly from below. But now our sons have to meet the artificial competition deliberately created by the Government, who are educating the children of the working man, at our expense, in order that they may take the bread out of our children's mouths.'[24]

Tawney's far-reaching influence resulted in him being embraced by both the left and right within the Labour Party. Hugh Gaitskell described him as 'the democratic Socialist *par excellence*',[25] while Michael Foot wrote in response, 'Those who might quarrel with Gaitskell about everything else would not dissent from that verdict.'[26] Tawney played a key role in the Labour Party in opposition after the General Strike as well as after the crisis of the 1931 National Government. He largely wrote the policy goals in *Labour and the Nation*, the major document set before the party conference in October 1928. These goals were overwhelmingly approved and included free education for all, the development of health and social services and the nationalization of many major industries, among them coal, power and transport. Tawney also drafted the 1934 manifesto document *For Socialism and Peace* under the very different leadership of George Lansbury. As Anthony Wright concludes, 'He was a leading party theorist and in every sense a party man.'[27]

The problem of unemployment

As both theorist and activist, Tawney also addressed the issue of unemployment, one of the most pressing social issues in the 1920s and '30s. He had become involved in practical unemployment relief at Toynbee Hall, but also argued to the Poor Law Commission that unemployment should be treated as an industrial disease – as it was in Germany – and not as the failure of the individual.

The reality of unemployment was a problem that would severely challenge successive Labour and Conservative Governments between the wars. From a pre-war boom, the number of unemployed had grown to over 2 million by the winter of 1921/2, falling only slowly throughout the 1920s. Behind these figures lay serious structural problems for heavy industry, since throughout that decade almost every heavy industry suffered a 20 per cent contraction in business from its pre-war heights. Shipping, steel, coal and textiles all saw a reduction in their workforces in areas where large-scale unemployment was already common.

Political arguments between the wars were therefore mainly about the best way to deal with the problems of unemployment and the economy. When Labour returned to power in 1929 it did so on a manifesto that promised more jobs for the unemployed and more social security for those without work. This would have been a huge challenge for any government, but the structural problems in heavy industry and the coming economic crash were to make it impossible for Labour.

Labour's return to power

Such failure was still in the future, however, when the Conservatives called a General Election in May 1929 after four and a half years in power, years which had included the General Strike. People's concern about jobs, plus the sense that Labour was now a party for the whole nation, resulted in success outside its traditional strongholds in Cheshire, Yorkshire and the West Midlands. Labour secured 37.1 per cent of the vote and 288 seats in the Commons. This left the Conservatives with 260 seats and the Liberals with 59. For the first time in its history Labour was the largest political party, with an agenda for reform. The party was jubilant in the immediate aftermath of the election, but within a few short years its jubilation would turn to despair.

In his second Government, Ramsay MacDonald appointed Arthur Henderson as Foreign Secretary, Philip Snowden as Chancellor, George Lansbury as head of the Office of Works and Margaret Bondfield as Minister for Labour, the first female Cabinet minister. For Margaret Bondfield, however, the appointment was a poisoned chalice. The combined difficulties of structural unemployment and the global economic downturn would bring an end not only to her career but also to the Government.

Margaret Bondfield

For Bondfield this was to be a particularly tragic end to what had been a pioneering career as a leader in the trade unions and in the Labour Party. Bondfield was not only the first woman Cabinet member and first woman Minister for Labour, but she had played an important role in the party since its foundations in the ILP and LRC. She was the first woman Privy Councillor and one of the first half-dozen women MPs. She had pioneered the role of women in the male-dominated culture of the trade unions, becoming the first female chair of the TUC and twice Chief Women's Officer of the General and Municipal Workers' Union. Throughout this remarkable career in politics and the unions she continued to benefit from her childhood faith in God. Her biographer Lockwood notes that 'she was sustained as always by the strong Christian faith which had been the mainspring of her public service and growing serenity'.[28]

Early background

Margaret Bondfield was unusual among Labour leaders, not only as a woman but in coming from the Southwest. Born in 1873 in Furnham, near Chard, she was the tenth child in a family of 11. While her family experienced overcrowding, they were never hungry because their cottage had a large fruit and vegetable garden attached to it. In common with other Labour leaders, Bondfield had a Christian upbringing and had actively embraced the Christian faith. Her family had been steeped in religion and politics for generations – her grandfather was a Wesleyan minister and her father an active Congregationalist and political radical. He was a supporter of the Methodist and Chartist tradition that had produced the Tolpuddle Martyrs (also in the Southwest) in 1834. At 13 Bondfield became a teacher/pupil at the Chard elementary school where she had been taught as a young child. Later she went to work and live in Brighton as a shop assistant, working up to 80 hours a week for an annual salary of between £15 and £25.

Political activism

It was in Brighton that the progressive Liberal and advocate for women's rights, Mrs Martindale, became Bondfield's mentor and began to influence her political direction. Bondfield moved to London in 1894 and experienced even worse conditions for shop assistants than she had suffered in Brighton. The 'live-in' system denied women workers any freedom and involved poor, cramped and unhealthy accommodation. Lockwood says, 'The injustice of the system fired Margaret with an enthusiasm to do something about it.'[29] When buying fish and chips one evening, Bondfield noticed a letter in the evening paper. It was written by the Union of Shop Assistants, Warehousemen and Clerks and urged shop workers to join in order to gain improvements in their working conditions. Bondfield immediately joined up and was soon active in the union. It was not long before she was elected to the London District Council and became a delegate to the union's national conference.

During this time she also met other London radicals, including Ramsay MacDonald, the Webbs and George Bernard Shaw. Their influence and arguments convinced her of the merits of Socialism and she soon became an advocate for the cause. Although initially attracted to the Social Democratic Federation, Bondfield never accepted their emphasis on violent class war, and instead she chose the Independent Labour Party as a means to combine her political radicalism and religious faith.

Bondfield's increasing involvement with the union led her to undertake some serious research into the conditions of shop workers. In 1898 the Women's Industrial Council published her report. The revelations about the harsh conditions and long hours endured by shop workers caused an outcry. It provoked a House of Lords enquiry in 1901 which formed the basis of the Shop Hours Act (1904). Bondfield found it increasingly difficult to get work because of her union activities, however, so instead she became the full-time secretary of her union. At the turn of the century membership grew rapidly from 3,000 in 1898 to 7,500 in 1900 as people began to see the union as an effective route to improving their conditions.

Bondfield also became a member of the Women's Trade Union League and in 1899 attended the Trades Union Congress as the only female delegate. She strongly advocated independent labour representation in Parliament and supported the meeting of trade unionist and Socialist societies on 27 February 1900. 'Her speech made a great impression ... she told them that the unions must get together for political action if they were to achieve their larger aims.'[30]

Pioneer for women

She continued to pioneer women's causes in the workplace and in politics. In 1906 Bondfield and Ramsay MacDonald started the Women's Labour League specifically to promote and educate women in

Labour politics. The growing support for women's suffrage did not secure universal support in the Labour Party, however, and a motion in favour of women's suffrage was defeated at the party conference in Belfast in 1907. The ILP was the first group to give the cause its practical support.

Outside the party there was growing militancy in the wider suffragette movement towards Prime Minister Bannerman's fine words but lack of action. When the split between the law-abiding and militant suffragettes occurred, Bondfield remained on the peaceful side and became a national officer of the National Union of Women's Suffrage Societies (NUWSS). Labour's 1912 conference finally voted in favour of adult suffrage, causing the NUWSS to back pro-suffrage Labour candidates in the by-elections before World War I. The war would have a dramatic impact on the place of women in society and in 1918 the Liberal Government granted the vote to all women over 30 (although this meant they were still not on equal footing with men).

At the start of the war Bondfield had resigned her role in the NUWSS over its attitude to the conflict and although she was not a pacifist she spoke against the war, opposed conscription and called for a negotiated peace. It was during the war that Bondfield first began to promote equal pay for women, as she saw women workers doing the same jobs as men but being paid less. She was to have a long time to wait for success on this front, however, as equal pay would not come until the Equal Pay Act in 1970, under a future Labour Government.

Early parliamentary roles

After the war Bondfield was elected to the Parliamentary Committee of the TUC and she travelled with the Labour/TUC delegation to assess the Soviet revolution. She also began to look for a parliamentary seat and in 1920 and 1922 stood unsuccessfully in Northampton. In 1923, however, she again stood as the Labour candidate there and this time was successful. During the campaign MacDonald pledged his personal support for her and George Bernard Shaw patronizingly described Bondfield as 'the best man of the lot'. In the same year she was elected the first woman President of the TUC General Council, but did not take up her presidency because of her election to Westminster. Both results reflect Bondfield's remarkable success in reaching the top of a male-dominated world.

As one of the first female MPs, Bondfield quickly established an effective role as advocate for women workers. In Labour's first Government of 1924 she was parliamentary secretary to the Minister for Labour, Thomas Shaw. It was a difficult job as she had to defend the Government's record in the context of rising unemployment, but she was also able to support rises in unemployment benefit and a large programme of relief work. Nevertheless, more than any other Labour leader Bondfield experienced the difficulties of delivering on Labour's promises of more jobs and better working conditions. In the General Election at the end of 1924 she lost her Northampton seat but, under the direction of Arthur Henderson, she was recommended for the constituency of Wallsend in a 1926 by-election. Lockwood describes the scene:

> ...20,000 people milled around outside the Town Hall waiting for the result. As the Returning Officer announced the Bondfield victory, bright summer bonnets were thrown into the air. Women danced in the street; men broke into song, and a general chant was heard: 'Maggie MP ... Maggie MP'. Housewives in one Wallsend block had made a special victory cake inscribed 'Maggie MP', a cake which cost the women more than they could really afford – such was their delight at the victory.[31]

Bondfield's time in Westminster would again be controversial, however. She became a member of a Commons committee established by the Conservatives to investigate the escalating costs of unemployment benefit. Its report recommended the lowering of the benefit and in some cases cutting it completely. In supporting the report, Bondfield appeared to collude with the enemy against the workers. The Conservatives later implemented its recommendations in the Unemployment Insurance Act (1927) and it was a bitter pill for the Labour Movement to swallow. There was outrage from almost everyone – the unions, Bondfield's constituency, the Labour Party and the TUC. Bondfield defended her position, believing that on balance the report was fair, and pointed to the fact that certain groups would now receive unemployment benefit for the first time.

Nonetheless, the controversy surrounding this issue led to Bondfield being challenged in her Wallsend constituency. Her reputation as a union woman, outsider and betrayer of the unemployed led the

National Unemployed Workers' Movement to field a candidate against her in the 1929 election. Despite this opposition, Bondfield retained the support of the unions and was returned with a majority of 7,105, one of the new Labour Government's 288 seats.

Minister for Labour

Labour's second Government started well for Bondfield, with her appointment as Minister for Labour and Britain's first female Cabinet minister. In those early months she achieved some minor successes by persuading the Treasury to increase contributions to the Unemployment Insurance Fund, ease qualification criteria and extend provisions for the long-term unemployed. Events were soon to overtake the good intentions of Bondfield and the Government, however. International markets would again affect domestic politics, just as they had done in creating the conditions that led to the General Strike. After the May election, MacDonald made an historic trip as the first British Prime Minister to visit the United States. Yet within weeks of his return a financial crash on Wall Street sent shock waves around the world from which MacDonald's Government would not recover.

Economic disaster

It was a rude awakening for Labour's reforming plans and the optimism of the late 1920s was soon replaced by despondency over growing unemployment. American business confidence had been shattered and its knock-on effect saw Britain's trade plunge. Within a year of the crash, unemployment had doubled from 1 million to 2 million and Labour's ability to deal with the economic crisis was limited. A.J. Davies records that Chancellor Philip Snowden was 'wedded to traditional ideas of free trade, the gold standard and *laissez faire*, and pinned his hopes on world economic recovery. When this didn't happen he was lost.'[32] Snowden and MacDonald appeared paralysed by the crisis that now engulfed them. The economic orthodoxy of the day demanded that the Government should cut costs, which included cuts in wages and unemployment benefits. At the same time the Government was caught between the twin pressures of rising unemployment costs and lower tax revenues from employees.

Cabinet member J.H. Thomas suggested large-scale road-building to tackle unemployment, but Snowden vetoed this as too expensive. By February 1930 another Cabinet member, Oswald Mosley, was appealing for import and banking controls and increased pensions to boost spending, but this was also rejected on grounds of cost. (Mosley later resigned from the Government to form a new party that would eventually become the British Union of Fascists.) As the effects of the global depression grew and unemployment continued to rise, Ramsay MacDonald personally took responsibility for the issue. He was still forced to rely on the advice of others, however, and was provided with no concrete proposals with which he could challenge the unyielding orthodoxies of Chancellor Snowden. In March 1931, in desperation and tacit admission of defeat, MacDonald set up a cross-party committee to seek agreement on the best way to tackle Britain's economic ills. The move reflected MacDonald's interest in co-operation for the sake of the country, but it was to prove a disastrous strategy both for him and for Labour.

The cross-party Sir George May Committee predicted a massive budget deficit and recommended an increase in taxes and a cut of £67 million from unemployment benefits. Most commentators now agree that this analysis was inaccurate and the committee's recommendations would do more damage than good. A minority report issued by two Labour members of the committee was in fact more realistic and helpful. Nevertheless, MacDonald and Snowden accepted the majority report and embarked on a desperate round of budget proposals, including cuts to teachers' and police pay and a 10 per cent cut in unemployment payments. The Labour Cabinet amended and then accepted the proposals, but the Conservatives and Liberals rejected the amendments as inadequate. The unions also rejected them, as they never accepted the May Committee's analysis in the first place.

The end of the second Labour Government

As the battle raged, MacDonald shuttled between Cabinet, unions, opposition leaders and eventually the King. In the summer of 1931, however, financial crisis overtook such political manoeuvring and immediate credits were needed from America and France. These would only be delivered if the British Government adopted radical cuts acceptable to both the Bank of England and the City of London. MacDonald went to the Cabinet for the last time to say that the cuts negated all Labour stood for, but were necessary for the sake of the national interest. The Cabinet split 11 to 9 on the issue and the resignation of Labour's second Government became inevitable.

Worse was to come. When MacDonald went to advise the King of his resignation, the King persuaded him to assume the leadership of a new National Government – an all-party coalition. MacDonald agreed and asked the current Cabinet for their support. Only three of them – Thomas, Snowden and Sankey – gave it. In his national broadcast in August 1931, MacDonald said in his own defence, 'I have changed none of my ideals. I have a national duty.'[33]

Although Margaret Bondfield did not follow MacDonald into his National Government, she was a political casualty of Labour's drastic electoral defeat in October 1931. Tragically her efforts as Minister for Labour had been frustrated by circumstances beyond her control. Nevertheless, she was guilty of accepting and even actively defending the Treasury's demand to balance the books and often said it was dishonest to borrow from the unemployment fund. As Hugh Dalton remarked in 1953, this was plainly bad advice from her officials. 'It was not sensible to try to balance the unemployment fund. Clearly this should show a deficit in years of heavy, and a surplus in years of light, unemployment.'[34] Bondfield never regained the confidence of the voters and when she stood for Parliament again in 1935 she was unsuccessful. Despite this less than glorious end to her career, she retained the remarkable claim of being Britain's and Labour's first female Cabinet member.

Following MacDonald's departure, R.H. Tawney also remained faithful to the Labour Party. In 1932 he published *The Choice before the Labour Party*, which contained his analysis on what had gone wrong in 1931. His belief was that Labour still had no firmly agreed set of goals for their political programme and needed a resolute commitment to Socialism. As Tawney himself had acknowledged, however, there were different kinds of Socialism and, as Labour headed off into opposition in 1931, it had plenty of time to explore them all.

Chapter 6

Unemployed

George Lansbury and Ellen Wilkinson:
1931–9

*A*fter MacDonald's defection, Labour was in a state of shock. Not only had it lost someone who had been a leader since 1900, but it also lost four-fifths of its MPs in the subsequent General Election. Only three former ministers remained: George Lansbury, Clement Attlee and Stafford Cripps. The party's choice of leader was first Arthur Henderson and then George Lansbury. This was consistent with its attempts to return to first principles. Lansbury was from the generation of Keir Hardie and one of the few remaining pioneers. Like a marathon runner, he had remained for the long haul and now in Labour's darkest hour he provided stability and consolation.

Lansbury served the Labour Party from 1892 to 1940, but was leader for only four of these years. The others were spent preaching Socialism in his distinctive evangelistic style, in streets, factories and churches and through his writings. He was a humorous and charismatic politician and A.J. Davies said of him, 'He was certainly one of the most attractive and appealing personalities that the British Left has ever produced. Photographs of him invariably show a happy smiling man whose obvious sense of humour contrasts with the severity of, say, Keir Hardie.'[1] Lansbury was also a Christian and for him Socialism was an expression of practical Christianity. 'I am a socialist pure and simple,' he said. 'I have come to believe that the power which should and which will, if men allow it, work our social salvation, is the power which comes from a belief in Christ and his message to man.'[2]

Lansbury would not take the party back to electoral victory, which earned him the title of 'ineffective leader' in Labour's official history. Yet he did save Labour from further decline, and he saved Britain from becoming *a one-party Conservative state. Clement Attlee said that Lansbury had inherited a demoralized party of just 52 MPs, but had turned them into an effective opposition. 'He was successful in inspiring and leading this little band, thus, as Mr Baldwin said at the time, saving Parliamentary Government.'*[3]

Repairing the damage

The first act of Ramsay MacDonald's National Government in August 1931 was to vote through its budget cuts. Twelve Labour MPs supported them, alongside 296 Conservatives and Liberals. Labour's national executive and the TUC denounced the cuts and voted to expel all supporting Labour MPs. The internecine war between former colleagues had begun and would culminate in Labour's dramatic collapse in the October 1931 General Election. Ex-Labour Chancellor Philip Snowden described Labour's election manifesto as 'Bolshevism run mad' and his departure from the party was especially bitter.

Yet in the dark days of 1931 it was not so much a party split as the straightforward departure of a leader and his closest allies. No trade union or affiliated organization had left the party. Labour's reputation as a serious party of government had been damaged nevertheless, and in the General Election its parliamentary presence was pushed back to 1906 levels. The Conservatives won an overwhelming 554 seats, leaving Labour with just 52 and the Liberals with 35. Labour had emerged almost *ex nihilo* to become by 1929 the largest parliamentary party. It had offered political salvation to the heavily laden workers, but had now abused their trust. The people turned on the people's party and abandoned them at the ballot box. In two short and miserable years Labour had experienced a political disaster equal to that of any financial crash. Now the party faced a new challenge: to rebuild or die. Could it ever gain the trust of the British people again?

Recovery in opposition

There was some hope amongst the hopelessness. If Labour had not yet become in any lasting sense the natural party of government, it had secured a role as the natural opposition. Labour's drubbing had not benefited the Liberals and the party was still well placed to fight another day. Although Labour's vote had fallen by almost 2 million since 1929, this was not the main reason for its collapse from 288 to 52 seats. The main difficulty was that Labour candidates had to fight against a united opposition on the National Government ticket.

In opposition one of the party's first tasks was to establish a National Joint Council. This would include Labour's national executive, the parliamentary party and the TUC General Council. It aimed to ensure that the party in Parliament would never again lose the trust of the wider Labour Movement and would never again fracture in the way it had so recently done. The party was determined to avoid the splits of the past and in 1932 the party conference passed a resolution overturning MacDonald's previous claim to be autonomous as leader of the parliamentary party. Future Labour leaders would take instructions from the national conference, and the 1932 conference also voted that Socialism and common ownership should be immediately implemented when Labour was back in power. The mood of the battered party was therefore a firm rejection of the perceived compromises of the past. In trying to emerge from the betrayal perpetrated by its parliamentary leaders, it sought to restate the certainties of old.

Before any new goals could be met, however, Labour had to choose a new leader. Although Arthur Henderson had lost his seat, the party turned to him in the short term before electing George Lansbury as leader in January 1932. At that time Lansbury was in his seventy-second year and it was an onerous task for such an old man. Despite his age, Lansbury was nonetheless still a strong and forthright speaker. Attlee described him as 'one of the most forcible speakers on socialist platforms ... his magnificent physique enabled him to undertake a tremendous programme in which his passionate sincerity had great effect.'[4] A.J.P. Taylor wrote that Lansbury 'was the obvious choice as leader ... His humble position as first commissioner of works did not represent his real standing in the Labour Movement. He had long been a national figure, who could command audiences as big as MacDonald's and would have been a member of Labour's Big Four or Big Five if it had not been for MacDonald's dislike of him.'[5]

George Lansbury

Lansbury was born on 21 February 1859 in a Suffolk tollhouse. His father worked on the railways and this later took the family to Sydenham, where Lansbury first went to school at the age of eight. The family then moved again, to Whitechapel, where at St Mary's School he developed his passion for books and also his flair for campaigning – by organizing a successful petition among the children for some playtime. As a teenager he worked with his brothers on night shifts for the Great Eastern Railway. This meant that his days were free, and he would either watch cricket or go to the House of Commons for a debate, an activity that betrayed his latent interest in politics. Work on the railways exposed him to the casualness with which workers' lives were treated and he personally knew four men who had been crushed to death as they coupled wagons by hand.

At this point in his life Lansbury was not religious and in fact admired the rationalist preachers who taught that religion was simply a means to keep the poor quiet. Then he met Father Kitto, an Anglo-Catholic priest who taught that Christianity was a practical religion expressed in what you did at work and at home. Kitto himself put his faith into action by serving and living amongst the poor and working class. Through Father Kitto, Lansbury was confirmed in the Church and immediately became involved in practical tasks and speaking at meetings. The Church became a focus for the development of his social work and campaigning activities. On Sundays he provided breakfast for the homeless and during the week encouraged his colleagues to join the union for protection against unscrupulous employers. By his late teens he was already a convinced pacifist and rejected the popular view that British colonialism in Africa and Afghanistan was justified.

Later Lansbury met and fell in love with Bessie Brine, a fellow Sunday School teacher, and the couple married on 29 May 1880. Following the death of his mother, the Lansburys' own three children were joined by two of George's younger brothers. Times were hard and a better life was offered in Australia, so in 1884 the family set sail for Brisbane. It was an unsuccessful venture, however, with no welcome and great difficulty in finding work. When the children fell sick the family were finally persuaded to take up Bessie's mother's offer of tickets home. Yet Australia had helped to crystallize Lansbury's thinking. On the journey out he saw exploitation in every port and experienced rejection himself as an immigrant, with the possibility of his family starving through lack of work. With no social security, desperate workers fought for often dangerous employment in unregulated businesses.

From Liberal to Labour

On his return to the East End of London things were little better, although Lansbury did get work in his father-in-law's yard. Despite the hardships in his own life, however, his eyes had been opened to the needs of others and he was determined to respond. He started with what he knew best and addressed a Liberal conference in 1886 on the need to combat the propaganda of emigration societies. His campaign was immediately successful and a deputation to the Liberal Government persuaded them to set up the Emigration Information Service. Lansbury met the influential Liberal MP Samuel Montagu, who saw in him the kind of person who could secure support for his party from the working class. Lansbury soon became Montagu's election agent as well as the unpaid secretary of the Bow and Bromley Liberals.

Lansbury's connections with Liberalism were short-lived. Against advice, he insisted on pressing the issue of an eight-hour working day at the 1889 national conference. For Liberal supporters of unregulated capitalism, this was too much to bear and Lansbury was hounded from the platform. Nevertheless, his appetite for politics had been whetted and he now looked for a new political home. Samuel Montagu refused to lose his young protégé so easily, however, and offered Lansbury a salary and a safe parliamentary seat. Lansbury later recalled the conversation:

> I told him I had become a socialist and wanted to preach socialism. He replied: 'Don't be silly, I am a socialist, a better socialist than you. I give a tenth of my riches each year to the poor.' I said: 'Yes, I know how good you are and respect you more than it is possible to say, but, my dear friend, we socialists want to prevent you getting the nine-tenths. We do not believe in rich and poor and charity. We want to create wealth and all the means of life and share them equally among the people.'[6]

Lansbury left the Liberals and formed the Bow and Bromley branch of the Social Democratic Federation after learning about the SDF's goal for worker representation in Parliament. This was the year of the London Dock Strike and Lansbury learned more about Socialism from the strike's leaders, Ben Tillet, Will Crooks and Will Thorn. After the strike Lansbury joined the National Union of Municipal and General Workers and enjoyed using the argument that 'the first strike I ever read of was that of the Children of Israel, who refused to make bricks without straw'.[7] Through the SDF Lansbury embarked on a career of preaching Socialism and seeking election. He was first elected in 1892 as a Guardian of the Poplar Union alongside Will Crooks. Together they transformed the Poplar workhouses and changed the way that England dealt with its poorest people.[8]

The Church Socialist League

Under the influence of the SDF's anti-clericalism, Lansbury withdrew his family from the Church. He had become disillusioned with clergy who denounced strikes and tolerated poverty. Yet according to his son, the years between 1890 and 1900 were not happy ones and Lansbury eventually returned to the Church. He began to integrate his politics and faith in a much more coherent way, helping to form the Church Socialist League in 1906.

The CSL was a predominantly Anglican society committed to economic Socialism. Its founding statement read, 'The Church Socialist League consists of Church people who accept the principles of socialism: the political, economic and social emancipation of the whole people, men and women, by the establishment of a democratic commonwealth in which the community shall own the land and capital collectively and use them for the good of all.'[9] It was the kind of definition that even Labour would not have until 1918. Despite its sacramental emphasis, the CSL also attracted Nonconformists. While some wanted to affiliate the CSL to the Labour Party, however, the majority remained in favour of nonalignment, seeing their business as simply converting Christians to Socialism.

Lansbury worked hard for the CSL as well as writing regularly in the religious press. In Halifax in 1912 he preached on the equality of all people in God's eyes. If working people understood this, 'they would not be content with the present conditions in which their women lived, and they would not be content to let their children go into the mills and factories at 12 or 13 years of age'.[10] During World War I Lansbury wrote *Your Part in Poverty* (1917), arguing that practical Christianity would lead to a Socialist state. In the book's foreword the Bishop of Winchester challenged Lansbury's argument, but expressed his desire to prevent 'churchmanship being bound up with Toryism'. While some agreed with Lansbury, others claimed that the Christian's duty was simply to obey those in authority, and still others that politics and Christianity should be kept separate.[11]

The attacks Lansbury made on Church complacency about poverty and unemployment took on greater significance now that he himself was back in the fold. His son wrote of that time, 'His regular attendance at Church and interest in the Parish filled some of his socialist friends with disgust. They had the common but erroneous notion that even real Christians were more concerned with the next world than with this.'[12]

MP for Bromley and Bow

Lansbury first stood as an SDF parliamentary candidate in Walworth in the 1890s and in Bromley and Bow in 1900. In 1903 he chose to stand under the newly formed Labour Representation Committee, and subsequently stood in Middlesbrough in 1906 and as the Labour candidate in Bromley and Bow in 1910. In the second election of 1910 he was successful and later commented on the elation he felt in finally achieving his dream of becoming an MP.

He chose to live among his constituents and receive complaints in person, 'even if this meant a brick through the window instead of a letter'.[13] His biographer Postgate described his role as a local MP: 'Almost daily the house in Bow was called at by men and women who were in legal, personal or financial difficulties and G.L. (the initials were by now commonly used) advised and helped.'[14] In Parliament Lansbury continued to campaign on poverty and unemployment and introduced an unsuccessful Bill to secure holiday pay for workers. He also took on wider issues and supported both Indian and Irish self-rule and the abolition of the hereditary House of Lords.

Champion of women's suffrage

The issue that stirred up most controversy for him, however, and 'almost eclipsed his devotion to socialism',[15] was his support for women's suffrage. In the Commons on 25 June 1912, Prime Minister Asquith was being questioned about the force-feeding of suffragettes when he dismissed the women as self-proclaimed lawbreakers. Lansbury later wrote, 'This so infuriated me that I rushed down the House in a white heat of passion, shouting to him that what he was saying was exactly what every tyrant said who had put reformers in prison. That he knew perfectly well none of these women, because of their creed and faith, could submit to the conditions which he laid down.'[16]

It was Christianity that connected Lansbury so deeply to the women's cause. His belief that everyone was equal in God's sight meant that he could not see men as superior to women. He continually challenged a Christian country that so systematically oppressed women. His frustration over the inadequate 1912 Suffrage Bill provoked him to resign his Commons seat and fight the election on women's suffrage. He failed to win the seat back and upset the Labour hierarchy in the process. It was a case of passion over political wisdom and his enthusiasm for the cause eventually took him to prison charged with sedition for supporting the destruction of property. In Pentonville Lansbury went on hunger strike while crowds cheered outside. Fearing a breakdown in law and order, the Government quickly ordered his release. It would not be the last time Lansbury went to prison.

The Poplar rates strike

Throughout World War I Lansbury preached Socialism and pacifism. No longer in the Commons, he continued as a councillor on Poplar Borough Council. In April 1919 Labour gained control of 39 of the 42 seats on the council and Lansbury was elected Poplar's first Labour Mayor. What to do with limited powers in the face of such high levels of poverty was a challenge Lansbury tackled in typically radical fashion over the next few years. The rating system in London meant that social care in the poorest boroughs was the responsibility of the poorest boroughs themselves. Poplar therefore had the biggest bills and the least ability to pay. Lansbury and his councillors appealed to the Government for assistance, but they remained intransigent. In frustration and desperation, the councillors adopted the radical tactic of calling an illegal rates strike. Poplar Council would refuse to pay its levies to other London bodies such as the Metropolitan Police and County Council until a similar London-wide body was established for social care. Local people would be allowed to keep the part of their rates that would normally go to these bodies.

Both the Government and the London Labour Party were infuriated at such tactics, but Lansbury was not for turning. Throughout the summer of 1921 legal action and counteraction proceeded against the councillors, but the law had not been designed to deal with such a confrontation. Eventually, in September 1921, Lansbury and his councillors were sent to prison – six women to Holloway and 25 men to Brixton. Support for their campaign had grown, however, and both Bethnal Green and Stepney Councils declared their intention to follow Poplar's lead. After six weeks in jail the councillors were released and a legal compromise was secured. *The Times* attacked Lansbury for leading a revolutionary movement, but the dispute had ended with Poplar and other poorer boroughs benefiting from the radical action.[17]

Return to Parliament

The 1922 General Election saw Lansbury returned to Parliament as the MP for Bromley and Bow. Despite his stature as a politician, however, MacDonald refused him a place in Labour's first Cabinet of 1924. Sidney Webb later recorded, 'The one glaring omission, so the Labour Party thought, was George Lansbury, who had certainly established a position in the party entitling him to Cabinet rank.'[18] MacDonald seems not to have forgotten Lloyd George's snide remark that it was Lansbury who appeared to be the leader of the opposition.

In Parliament but outside the Government, therefore, Lansbury was able to focus on the wider world and helped form Labour's Commonwealth Group, set up to pursue equality in relationships throughout the British Empire. He also demanded that 'Scotland, Wales and England should each have their own Parliament with a joint committee for matters concerning them all'.[19]

The Office of Works

Lansbury did make it to Labour's second Government in 1929 as First Commissioner of Works. Holman comments, 'To the civil servants, the brief of the Office of Works was to conserve and maintain old buildings and royal parks. To Lansbury, it presented the opportunity to promote play and recreation.'[20] Lansbury's reforms won favourable reviews describing him as the busiest member of the Government. His advocacy of the all-British Lido led the magazine *Time & Tide* to say in its editorial on 29 September 1929 that 'Mr Lansbury is a dreamer and his persistency makes dreams come true. He will be remembered as the First Commissioner for Good Works.'[21]

Despite being a lifelong teetotaller, Lansbury defended others' right to drink. As First Commissioner he granted a drinks licence to the restaurant at Hampton Court, despite a barrage of criticism from prohibitionists in the Commons. A commentator in the *Sunday Express* wrote, 'I hope Mr Lansbury's lead will be followed by municipalities all over the land, so that soon all Britons will enjoy the liberty to drink a glass of beer in their public parks, like Germans, French, and other civilized people who can drink without becoming drunkards.'[22]

The 1931 crisis and beyond

Lansbury was also at the centre of the Government crisis in 1931. MacDonald appointed him, along with Oswald Mosley and R.H. Thomas, to a committee charged with tackling unemployment. Lansbury presented Mosley's proposals to the Cabinet and, like Mosley, was frustrated at Chancellor Snowden's inflexibility. He later wrote of Snowden, 'Once he has been told what to say and do by Treasury officials he never budges.'[23] Lansbury could not support the budget cuts and persuaded Henderson to join the half of the Cabinet which argued that the financial crisis could be dealt with by taxing the rich, not cutting benefits to the poor.

Following the devastation of the 1931 election, Lansbury was one of the few Labour MPs who held his seat, and the only previous member of the Cabinet to do so. With the party traumatized by near destruction, it was to the 72-year-old Lansbury that the 52 remaining MPs now turned for leadership. As Postgate comments, 'The party did not want another

Olympian autocrat, or a Parliamentarian who could slur over difficulties by wordy formulas; it was reeling from the double shock of treachery and defeat. It wanted someone who could restore its confidence in human decency and its belief in its future.'[24]

The future of the party looked bleak, however. It had lost most of its major speakers and its Commons defeats became enormous compared to the past. Then, to add insult to injury, the ILP, the party of Hardie and the pioneers, disaffiliated in 1932 on the grounds that Labour was not sufficiently Socialist. Given this inheritance, it is a wonder that Lansbury was able to build an effective opposition at all. Nevertheless he did and, although Labour was unable to pass any legislation, Lansbury re-established the party as an advocate for the poor and unemployed. In the face of Chancellor Chamberlain's complacency and consumer statistics, Labour again spoke for the millions who were missing out on Britain's so-called prosperity. Despite the powerlessness of opposition, Lansbury succeeded in raising unemployment in the nation's consciousness and conscience.

In 1933, despite the loss of his wife, the 74-year-old Lansbury was still pursuing his Socialist mission. Holman notes that in the country, ordinary Socialists who had been devastated by MacDonald's betrayal took heart from Lansbury's dogged performance as he pressed and challenged the Government. Lansbury appeared to be the ideal leader when unemployment and the economy were the dominant issues. When international affairs took centre stage, however, things were rather different.

Pacifism and the party

In January 1933 Adolf Hitler became Chancellor in Germany. Immediately he made his intentions clear by withdrawing from disarmament agreements and the League of Nations. Lansbury's pacifist stance led Labour's conference of 1933 to vote against rearmament and to agree on a general strike in response to any future war. These views reflected a popular desire for peace and 1933 also saw the Oxford University Union declare, 'This House will in no circumstances fight for its King and Country.' Lansbury became one of the founders of the Peace Pledge Union, which by 1936 had 100,000 members pledged against fighting.

Not everyone in the Labour Movement was pacifist, however. Ernest Bevin of the Transport and General Workers' Union and Hugh Dalton, the Eton- and Cambridge-educated economist, saw Labour's position and Lansbury's leadership as naïve and ineffective. Bevin and Dalton worked hard behind the scenes and at the 1935 conference Bevin ridiculed Lansbury's position during a motion on British rearmament. In response to Lansbury's principled pacifism Bevin accused him of 'hawking your conscience around from body to body asking to be told what to do with it'.[25] The party conference backed Bevin and rearmament this time, and Lansbury was forced to resign as leader. Later, in response to a suggestion that he had been too hard on Lansbury, Bevin replied, 'Lansbury has been going around dressed up in saint's clothes for years waiting for martyrdom. I set fire to the faggots.'[26]

Ernest Bevin

Ernest Bevin had no sympathy for Lansbury's Christian pacifism, despite having once embraced Christianity himself. In 1902 Bevin was baptized in Manor Hall Baptist Church where he worshipped. He was an active member there until 1905 and assisted in its evangelistic campaigns by speaking at the open-air meetings.[27] Even as late as 1909, when Bevin was 28, he contemplated becoming a missionary – at the same time as he first became an organizer for the Dockers' Union. However, the sense of belonging and purpose he had previously found in the Baptist chapel was soon found in his union activities instead. Gradually Bevin came to regard Nonconformity as inadequate, perhaps especially in its response to social injustice.

His later antagonism towards the Church in general was seen in his leadership of a march by the unemployed to Bristol Cathedral. A great crowd of men had assembled in Horsefair, Bristol, and with Bevin at their head they marched to the cathedral for the morning service. They took up places along every aisle and remained there, motionless, throughout the service. Francis Williams describes their prophetic presence, 'many of them clearly in great distress from hunger, all of them poorly clad; a mute challenge to the Christian conscience of every worshipper'.[28] The men filed out at the end of the service and, after a benediction from Bevin, proceeded home without disturbance. Bevin and Lansbury had shared similar journeys of faith, both accepting and then rejecting it. At least part of this rejection was because of the Church's complacency towards social injustice. They both rejected a religion that did not work in real life. Lansbury, however, found his way back, while Bevin remained outside.

Ellen Wilkinson

Throughout the 1930s unemployment remained the dominant political challenge for Britain. It was aptly called 'the devil's decade'. Unemployment figures rarely dropped below 1 million, rose to 2 million in 1931 and peaked at 3 million in 1933. These were wasted years for millions of people – often the same people in the same areas year on year. By the mid-1930s unemployment was concentrated in the industrial areas of the Northeast, Scotland and South Wales and it was often the leadership of Labour MPs in those areas that galvanized the people's spirit and challenged the nation's conscience.

One such MP was Ellen Wilkinson, the Member for Middlesbrough East from 1924 to 1931 and for Jarrow from 1935. Kenneth Morgan describes her as arguably Britain's most important female politician, who made the role of women in high politics credible and effective as no one else had done before. She 'had a dramatic, perhaps decisive, impact on the public conscience, long before the new egalitarian passions of the Second World War'.[29] Donald Soper once claimed that, 'as a result of the Jarrow Crusade, Ellen gave to the Labour Movement and to the political world the concept that unemployment is intoler-able'.[30] Wilkinson's biographer, Betty Vernon, describes her determination and motivation: 'By sheer ability and a driving capacity for hard work Ellen won her way from a humble background to Parliament, the Privy Council and the Cabinet. But behind that ability lay a strength of purpose derived from the Methodist precept to "go for those who need you, especially those who need you most".[31] Morgan also recognizes that Methodism had an enduring impact on Wilkinson's politics: 'This was a lifelong commitment, not merely a phase of adolescent revivalism.'[32]

Faith, education and politics

Ellen Wilkinson was born in Manchester on 8 October 1891, but her mother did not receive proper treatment at Ellen's birth and suffered for the rest of her life. This is one reason why Socialism appealed so greatly to Ellen. Poverty had denied Ellen's mother the medicines and treatment she needed, and had condemned her to a life of pain. The philosophy of Socialism – that all were equal and should receive equal treatment regardless of their wealth – was therefore attractive to Ellen in the light of very personal experience.

Methodism was in the family blood and the chapel in Grosvenor Street, Ardwick, influenced the future of the whole family. When Ellen was unable to go to church she would hold services at home with her grandmother and after singing, she would take the role of the preacher, her grandmother listening intently while her mother looked on, horrified at the irreverence of it all. It was at the Methodist Sunday School foreign missionary festival that Ellen first learned to speak in public.

Her father had also preached, and instilled in his daughter both a Methodist morality and a respect for education. The whole family's commitment to education was demonstrated by her brother Richard's willingness to become a joiner in order to help pay for Ellen's university fees. Afterwards he too went to university, studied theology and became a Methodist minister.

At the age of 15 Ellen won a teacher-training bursary which allowed her to teach half the week at Oswald Road Elementary School and spend the other half at Manchester Day Training College. During this time she read Robert Blatchford's *Merrie England*[33] and was converted to Socialism. She also went to an ILP meeting where, among the rows of men, the diminutive Kathleen Glaiser (Bruce's wife) stood up to speak, transfixing the crowd with her passionate talk on 'Socialism as a religion'. At 16 Wilkinson joined the ILP and threw herself into campaigning for the cause, selling copies of the *Clarion* and handing out leaflets at every opportunity.

In 1910 she went to study history at Manchester University and met Walton Newbold, the son of a wealthy Liberal Irish Quaker. Both of them were politically active, Wilkinson in the University Socialist Federation and Newbold as director of the University Fabian Society. They became engaged despite their family's disapproval and, although the engagement did not last, they were to remain friends and fellow activists. While Wilkinson was committed to the Labour Party, she was also sympathetic to the more radical politics espoused by Newbold. She joined with him and others to found the British Communist Party in 1920, although she left within a year. Newbold himself went on to become a Communist MP.

A determined campaigner

At the height of the women's suffrage struggle before World War I, Wilkinson joined the National Union of Women's Suffrage Societies (NUWSS). She became an able organizer and speaker with an ability to face hostile crowds and deal with heckling through the warmth and wit of her personality. As a pacifist she also supported the Non-Conscription Fellowship during the war and later, in 1934, she was to become a founding member of the Peace Pledge Union. Her pacifism could not be sustained, however, and she eventually withdrew from the PPU, citing the necessity of fighting Fascism.

After leaving university in 1915 she worked as the first female organizer of the National Union of Distributive and Allied Workers (NUDAW). This enabled her to become active in local politics and in 1923 she was elected to serve on the Manchester City Council. Parliament was now Wilkinson's goal, however, and she tried for a seat in Ashton-under-Lyne in 1923 and again in Middlesbrough at the General Election in 1924. That time, despite being up against able male candidates, Wilkinson was selected as Labour's candidate and won with a majority of 927 votes. With Margaret Bondfield now gone and the other female MPs representing other parties, Wilkinson was Labour's only female MP. She became known as 'Red Ellen', both for her politics and for the colour of her hair.

Fights for women

In Parliament Wilkinson immediately became involved in campaigning on women's issues, not least concerning her own conditions at Westminster. The cramped and inadequate facilities meant she had to share an office with two others, Lady Nancy Astor and Mrs Philipson, while the Duchess of Atholl had her own office as a junior minister. The

Commons up to that point had been the most prestigious gentlemen's club in London and the arrival of the opposite sex had not only shocked the gentlemen but had highlighted the extremely limited provisions for women – which included a convoluted route through the precincts of Westminster to the ladies' toilet. Wilkinson complained and began a long-running battle with the authorities about services for female MPs. Parliamentary protocol was cited as the reason for male preference in restaurants and other facilities, so she set out doggedly to change the protocols of centuries.

Wilkinson's fights on behalf of women extended especially to those disadvantaged by legislation. She was particularly active on the Widows' and Orphans' Pensions Bill and the Unemployment Insurance Bill. The Widows' Bill was full of injustices and prejudices towards some categories of women. She argued on behalf of those women who had paid contributions for years but were denied payments because their children were now too old, or some other arbitrary criteria.

Her feminist credentials ran deep and involved her in arguments for more women police officers and in a successful campaign to enable women who married other nationals to retain their British citizenship. She also tackled the ridiculous refusal to allow women to serve as diplomats, which had been established on the grounds that a woman could not keep a secret. After the passing of the 1928 Equal Franchise Act that finally gave women the vote on the same basis as men, she paid credit to those who had struggled to see this day: 'Women have worked hard; starved in prison; given of their time and lives that we might sit in the House of Commons and take part in the legislating of this country.'

The battle for Jarrow

Following the 1929 election and Labour's return to power, Ramsay MacDonald appointed Wilkinson as parliamentary secretary to the Minister for Health. She opposed MacDonald's National Government and then lost her seat in the disastrous election of 1931. She had, however, established a good reputation in Parliament and many wanted her back. Wilkinson was selected as the Labour candidate for the shipbuilding town of Jarrow on Tyneside in the run-up to the 1935 election.

During the campaign the Conservatives made many overtures and promises about regeneration and tackling the endemic unemployment in areas such as Tyneside. The 1935 election brought a partial recovery for Labour with the return of 154 MPs, including Wilkinson in Jarrow with a majority of 2,350. Like many others, however, Wilkinson was to experience deep frustration and anger when Conservative Government promises of help to her constituency were betrayed. Jarrow's unemployment figures were worse than most, with nearly 80 per cent of the working-age population out of a job and only 100 of the 8,000 skilled manual workers in employment. Little sympathy was forthcoming from the Conservative Walter Runican, President of the Board of Trade, who said, 'Jarrow must work out its own salvation.'[34]

In desperation and defiance Jarrow Borough Council began to do just that. They drew up a petition asking for Government help and decided to march to London to present the petition personally. All physically fit men were encouraged to participate, but the women were discouraged from doing the same. This did not dissuade Ellen Wilkinson, however, and she walked large sections of the journey to London alongside the 200 men who set off on 5 October 1936. The Bishop of Durham described the march as 'revolutionary, because it substituted organized mob pressure for the provisions of the constitution', but the Bishop of Sheffield blessed the march and said the marchers were doing a 'most English and constitutional thing'.[35]

Each night on the journey Wilkinson spoke at public meetings, articulating the jobless frustration of the men of Jarrow and their passion for work. They received no welcome in Westminster, however. The Government condemned the march and refused to meet its representatives, claiming instead that grievances should be made through MPs. Wilkinson accused the Government of making a fetish out of precedent and Chuter Ede, another Labour MP, declared, 'I am not in the House to preserve precedents that deny the rights of humanity.'[36] Perhaps through embarrassment or because the march had struck a chord with the public, the Government recanted and eventually agreed to meet a delegation for the unemployed.

The Jarrow Marchers entered the nation's consciousness as a dignified protest against inaction on mass unemployment. For those for whom the 1930s did provide work and money to buy all the new consumer goods, the Marchers provided a window to another much tougher world inhabited by their fellow citizens. Vernon comments, 'It disturbed the middle classes. Many, becoming guiltily aware of the madness of want amid plenty, began to ask questions and for the first time veered towards socialism.'[37] Morgan says of Wilkinson's role, 'She was a crucial figure in giving the movement new inspiration and zest for the good fight throughout that unhappy decade.'[38] In her book *The Town That Was Murdered* (1939), Wilkinson wrote about her beloved Jarrow and referred repeatedly to the influence of Primitive Methodism on its fight against poverty and unemployment.[39]

Many-sided involvement

Ellen Wilkinson was also involved in the start of the *Tribune* weekly newspaper, designed to be the voice of the left in the Labour Party. She collaborated with Stafford Cripps, Aneurin Bevan and others in supporting calls for a 'Popular Front' of political groups to defeat the Conservatives in Britain and Fascism in Europe. She led calls at the 1936 party conference for practical support to be given to the Spanish Government in its fight against General Franco, and in December 1936 she travelled to Spain with Clement Attlee, where they both witnessed the German bombing of Madrid. Neither Hitler nor Mussolini felt any reluctance about backing Franco against the Spanish Government.

Back in the Commons, Wilkinson tackled the much more down-to-earth issue of consumer rights. She believed that large numbers of working-class people were vulnerable to misinformation and repossession of hire-purchase goods, and therefore needed greater protection. In 1938 she saw the passage of the Hire Purchase Act which required greater transparency from shops on hire-purchase costs and offered some protection against repossession.

Success at the highest levels

When Winston Churchill replaced Neville Chamberlain as Prime Minister after the start of World War II, Wilkinson was appointed as parliamentary secretary to the Minister of Pensions in the Coalition Government. During the war she also served in the Home Office team under Herbert Morrison.

She reached the peak of her career in Labour's 1945 Cabinet as the first female Minister for Education. Against the opposition of Treasury ministers she secured extra spending on education, a rise in the school-leaving age from 14 to 15 and the introduction of the School Milk Act (1946) which provided free milk to pupils. Nevertheless, in these last years before her early death, she was constrained from instigating further reforms by the mammoth Butler Education Act of 1944, which had been broadly endorsed by Labour. Despite her successes, Wilkinson became depressed by an unwarranted focus on her failures. Her response was to take a drug overdose, from which she died in 1947.

Strength of character

Although Ellen Wilkinson never married, it was not for want of male friends. She had a vivacious and forthright character, and her confidence perhaps intimidated some men. She also had a fierce temper and when her secretary once allowed a neighbour to use her flat to place a gambling bet, Wilkinson erupted in righteous indignation. She told a Left Book Club meeting in March 1939, 'I am still a Methodist, you can never get its special glow out of your blood. I still keep up my membership at Grosvenor Street and when I can, attend Longsight Chapel where my brother was the Superintendent.'[40]

After her death Jack Lawson MP wrote in the *Methodist Magazine*, 'Vivid and resolute, Ellen drove herself like a fury, bringing colour and courage to the Labour Movement she loved. Her life force was rooted not in egotism or the desire for power as an end in itself. Quite simply it arose from the urge of compassion for mankind and a vision of the world that might be.'[41] The *Times Educational Supplement* said on 8 February 1947, 'Had Ellen Wilkinson lived longer, there is little doubt that the children of England and Wales would have had reason to bless her name. She would have made mistakes; she would have provoked bitter antagonism; but she would have seen to it in fact, as well as promise, no child would be denied the opportunity that was his due.'

The coming of war

There is irony in the twin themes of peace and unemployment that characterized the 1930s. What Ellen Wilkinson wanted and fought for was jobs and regeneration for the depressed areas of the Northeast. This was what many Labour MPs wanted, including George Lansbury, and it was what they eventually got. However, it was secured not because of government-driven regeneration but because of war. Rearmament and the war economy provoked the momentum and investment that brought life back to the depressed communities of the Northeast and other industrial areas of high unemployment.

When Lansbury was forced to resign because of Bevin's political realism, he continued to be motivated by his ideals. In 1936, at 77 years old, he lobbied President Roosevelt and spoke in 26 US cities over a period of six weeks in a crusade for peace. Speaking about it in the Commons on his return, he was heckled to 'go and tell Hitler' – and to everyone's surprise he did, meeting Hitler in Berlin on 19 April 1937. Lansbury's efforts were in vain, however, and within a year Hitler had annexed Austria and in March 1939 invaded Czechoslovakia. Sadly, Lansbury's pacifism had reinforced Britain's failure to prepare for war and deal firmly with the Fascist alliance of Germany and Italy. As the Labour Party remained split over the issue of war, it sent mixed messages to Chamberlain, who pursued appeasement with Hitler until Britain was finally forced to declare war after the invasion of Poland in September 1939.

While Lansbury may have rescued parliamentary democracy, therefore, his pacifism risked delivering the nation to a Fascist invader. Throughout the winter of 1939/40 British and French troops remained stationary while German troops marched on into Poland, Denmark, Norway, the Netherlands, Belgium and Luxembourg. It was not until May 1940 that Churchill succeeded Chamberlain as Prime Minister and Labour joined the Coalition Government. In the same month Hitler invaded France and British troops were forced back across the sea from Dunkirk. On 10 June 1940 Mussolini joined the war in support of Germany, and Britain stood alone against the massed armies of European Fascism.

CHAPTER 7

Coming of Age

STAFFORD CRIPPS AND LEAH MANNING:
1939–51

Clement Attlee's reforming Government of 1945 was Labour's high point. It included massive progress on welfare, nationalization and the creation of the National Health Service. Many believe it was a watershed for Socialism, realizing much of what Hardie and Labour's pioneers had set out to achieve. A.J. Davies believes it marked a move from 'phase one' of the Labour Movement into 'phase two'. This new period demanded administrative and bureaucratic skills over ethical assertion,[1] an ability to deal with the detail rather than simply pronounce on good and bad.

Ethical assertion would not be entirely absent, however. George Thomas (Viscount Tonypandy) said of Attlee's views on religion, 'He was very shy and reticent when conversations turned to religion but he held deep Christian convictions.'[2] Attlee's administration contained many Christians, including the Methodists George Tomlinson, George Isaacs, Arthur Henderson Junior and Jack Lawson, the Secretary for War. Its Congregationalists included Harold Wilson and James Griffiths and there was a Baptist, A.V. Alexander, as well as the Roman Catholics R.R. Stokes and Lord Pakenham. There was also the High Anglican Sir Stafford Cripps, nicknamed 'the Red Squire' because he owned a mansion in the West Country.

Cripps was an idiosyncratic character and his style of politics saw him ejected from the party in 1939, but rehabilitated in 1945. Cripps remained provocative and later asked Attlee to stand down as Prime Minister. Chris Bryant comments, 'This was vintage Cripps. It was brave, ambitious, fool-hardy, arrogant, ill-considered – all the things he had been throughout the thirties and in 1942. Another Prime Minister would probably have sacked him on the spot. Attlee decided to promote him instead.'[3]

During the 1945 election campaign Cripps travelled throughout the country and presented one of Labour's 10 radio broadcasts. This was perhaps the last specifically Christian party political broadcast in Britain. In the broadcast he said, 'Let those of us who boast the proud title of Christian follow the precepts of our great Teacher and make ourselves the selfless guardians of our neighbours, unconcerned with private wealth and interests, but anxious only to place all at the service of the community. Economic recovery is only half the task, for it is not new machines or fresh political expedients that we need so much as decent moral principles.'[4]

Moral principles and practical action were characteristic of Stafford Cripps. His pre-war principles got him into trouble, but his post-war actions would aid Attlee's Government and Britain's recovery.

———————

Wartime government

In the summer of 1940 Hitler was preparing to invade Britain. Europe had entered its darkest days and Britain her darkest hours. The war came starkly home to MPs when a bomb destroyed the chamber of the House of Commons. In the Battle of Britain, however, the skill of the RAF and 'total war' (as complete mobilization was known) won through. Over British skies in August 1940 German aircraft losses occurred at twice the rate of those suffered by the RAF. On 16 August all RAF squadrons were engaged with the enemy while repeated new waves of attackers crossed the Channel. Martin Gilbert notes, 'At the very moment when no extra British planes were available to go up against them, no further wave of attackers crossed the coast. It had been the closest imaginable margin of safety – and survival.'[5]

In late 1940 Churchill's Coalition Cabinet replaced the beleaguered Chamberlain. The new Cabinet included Labour leader Clement Attlee and deputy leader Arthur Greenwood. Churchill also mirrored Lloyd George's World War I co-option of Arthur Henderson by appointing the trade union leader Ernest Bevin as Minister for Labour, despite the fact that Bevin was not even an MP.

'Total war' in Britain meant a transformation of all aspects of society. It included central planning, investment and full employment, all of which were characteristics of Labour's pre-war policies. Fire, health,

GOD'S POLITICIANS

education and social services were centralized to provide for everyone in
the fight against Fascism. As Minister for Labour, Ernest Bevin oversaw
wartime production, but he also secured improvements in factory conditions. Women were required to work, but this in turn necessitated
nursery provision. World War II would effectively implement Labour
policy by stealth.

There were psychological consequences too. Rationing highlighted
the very Socialist concept that everyone, however rich or poor, received
adequate amounts of essential supplies and endured equal trials. Nights
in air-raid shelters and the evacuation of children to the countryside
created a sense of unity. Like World War I, this war would change
Britain in ways unimaginable in peacetime, and it also altered political
views. Research from the Mass Observation Unit at the end of 1942 concluded that two out of five people had changed their political outlook.
Soldiers and civilians alike concluded that their efforts for victory
should not mean a return to the social divisions and unemployment of
the 1930s.

The 1945 landslide

Given this analysis, it should have been no surprise that the General
Election of 1945 produced a landslide for Labour. In the aftermath of a
Conservative-led wartime victory, however, it *was* a surprise. Davies
comments, 'Few on the British left fully realized what changes in the
political climate had been wrought by the war.'[6] Labour's 1945 manifesto, 'Let us Face the Future', had captured the hopes of people
emerging from war. Its proposals included large-scale nationalization,
the creation of a National Health Service and a commitment to tackle
the five giant evils of want, squalor, disease, ignorance and unemployment. Labour secured 48 per cent of the vote and 393 seats in
Parliament, a people's mandate for its most radical programme ever.
Conservative losses were on an equally grand scale, with only 213 MPs
returned from their wartime total of 418. Meanwhile the Liberal vote fell
further to just 12 seats.

Labour's Clement Attlee, a diminutive, bespectacled man, seemed the
most unlikely of Prime Ministers. During the election Churchill had
campaigned in magisterial fashion while Attlee's wife drove him around

128

in the old family car. The public, however, had viewed Labour as more united and more youthful, and almost two-thirds of first-time voters voted for Labour. The image of unity was only an image, nevertheless. Many believe that Attlee's biggest achievement in the 1945 Government was to keep his Cabinet together for long enough to implement change. Despite his victory, Attlee's own position was immediately threatened in an attempted coup. Indeed, it was his failure to maintain unity that resulted in Labour's failure to secure a full second term in 1950. One of the deepest rivalries was between Foreign Secretary Ernest Bevin and the Minister for Health and Housing Aneurin (Nye) Bevan. When someone commented that Nye Bevan was his own worst enemy, Ernest Bevin replied, 'Not while I'm alive, he ain't.'[7]

Labour's post-war Government faced many similar challenges to the Liberals after World War I. While Britain had won the war, the economy had been shattered and the country's role as a global power had been irreparably damaged. The war had created massive debt and Labour's programme demanded massive investment. Britain once again turned to America for the loans it needed for national renewal. Three major pieces of welfare legislation were introduced from 1946 to 1948. These created the minimum standards envisaged by Sir William Beveridge in his 1942 report. In Health, Nye Bevan built on the central medical services set up during the war and, against the wishes of the Conservatives and the doctors, pushed through the National Health Service Act (1946). Bevan also took on Housing following Attlee's failure to fulfil a promise to create a separate ministry. This was one reason why only 230,000 homes were built in 1948 compared to 350,000 in 1938.

Stafford Cripps

Sir Stafford Cripps was appointed President of the Board of Trade, in part because of his wartime experience (in both world wars) in management and production. He worked tirelessly to promote industrial production and exports before becoming Chancellor in 1948.

Cripps had always seemed destined for greatness. He secured his knighthood as the Solicitor General in Labour's 1929–31 Government, despite having only joined the party a year before. His self-confidence – some would say arrogance – was evident as early as his student days, when he was president of his University Union. This had more to do with his skill at organizing good social events than with his political prowess, however. Cripps was a latecomer to Labour politics and when he eventually did join, it was not as a foot soldier but with a view to becoming a minister.

Background in law

Politics and law were in the family blood when he was born the youngest of five children in 1889. His father Alfred was a Conservative MP before becoming Baron Parmoor of Frieth in 1911. Alfred was also a leading lay Anglican and friend of Archbishop Davidson. During World War I he aligned himself with the pacifist-leaning clergy and this brought him closer to the views of MacDonald and Snowden. While the Cripps family's wealth and history rendered them unlikely Labour sup-porters, the relationship with Beatrice and Sidney Webb had already exposed them to Labour values and thinking, and when MacDonald offered Alfred a position in Labour's 1924 Cabinet, it provoked a firm decision to transfer from the Conservatives to Labour.

Although the young Stafford followed his father into law, it remained unclear whether he would do the same in politics. When his political views did eventually emerge, they were more ideological than practical, in part because he had not faced the same kind of practical challenges as many other Labour leaders. While he had lost his mother at the age of four, he had also had everything money could buy, including a privi-leged education at Winchester College. It was there that the family ethic of social leadership was reinforced, as well as an inclination to excel in chemistry, but he also gained a reputation for spending time in The Green Man pub.

His chemistry work came to the attention of Sir William Ramsay, who invited Cripps to join him at University College in London. From 1910, however, Cripps began to train for the Bar and never did complete his chemistry degree. A further distraction was his marriage to Isobel Swithinbank in July 1911 and the rapid arrival of their first two children. Although he volunteered for military service in 1914, Cripps was refused on medical grounds. Instead he drove for the Red Cross in France before being sent to an explosive factory in Chester to use his chemistry expertise. As manager on a production line, Cripps learned lessons that he would one day take to the Board of Trade. In 1916 he fell seriously ill and remained an invalid for the remainder of the war. Bryant says of this time that Cripps' resources were his fortitude, his family and his faith. Gratitude to God for survival and a view of public service as a Christian calling were convictions that he developed at around this time.[8]

A latecomer to politics

In 1919 Cripps started work in the Middle Temple and by the mid-1920s had established a large and successful law practice. His father and his uncle Sidney Webb had become ministers in Labour's 1924 Government, but there was no similar commitment from Stafford. He still believed that the Church offered the best hope for changing the world and was active in the World Alliance for Promoting International Friendship. There he worked with his former Winchester warden Hubert Burge, by then the Bishop of Oxford. Cripps believed the Church had a role in the new international order, but its failure to act decisively in the General Strike and in other international issues finally caused him to turn to politics. Writing to a friend, he said, 'I must really make up my mind to do my share of work besides earn money.'[9]

By 1928 Cripps had decided to become a politician and by 1929 he had joined the Labour Party. It is not clear whether this was in support of its policies or whether 'he simply succumbed to the persistent pleas of Herbert Morrison, the new Minister of Transport'.[10] Whatever the motivation, it was understood by all concerned that Cripps was joining the party with a view to being elected. He was selected as a candidate and campaigned for West Woolwich, but his legal work and appointment as Solicitor General in 1930 meant that he really had to be found a seat immediately. With the support of Arthur Henderson, and against the wishes of rival candidate Leah Manning, he was selected and elected for Bristol South East. Almost immediately his allegiance to the party was tested when MacDonald left to establish his National Government. Cripps stayed on and despite the electoral catastrophe of 1931 he held Bristol South East with a majority of 429.

Labour had been reduced to a rump in the Commons and both Cripps and Attlee took leading roles in supporting Lansbury and rebuilding the party. Attlee said of Cripps, 'Many great lawyers have failed to adapt themselves to the House of Commons, but from the start Cripps showed that he was the exception. He brought to our ranks wide knowledge, fine debating powers and a first-class mind.'[11] Cripps himself was impressed by the single-minded commitment of party leader George Lansbury. Bryant comments, 'He caught Lansbury's infectious idealism, enthusiasm and sense of Christian vocation.'[12] This inclination for idealism would lead to the growth of his popularity in the party, but also to his expulsion from it.

The dangers of idealism

With Labour languishing in opposition throughout the 1930s, the attractions of utopian ideals – whether Fascist, Communist or pacifist – were great. Cripps had achieved his political prominence with little sacrifice and he seemed rather reluctant to accept the perseverance that parliamentary politics demanded. This made him susceptible to notions of quick-fix solutions or even revolution. From 1931 his views became increasingly extreme and in 1932 he helped create the Socialist League, a radical voice within the party. Its language was consistent with Labour's return to the 'pure' Socialism of Lansbury and League members wanted a Socialist commonwealth established by a Socialist working class. Cripps became chair of the League and others such as Aneurin Bevan joined him. Nevertheless, he began to frighten his parliamentary colleagues with his call for a 'temporary dictatorship' in a lecture entitled 'Can Socialism come by constitutional methods?'

While the Conservatives regarded Cripps' rhetoric as an electoral gift, it did also secure him popular support within Labour. As a result he was elected to the national executive in 1934, but for many he was not a true 'Labour man' and Michael Foot said of him, 'He knew little of the Labour movement, less of its history and amid all his other preoccupations had little time or inclination to repair the deficiency by a reading of socialist literature. His marxist slogans were undigested; he declared class war without having studied the contours of the battlefield.'[13]

Call for a 'United Front'

Cripps' Socialist League called for a vigorous response to the Fascist governments of Hitler and Mussolini – yet its ideological obsessions meant it would not support Britain or the League of Nations as partners in any such response. The League was happy enough with the idea of war, but not a capitalist war. Cripps therefore resisted League of Nations sanctions against Mussolini for his invasion of Abyssinia in 1935. He also supported the affiliation of the Communist Party to Labour against the wishes of the wider party. In addition, as if his work with the Socialist League was not provocative enough, Cripps started to build what he called a 'United Front', to include Communists in a fight against capitalists and Fascists. He proposed the idea to the 1936 party conference and although they voted it down, Cripps decided to work for it anyway.

A 'United Front' against Fascism was duly announced on 1 January 1937. The Front was a coalition of the Communist Party, the Independent Labour Party and the Socialist League, but it was unacceptable to the Labour Party itself. Labour's national executive warned that any party member involved risked being expelled and they began to make moves against Cripps. He managed to hang on, thanks to his legal work and his popularity in the party, but he found himself increasingly marginalized. Then the national executive announced that all Socialist League members would be ineligible for party membership from 1 June 1937. Cripps adopted delaying tactics until the 1937 conference could have a chance to vote on the United Front. He temporarily disbanded the Socialist League and for a time did not speak on platforms with the ILP or the Communist Party.

The 1937 conference refused to endorse the United Front – although Cripps did get Labour to change its policy of nonintervention in the Spanish Civil War. While Mussolini and Hitler supported Franco against the Spanish Government, the Governments of Britain and France had chosen not to intervene. As a result, around 2,000 British Communists and Socialists voted with their feet and joined the International Brigade to fight in Spain against Franco, and over 500 of them were killed. While Labour's policy change was an endorsement of their efforts, however, the British Government itself remained neutral.

Expulsion

Throughout 1938 Cripps pursued his twin objectives of defeating the Government and securing an alliance to fight Fascism. He decided to change tack by supporting the political campaigns of a wider 'Popular Front' proposed by his friend and Communist Party member Henry Pollitt. The Popular Front would include Liberals and non-aligned opponents of Fascism. As chair of the *Tribune* newspaper, Cripps adopted this as a new editorial policy, provoking the resignation of its editor and two young journalists, Michael Foot and Barbara Castle. Cripps' argument was that a coalition such as the Popular Front was necessary since electoral statistics proved that the current Government was unbeatable otherwise. He approached Labour's national executive with the proposal, but it was rejected.

When Cripps went to the media with the story, the executive demanded a retraction, threatening expulsion if he did not comply. Cripps stood firm, however, and on 25 January 1939 he was expelled from the Labour Party. His colleague Nye Bevan said, 'If Sir Stafford Cripps is expelled for wanting to unite the forces of freedom and democracy they can go on expelling others. They can expel me. His crime is my crime.'[14] As a result of this stance, Bevan was also expelled from the party. Both Beatrice Webb and R.H. Tawney were dismayed at Cripps' brilliancy and charm 'but inability to take counsel with fellow workers, and instability in ends and means'.[15] Labour's conference that year upheld Cripps' expulsion and overwhelmingly rejected his proposals for a Popular Front. Ellen Wilkinson wrote, 'He forgets that party government is an essential instrument of political liberty in a democracy. Yet by his sheer honesty and selflessness Cripps can always command loyalty. He is a bad leader but a magnificent lieutenant.'[16]

Influential wartime career

By December 1939 Bevan had been readmitted to the party, but Cripps remained an Independent MP throughout the war. Ironically, his Popular Front against Fascism eventually came about not because of an electoral pact but because Hitler's troops marched across Europe. Prime Minister Churchill recognized the need to secure Russian support against Hitler and turned to Cripps as someone who might provide useful insights and establish trust with Stalin. In a highly unusual move for a sitting MP, Churchill dispatched Cripps to Moscow as Britain's ambassador, where he spent 18 months trying to influence Russian opinion towards an alliance with Britain.

On 12 July 1941 he was finally successful and Stalin and Molotov, along with Cripps and the head of Britain's military mission, signed the Anglo-Soviet agreement against Hitler. Cripps' experience of Communism in Russia, however, caused him to reflect on his revolutionary ideals. He wrote to a friend from Moscow, 'One thing has been proved here so far and that is that you cannot leap into Utopia in one bound.'[17]

Cripps' popularity remained strong in Britain and when he returned from Moscow he stubbornly refused a role in government unless it was in the Cabinet. By early 1942 the war was going badly, with the loss of Hong Kong, Malaya and Singapore to the Japanese. Churchill's own popularity was low and any support for Cripps was support he could use. He therefore created the post of Leader of the House and Lord Privy Seal, an amalgamation of Churchill's and Attlee's previous roles. Attlee became Deputy Prime Minister, Churchill concentrated on the war and Cripps secured his place in the Cabinet. He was now at the height of his popularity and in April 1942 an opinion poll put him as favourite, second only to Anthony Eden, to replace Churchill in the event of his demise.

His enjoyment of such popularity was short-lived, however, and when Churchill shuffled his Cabinet in November 1942 he sent Cripps to the Ministry for Aircraft Production. Cripps remained in this post for the next two and a half years, at a time when controversy surrounded the tactics of the RAF. Air power had become a formidable but ethically questionable weapon by the latter part of World War II, and Bishop Bell of Winchester was an outspoken critic of it. The RAF were engaging in night-time saturation bombing of German cities while the US Air Force bombed them during the day. An RAF chaplain at Bomber Command in High Wycombe once asked Cripps to speak to the pilots engaged in the nightly and often inaccurate bombing. He agreed and then, true to controversial form, proceeded to question the ethics of commanders who sent pilots on morally doubtful and tactically flawed missions. What Cripps actually said is now lost, but his remarks were interpreted as undermining discipline and senior officers were furious about his lecture.

Reconciliation with the party

By early 1945 it was apparent that the war would soon be over and Cripps would shortly be up for re-election. This focused his mind and in February 1945 he made a formal application to Labour's national executive, who accepted his readmission to the party. At the 1945 conference in Blackpool, his speech was received with prolonged applause. Following Germany's surrender, Churchill called an election for 5 July 1945. The party political broadcast that Cripps delivered during the campaign demonstrated that his ideals remained intact. He argued that 'the basis of Labour's stance was ethical, rooted equally in Christian Socialism as in the working class movement and it was its inspiration "by the spirit of comradeship and moral purpose" that recommended it'.[18]

Attlee's acceptance of Cripps into his Government recognized his valuable contribution. Britain needed to rebuild its economy and Cripps had run Britain's largest industry for a large part of the war. Attlee appointed him as President of the Board of Trade and Cripps set off on an extensive tour of the factories to encourage workers towards the goal of rebuilding Britain. His language was infused with Christian exhortations and he believed that Britain needed a new moral purpose. 'Our industrial morale is low,' he said, 'because a merely materialistic, self-centred outlook on our work cannot give us a high morale. Inducements of a material kind can never and will never replace the spiritual urge which transcends our own personal interests.'[19]

A vital role in post-war government

Cripps had a central role in the early days of Attlee's Government. He sat on the committee that oversaw the process of nationalization and was intimately involved in the financial arrangements surrounding American and Canadian loans. Throughout 1946 the Government maintained its momentum on legislative reform and high levels of employment, yet despite the loans the economy began to falter. The loans had paid for the first wave of nationalization, but a hard winter in 1946/7 resulted in lost production and coal shortages. By the summer of 1947 over half of the loans designed to last until 1951 had gone. At this point the decision was taken to make the pound convertible, a condition of the original loan agreement. It had disastrous consequences for the economy, however, and resulted in a run on the pound that required the suspension of convertibility.

In the midst of the crisis Cripps approached Attlee and asked him to stand down as Prime Minister, believing that Ernest Bevin would be best placed to tackle the economic challenges. Attlee famously phoned Bevin and said, 'I've got Stafford here, he says you want my job,' but Bevin would not confirm the suggestion. Rather surprisingly, instead of sacking Cripps, Attlee promoted him to Minister of Economic Affairs at the Treasury.

Within months of this, Chancellor Hugh Dalton resigned following his self-disclosed budget leak to a journalist. In November 1947 Cripps became Chancellor in his place and immediately changed Britain's economic direction from one based on growth to greater fiscal austerity and wage restraint. Cripps' decision to devalue the pound also provided momentum for Britain's exports. In 1950, however, Cripps had to resign both as Chancellor and MP because of cancer and it would be just two short years before his death. Two weeks after his resignation the 25-year-old Tony Benn was selected for Cripps' seat, Bristol South East, and Cripps wrote of his delight at Benn's selection in the *Bristol Evening World*.

Upholder of Christian values

Throughout his time in the 1945 Government, Cripps was in high demand as a public speaker and continued to write pamphlets. These were mainly Christian Socialist tracts and included *Towards Christian Democracy* (1945), *Democracy Alive* (1946) and later *God in our Work* (1949). In *Towards Christian Democracy* Cripps argued that Christianity must be a living reality and must express itself in what he called 'social salvation'. He stressed that the Church, while not aligning itself with a particular party, must nevertheless engage with all aspects of everyday life. What mattered most to Cripps was the need constantly to translate the message of Sunday worship into Monday work. He continued to believe that political leadership should not consist of trying to interpret and then follow the wishes of the majority, but rather that it should actively try to lead popular thinking within truly Christian values.

Following his death in 1952, an obituary in the *New Statesman* said that all of Cripps' life and ways stemmed from his faith. Victor Gollancz described him as 'one of the few real socialists of our time … he will rank with Schweitzer as one of the two great Christians-in-action that the last half century has produced'.[20] Bryant concludes that Cripps was both an idealist and a pragmatist who realized that purity without power was impotence, and this meant that 'throughout his diplomatic and ministerial career he tried to combine idealism with power, defying the cynical cry that power must of its nature corrupt'.[21]

Leah Manning

One of the people for whom electoral success in 1945 came as a surprise was Leah Manning, the woman Stafford Cripps had displaced from the Bristol South East constituency in 1930. She had briefly been an MP before the war, but had lost her Islington seat in the 1931 election. In 1945 she won Epping for Labour, the one-time constituency of Winston Churchill, who had moved to the neighbouring constituency of Wanstead and Woodford.

Euphoria reigned among the victorious 1945 Labour MPs, and Manning records something of the momentum for reform in her auto-biography. 'Yesterday it was coal. Hugh Dalton began in moving the Second Reading of the Cable and Wireless Bill. Today it is Cables. The socialist advance continues. And we went swinging through the lobbies, singing The Red Flag and Welsh hymns. The Tories thought this sacrile-gious, but in 1946 we were in high spirits.'[22] George Thomas recorded similar incidents and described how each night, as MPs trooped through the division lobbies, he was often asked to strike up a note. He would start to sing 'Guide me, O thou great Jehovah' and recalled that 'instantly there would be a mighty choir singing its way through the lobbies'.[23]

Manning was another whose Christian faith had motivated and maintained her Socialism through the dark years of Labour opposition. Fellow MP Tom Skeffington-Lodge said of her, 'From an early age she felt that her Christian beliefs could best be expressed in a practical way through membership of the Labour Party. Throughout her life she sought to insist that it should base its policies on a clear moral purpose designed to bring about human betterment at home and abroad.'[24]

Early influences

Manning grew up under the influence of the Salvation Army and Methodism. She was born Elizabeth Leah Perrett in Droitwich in 1886, the first of 12 children born to Charles and Harriet Perrett, officers in the South Hornsey Salvation Army Corps. When she was two her parents were sent to Canada with the Army and left Leah with her maternal grandfather. It was from him that the Methodist influence came. Stan Newens comments, 'For him the politics of Gladstone and his successors in the Liberal party followed automatically from the teachings of his church. Inevitably, Leah, who adored him, was deeply influenced. She was in addition affected by the books provided for her by her step grandmother, which emphasized faith, temperance and morality but also compassion for the victims of poverty and misfortune.'[25]

Manning's education in London brought her into contact with the Revd Stewart Headlam, a member of the London School Board. At Cambridge Headlam had embraced the teachings of the early Christian Socialists F.D. Maurice and Charles Kingsley. Now, as an Anglican priest in central London, he was known for his extrovert character, radical theology and understanding of the theatre. It was Headlam who established the first Christian Socialist organization in England,[26] but he remained hostile to the idea of a Socialist political party and never joined the Labour Party.

Through her contacts with Headlam, Manning was introduced to Christian Socialism, the theatre and High Church worship – all to the horror of her strict, Nonconformist grandparents. As a teenager she attended St Margaret's Church, Westminster, the church of Parliament to which 40 years later she would return as an MP. It was Headlam, too, who suggested that Manning should go to Homerton College, Cambridge, to train as a teacher. This decision would determine Manning's future both as a teacher and as a leader of teachers.

Socialist convictions

In her early days at Cambridge she received an invitation to the University Fabian Society from the future Labour Chancellor Hugh Dalton. Headlam had specifically asked Dalton to invite Manning, and she later saw the note he had sent. It said she was from a stuffy middle-class family, Methodist and Liberal in politics, but she had the makings of a good Socialist. Manning's character was such that she did not do things by half and shortly after her introduction to the Fabians she joined the society, as well as the ILP and the Guild of St Matthew. The Fabians opened up a world she had not known existed, and she commented, 'I had never heard of homosexuality, but a frank, open debate on the subject … made me understand suddenly my grandfather's outraged feelings at the sentence on Oscar Wilde.'[27]

Manning did well in her teacher training, was placed on the 'List of First Appointments' and anticipated a return to London. She was delighted to be offered a job in Cambridge instead, but crestfallen to discover it was at New Street, the school everyone regarded with horror because of the low morale and poverty among its pupils. Manning's lecturer challenged her, 'Do you, a Socialist, think yourself too good for those poor children?' She recalled, 'Somewhere, faintly, my conscience whispered, "You say you never do anything by halves. Here's your chance to prove you're a socialist and not only in name."'[28] She therefore stayed in Cambridge, where she met and married Will Manning in 1914, as well as becoming secretary of the Cambridge ILP.

Displaced candidate

By 1929 Manning had performed successfully in her chosen profession and had become president of the National Union of Teachers (NUT). It was on their recommendation that she pursued selection as the Labour candidate for Bristol South East. A fellow member of the National Association of Labour Teachers suggested that her nomination was secure, but when she met him at Bristol Station he reported, 'A snag has come up and Uncle Arthur wants the seat for some lawyer chap called Cripps.'[29] Cripps' recent appointment as Solicitor General meant that the party quickly needed him in Parliament. Manning, however, would have none of it and with the support of the NUT – who were keen to gain teacher representation in Parliament – she continued her fight for the nomination. Her old friend Hugh Dalton was sent to persuade her to stand down. She recalls the pain of the decision in her autobiography:

He needed to use only one simple phrase, 'Uncle Arthur asks me to tell you that he will make this a test of your loyalty to the Party.' Loyalty to

the Party, to my friends, to institutions, had been a guiding principle all
my life. Those words broke my stubborn resistance; they also broke my
heart, for I had counted on Hugh supporting me all the way in my fight.
I can remember only a very few times when I have given way to tears –
this was one of them.[30]

Afterwards Manning was told that Uncle Arthur would do everything
possible to secure her the next by-election. This is what took Manning
to East Islington, a seat she temporarily won before losing it again in
Labour's 1931 election disaster.

The Spanish Civil War

Manning was active in the Spanish Civil War of 1936–9. In the Spanish
General Election of 16 February 1936 the Parties of the Left secured 265
seats to the 165 seats secured by the Parties of the Right. Despite this
democratic mandate many within Spain, including the majority of the
military, refused to accept the result. Widespread violence precipitated a
collapse in public order and in July 1936 General Franco led the army in
its challenge of the Government. Spain's war typified the wider Fascist/
anti-Fascist struggles of the 1930s and was to become a forerunner for
World War II. It was a different kind of war from the type of conflict in
which the weak simply give up territory to the strong. This was a political war – or, as the Frenchman Antoine de Saint-Exupéry wrote, 'You
have been captured. You are shot. Reason: your ideas were not our
ideas.'[31] These ideas caused thousands of volunteers from many countries to join the International Brigade in Spain, but their enthusiasm was
no match for the professional soldiers of the Spanish, German or Italian
military.

Leah Manning was in Russia when the Civil War broke out in 1936.
She immediately flew to Madrid, where she met with Spanish Socialists
to see how she could help. On her return to Britain she arranged an all-
party meeting in the Commons through her parliamentary contacts and
set up the Spanish Medical Aid Committee to take out lorry-loads of
badly needed medical supplies. However, it was the siege and bombing
of Bilbao by Franco that took Manning back to Spain. She was asked to
help with the evacuation of starving children from Bilbao and, using
her Spanish contacts, she flew into the besieged city. While there she

witnessed the German bombing of Guernica, a quiet market town outside Bilbao and renowned home of Basque nationalism. Franco was making the point that there would be no Basque nationalism under his rule. Manning later wrote:

> *Helpless to do anything we watched from the hills. Until nearly eight in the evening, incendiary bombs and high explosives rained down every twenty minutes. The town was open and defenceless; it was crowded with market day visitors and as people fled from the destruction they were dive-bombed and machine-gunned from the air. The roads out of the town were jammed with dead and injured; 1,654 killed; 889 injured. It cannot be described in words; only Picasso's 'Guernica' can depict its stark horror.*[32]

Manning set about managing the evacuation of 4,000 children from Bilbao – and in the process had to outmanoeuvre both the British Consul in Bilbao and the Government at home in order to get the children to safety in Southampton. The British Government maintained its noninterventionist position on the war and was therefore reluctant to become involved in any matters that might be interpreted as support for one side or the other.

1945 euphoria

During World War II Manning continued to work for the NUT and represented them in the huge task associated with the 1944 Education Act. She had not planned to fight the 1945 election and was not an official candidate of her union, but in the summer of 1945, buoyed up by the wave of national euphoria, she decided she wanted to fight the Conservatives. She was selected for Churchill's former seat of Epping and, despite the recent boundary changes precipitated by population growth in the suburbs, she was expected to lose. It was Churchill's own decision to allow soldiers to vote that swung the Epping constituency Labour's way.

The memory of the demobilization muddles of World War I provoked many parents to write to their sons and encourage them to vote Labour. Ernest Bevin's promise of civilian clothes and a civilian job for the returning soldiers, instead of the unemployment of the 1930s,

Keir Hardie addressing a peace rally in Trafalgar Square at the outbreak of World War I, 2 August 1914. *The Hulton Getty Picture Collection*

The Independent Labour Council in 1899. With representatives of the Trade Union Movement they formed the Labour Representation Committee (later the Labour Party) at the Memorial Hall, Farringdon, on 27 February 1900. *National Museum of Labour History*

Early Labour MPs outside the House of Commons in 1906. Front row, left to right: Arthur Henderson, J. Ramsay MacDonald, Keir Hardie, D. J. Shackleton. Back row, left to right: G. H. Barnes, Philip Snowden, John Hodge, Will Crookes, J. O'Grady. *National Museum of Labour History*

Canvassers and clergy for Labour. Keir Hardie, Mrs Bernard Shaw, Revd Geoffrey Ramsey and George Bernard Shaw at Merthyr Tydfil during a 1910 General Election. *National Museum of Labour History*

Post-World War I Labour election posters. World Wars I and II changed Britain dramatically, and Labour benefited from the mood of optimism and progress after the wars. *National Museum of Labour History*

1922: James Ramsay MacDonald (on left) returns as Labour leader, having lost his seat in 1918. With 'Uncle' Arthur Henderson, Party Secretary 1912–35. *National Museum of Labour History*

Labour's first Cabinet in 1924. *National Museum of Labour History*

Margaret Bondfield, Britain's first female Cabinet Minister, a Labour Party member and a Christian. © *Popperfoto*

George Lansbury was the East End's local hero, and, as leader of the Labour Party, rescued democracy at a time of political extremes. *The Hulton Getty Picture Collection*

The Jarrow marches approaching Luton in October 1936, with Ellen Wilkinson MP taking two steps to everyone else's one. *The Hulton Getty Picture Collection*

Revolutionary economics. Stafford Cripps, anti-fascist campaigner and Communist sympathizer, manages the money for Attlee's 1945 Government. © *PA*

The Gang of Five: Harold Wilson, Nye Bevan, Ian Mikardo, Tom Driberg and Barbara Castle at Labour's 50th party conference in 1951.

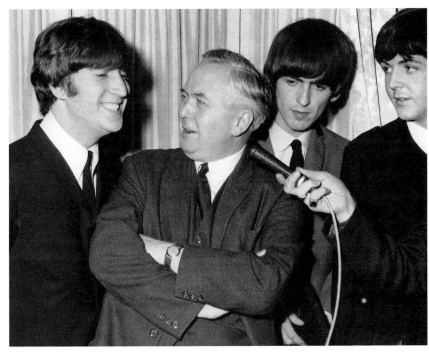

Harold Wilson's first Government in 1964 caught the mood of the British people. Even the Beatles joined the party. *The Hulton Getty Picture Collection*

Revd Donald Soper, Chaplain to the Labour Party?

Michael Foot and Tony Benn share a rare smile during the Thatcher years. *The Hulton Getty Picture Collection*

John Smith, the Prime Minister we never had. He rehabilitated Labour, reclaimed the moral ground and restored the party's faith. © *Stefano Cagnoni/CSM*

Chris Smith, Keith Vaz, Jack Straw and Hilary Armstrong at a Christian Socialist Movement service at St Martin-in-the-Fields, 1994. © *Maggie Murray/Format*

CSM Chair Chris Bryant (right) and CSM Co-ordinator David Cairns provide shelter for Tony and Cherie Blair as they arrive for the 1994 conference service in Blackpool.

also secured votes. Thus the soldiers' vote won Epping for Manning as well as many other constituencies for Labour. It was a revivalist-style election. One party organizer commented, 'Not since the field-preaching of the Wesley brothers has such a surge of "revival" swept the hamlets and county towns of Southern England. Villages steeped in century-old Tory tradition bloomed with Labour posters.'[33]

Manning threw herself into parliamentary life with characteristic enthusiasm. Her optimism never faded during that first session and when she became a member of the Estimates Committee, she even made some friendships on the opposite side of the House. She joined two parliamentary groups – Agriculture, since Epping was largely an agricultural constituency, and Foreign Affairs, which was her first interest.

Christian Socialist colleagues

Her closest friends in Parliament were members of the Parliamentary Church Council of St Margaret's Church. As a group they tried to attend prayers each day and received Communion on saints' days. Manning was also an active member of the Parliamentary Christian Socialist Group, formed shortly after the 1945 election with Tom Skeffington-Lodge, MP for Bedford, as its chair. Other members of the group included Harold Wilson, Roy Jenkins and Arthur Henderson Junior. Manning was an active member among more than 100 others, and they would meet in the Commons and also organize fringe meetings at Labour's party conferences. She was also closely involved with the 1945 Christian Socialist manifesto, 'In This Faith We Live'.

Despite sharing her faith and a place in the Commons with Stafford Cripps, Manning's views on her mercurial colleague were never really warm. She wrote that after analysing her feelings, she felt this was not because she still held a grudge about Bristol South East, but because she regarded Cripps as sanctimonious. She believed he had done the wrong thing by voting against sanctions at the time of the Abyssinian crisis and she also felt he was willing to tell an expedient lie. While she was able to forgive other colleagues for political errors, she felt unable to do the same for Cripps. She concluded, 'When Cripps publicly denied that he had devaluation in mind, and then devalued within a few days, I felt that that was unforgivable behaviour in one who professed complete probity in public life.'[34]

Labour's loss of power

Attlee's 1945 Government was ultimately only a qualified success. Its achievements included radical reforms such as the establishment of the NHS and the welfare state, and it had broadly delivered full employment throughout its time in power. These achievements remained secure even under successive Conservative Governments who, while trying to undermine them, were never able to abolish them. Despite economic problems, Attlee's Government successfully raised industrial production and exports almost trebled between 1945 and 1949. However, as Dudley Seers argues in his book *The Levelling of Incomes since 1938*, it achieved no noticeable impact on a trend towards equality of distribution.[35]

The post-war national euphoria could not be sustained and Labour's 1945 majority was reduced to just five seats in 1950. Attlee's problems continued, with the left of the party angry at Britain's involvement in the Korean war and trade unions angry at wage controls. He called an early General Election in 1951 and, although Labour secured more votes overall than the Conservatives, the electoral system meant that it secured only 295 seats to the Conservatives' 302. Labour had revolutionized Britain, but in the process had run out of steam. It would be 13 long years before the party was back in power.

CHAPTER 8

Making a Stand

DONALD SOPER AND TOM DRIBERG: 1952–63

*T*he anti-Nazi alliance of America, Britain and Russia did not continue after the war. No sooner had Hitler been defeated than a cold war descended on East–West relations. This new ideological struggle was to have a direct and debilitating effect on the Labour Party. Controversies in foreign policy had added to Labour's demise in 1951, and party disputes about the atom bomb would dominate its time in opposition. Many of the leading protagonists during this period were Christian, including Donald Soper and Tom Driberg MP. Soper's Christian pacifism informed both the Labour peace movement and public causes such as the Campaign for Nuclear Disarmament. Britain's decision to manufacture its own atomic bomb was met with Nye Bevan's criticism inside the Commons and Soper's criticism outside. For many the nuclear age had redefined war. Weapons that indiscriminately killed and contaminated the environment could no longer be justified on any moral grounds. In the 1950s, amidst growing public concern over relations with Russia, Soper's message seemed not only acceptable but prophetic.

Yet another war was going on too, for the very nature of Socialism. Soper's Socialist absolutism conflicted with the revisionism of Hugh Gaitskell and Tony Crosland, who believed in a modern Socialism for a modern generation. As the conflict raged within Labour, the Conservatives swept to victory at three successive General Elections. Britain was changing and the Conservatives changed with it. Labour's challenge was to marry its Socialist ideals to this changing world – to pursue, if it could, a principled realpolitik.

Post-war tensions

After World War II the League of Nations was relaunched as the United Nations. This event, which took place in London in 1946, reflected the Labour Government's efforts for international reconciliation and 51 nations attended the UN's opening session at Methodist Central Hall. In his speech King George VI challenged the UN 'to lay the foundations of a new world, where such a conflict as that which lately brought our world to the verge of annihilation must never be repeated; where men and women can find opportunity to realize to the full the good that lies in each one of them'.[1] The UN expressed the hope of a new kind of internationalism where individual nations would be mutually accountable in order to protect against future wars.

The hope of those early days was soon to disappear, however. The Russian delegation proposed their own candidate for the UN presidency and, although they were defeated by 28 votes to 23, it revealed the fault lines in the post-war world. A key challenge for the fledgling UN was how to deal with the atom bomb. America alone had used the bomb in anger, and now urged the world to move towards its rejection. Talk of disarmament proved short-lived, however. Just four weeks later Stalin declared the impossibility of international peace and announced the rearmament of Russia. This would include the rapid development of Russia's atomic bomb. By early 1947 Russian foreign policy was a clear cause for concern. Russia's involvement in Poland's elections provoked America to accuse her of aggression and expansionism – although the Russian perspective was that it was all to do with consolidation and defence.

Following the drive against Hitler, Communist forces now controlled Czechoslovakia, Yugoslavia, Hungary, Romania, Bulgaria and Albania. In southern Europe, Greece and Turkey remained vulnerable to internal revolution and Labour's Foreign Secretary Ernest Bevin declared that Britain was no longer able to guarantee the security of Greece. By May 1947 US President Truman accepted the need to support the remaining democracies of Europe. Congress passed a Bill to allow economic and military aid to Turkey and Greece, and a wider aid package was planned by US Secretary of State George C. Marshall.

The Marshall Plan

The Marshall Plan was to reinforce the gulf between American-leaning nations and Soviet-leaning nations. Supposedly a reconstruction package for all countries, Russia saw it rather as an American attempt at post-imperial domination. Russian Foreign Secretary Molotov warned Britain and France to reject the Plan or face grave consequences. Bevin replied, 'My country has faced grave consequences and threats before and it is not the sort of prospect that will deter us from doing what we consider to be our duty.'[2] By 1949 the Marshall economic plan had spawned its military counterpart, the North Atlantic Treaty Organization (NATO), and Britain was one of the 12 European nations who – along with America – signed a military assistance agreement against potential aggressors.

Loss of confidence in Labour

Meanwhile, Bevin was strongly criticized by the left of the Labour Party for aligning so clearly with America. Labour retained its sympathy for Soviet ideals and remained suspicious of American imperialist ambitions. In 1946 the 'Keep Left' group of MPs argued that Britain should remain 'equidistant' in its relations with Moscow and Washington. Public concern was heightened when Russia tested an atom bomb in 1949 and potential conflict became a factor in the elections of 1950 and '51.

The Conservative leader Winston Churchill had successfully dealt with Stalin in World War II, and there was a feeling among voters that he would be more capable than Attlee of delivering stability in foreign affairs. When Churchill won the election in 1951, he accepted this stabilizing role and led renewed efforts to establish trust between the Russians and Americans. Among the many reasons for Labour's defeat in 1951 were internal divisions on foreign policy, both in the Cold War and the Korean War. In opposition, foreign policy and the atom bomb would continue to play a prominent part in the party's internal battles. In particular, policy on nuclear weapons would become a touchstone issue.

The Bevanites

As Labour went into opposition Nye Bevan, the creator of the NHS, emerged as the leader of the party's left wing. The left's primary beliefs were that nationalization had not gone far enough and that Britain was too dependent on American foreign policy. When the Conservatives proposed rearmament in 1952, Attlee accepted it, but Bevan led a group of 57 MPs in a rebellion against the proposals, demonstrating how vocal and organized the 'Bevanites' had become. The Bevanites also secured places on Labour's national executive and the Tribune newspaper became the vehicle through which they advocated nationalization and nuclear disarmament.

Bevan continued his anti-militarist protests when Britain and America supported German rearmament in 1954. He led a revolt in the parliamentary party, only narrowly losing the vote by 113 to 104. He then took the struggle to the party conference and again narrowly lost by 3.2 to 3 million votes. Bevan's response was to stage a dramatic resignation from the Shadow Cabinet, arguing that he could best serve the party from outside its leadership. He became an established thorn in the leadership's flesh and rebelled again in 1955 when Labour's leadership supported Churchill's decision to develop Britain's atom bomb. Not only did he lead an abstention to the vote in the Commons, but he also interrupted Attlee as he summed up the debate for Labour. For this Bevan had the whip removed and only just avoided being expelled from the party, with the national executive voting 14 to 13 in his favour.

CND

Nye Bevan and the Labour left believed they were reflecting widely felt public concern about atomic weapons. The 1950s and '60s were a time of growing Cold War tensions and there was a widespread belief that nuclear war was possible. After Stalin's death in 1953, Nikita Khrushchev pursued his own revised Communist philosophy. By 1961 East Berlin was haemorrhaging over 4,000 young and skilled workers to the West every week. On 12 August that year the exodus reached its peak when 2,400 people crossed from East to West Berlin in one day. The East German Army responded on 13 August by stationing troops along the border of the Soviet zone and beginning to build a wall to block off access to the West. The Berlin Wall would be the site of many deaths and would stand as a symbol of Cold War tensions for nearly 30 years.

In Britain these tensions were expressed in the creation of the Campaign for Nuclear Disarmament (CND) in 1957. It soon attracted a membership of over 20,000 and in September 1961 its chair, Canon John Collins, led a protest march of 12,000 people from St Paul's Cathedral to Trafalgar Square. Over 1,300 demonstrators were arrested following their nonviolent direct action. Collins believed the question of nuclear war was the supreme moral issue of the day.

Donald Soper

Among the founders of CND was Methodist minister and Labour activist Donald Soper. It was Soper's arguments that underpinned much of Labour's support for the peace movement and its antagonism towards nuclear weapons. His long career as an open-air preacher and agitator had courted controversy and his views were denounced and admired with equal intensity. As President of the Methodist Conference, Soper condemned the nature of atomic warfare and argued that, whatever the dangers faced, nothing could justify the use or threat of such weapons. He inflamed debate by declaring that he would rather see a world overrun with Communism than countenance a third world war.

Development of faith and politics

Like many Labour activists Soper had grown up in a Nonconformist home – his mother was a Congregationalist, his father a Methodist. As a young man, however, neither politics nor the realities of London's poor troubled his sheltered Wimbledon existence. The family attended St John's, Wandsworth, where the young Soper was taught a rigorous personal religion that had limited application to the wider world. It was his later involvement with the national Temperance Movement that broadened his horizons and provided him with the speaking opportunities which so defined his later life.

By the age of 15 Soper, like many others, had accepted World War I's patriotic call to arms. In 1918 his skills as a bayonet instructor led to his promotion in the Cadet Corps. Here he would teach men twice his age the art of hand-to-hand combat and killing. Yet even at 15, Soper had misgivings about war. He was shocked by the violence of the trenches, and when he took part in the first two minutes' silence after the war his attitude was profoundly changed by this corporate act of remembrance. A tragic incident on a cricket pitch – Soper bowled a ball that struck a colleague, who then died on the pitch before his eyes – reinforced in him the horror of violence.

In 1921 Soper went up to St Catherine's College, Cambridge, where for the first time he questioned the Christian faith of his childhood. He began to distance himself from a Christianity that was merely a system and embraced instead a faith that would become a way of life. This produced what Soper called a 'measured faith', one that included doubts but primarily expressed itself in action. Both Dean Inge and William Temple influenced his theology, Inge emphasizing the absolute nature of private morals and Temple impressing on him that morality must also be applied to public issues.

Soper's efforts to apply his faith to real life took him to a Student Christian Movement meeting in the factories of Derby in 1924. For the first time he was exposed to the appalling labour conditions suffered by factory workers. Soper reflected on this experience as a kind of conversion like any that Billy Graham could provide, and he left the factory a Socialist, committed to an involvement in politics.

Methodist ministry

By 1925 Soper could no longer refuse his call to the ministry and began to train at Wesley House, Cambridge. The 1926 General Strike split opinion among his fellow students, but his own support for the strikers was clear. By late 1926 he decided to put his theology into practice and left the cloisters of Cambridge for a Methodist mission off the Old Kent Road in South London. It was here that Soper's measured faith was applied to the daily reality of poverty in the lives of his neighbours. Many were unemployed and those who worked often did so in dreadful conditions. Alcohol provided one of the few escapes from life's harshness, but it also fuelled the conflicts and poverty that marred the lives of many families. One man threatened suicide in front of his frightened children and was only stopped by Soper's insistence that he was loved and needed.

It was Soper's more public ministry that would catch people's attention, however, when he started his open-air speaking at Tower Hill in 1927. His popularity developed immediately and within a year he was attracting regular crowds of up to 2,000 people. Then the summer of 1929 was doubly eventful for him, when he was ordained on 30 July and married to Marie Dean on 3 August.

Pacifism

Throughout the 1930s Soper continued to minister to his growing church and to preach at Tower Hill. His pacifist activity grew against the backdrop of Hitler becoming German Chancellor and the rearming of Britain. Soper's pacifist convictions were by this time deeply rooted in his Christian beliefs, and he would often resort to the simple and disarming argument that Jesus did not kill and therefore neither should his followers. It was an argument that infuriated and confounded his critics, especially as war approached in 1939. In an article in the *Daily Herald* he wrote, 'I could not conscientiously refuse to fight if I did not believe that this is God's world and that Jesus is the way.'[3] Once war was declared, the authorities regarded Soper's views as damaging for morale and he was banned from the media. Nevertheless, he continued to speak in the open air and from March 1942 he preached regularly at Hyde Park Corner – receiving enormous abuse in the tense wartime atmosphere.

The Church of Scotland's own radical priest, George McLeod, was also banned from the airways during the war. McLeod was the first non-Anglican to preach in St Paul's Cathedral following an invitation from Canon John Collins, who regarded him as 'a modern prophet, perhaps the only real prophet we have today'.[4] McLeod had led the arguments against supporting war at the 1933 General Assembly, but he later described himself as 51 per cent pacifist with an emphasis on pursuing peace rather than ruling out the necessity of war. McLeod had a global theology in which faith had to relate to issues of hunger, the atomic bomb, the economy and the environment. He preached what R.H. Tawney had taught – that 'the Cross be raised again at the centre of the market-place as well as on the steeple of the Church ... recovering the claim that Jesus was not crucified in a cathedral between two candles but on a cross between two thieves, on the town's garbage-heap'.[5]

Political action

A global theology required global solutions, and both the UN and the World Council of Churches were regarded as means through which God was working in his world. The strengthening of the UN became a recurring theme of the peace movement and Soper regularly spoke on this at Labour party conference fringe meetings. Soper's career was increasingly characterized by his argument for Christian involvement in politics and, like Tawney, he believed the economy was a religious subject. He believed that some issues could only be dealt with through politics and that politicians needed the inspiration of the Church. Soper repudiated a gospel which was exclusively spiritual, which demanded only a good death and not a good life. Such thinking, he said, was captured in a hymn he had sung in Sunday School, 'I am but a stranger here, Heaven is my home'.[6] At the party conference service in 1953 he told delegates that it was nonsense to ask the Church to 'keep out of politics'.[7]

In 1954 Soper started a regular column in *Tribune* under the editorship of Michael Foot. Through the newspaper his views would permeate the left of the party in a way that many Government ministers would have envied. His columns included political news or analysis, practical lessons on how to apply Socialist values, or comments on the inadequacy of Conservative values. Soper was not afraid to argue that Conservatism was inconsistent with Christianity. In doing so he incurred the wrath of leading Conservatives, including Lord Hailsham, who wrote a *Spectator* article entitled 'Is Dr Soper consistent with Christianity?'[8] Soper argued that the New Testament emphasis on community and self-sacrifice was incompatible with Conservative notions of individualism and appeals to self-interest. Despite this antagonism towards Conservatism, however, he did acknowledge that some Christians were Conservatives. While Conservatives and Socialists might be equally sinful as individuals, he said, the system they supported must also be judged.

Soper pursued his priorities of common ownership and nuclear disarmament within various groups. He was prominent in the 1958 Victory for Socialism group that argued for the implementation of the 'common ownership of the means of production' once Labour had secured power again. Labour would first need to win, however, and throughout the 1950s this seemed increasingly unlikely. Following Churchill's resignation, the new Conservative leader Anthony Eden called the May 1955 election at a time of major industrial unrest. Labour's association with the trade unions was seen more as a liability than a solution and its vote fell again, this time by 1.5 million to 46.4 per cent and 277 seats.

Changing direction under Gaitskell

Attlee resigned as leader in the wake of this poor performance, and the revisionist Hugh Gaitskell defeated Nye Bevan in the contest to replace him. Gaitskell cleverly secured a degree of unity in the party by appointing Bevan as Shadow Foreign Secretary and Harold Wilson as Shadow Chancellor. Bevan had become a safer pair of hands since renouncing his unilateralist position on nuclear weapons. He had come to believe that even if Britain did destroy its weapons, it would make no difference to the American and Russian positions. At the 1957 party conference Bevan famously described unilateralism as tantamount to 'sending a British Foreign Secretary naked into the conference chamber'.[9] Soper and Bevan maintained a mutual respect despite Soper's struggle to forgive Bevan for abandoning unilateralism. Soper continued to believe that only the unilateralist left could provide the foundation for Labour to move forward, and he accused the right wing of the party of undermining unity – the very accusation that the right was making towards the left of the party.

Nevertheless, under Gaitskell's leadership the Labour Party was moving further away from Soper and the left on the issues of nationalization and disarmament. Even Soper grudgingly admired the 1959 policy compromise which meant that a future Labour Government would support a non-nuclear club of nations while using Britain's weapons to bargain with. It was a policy specifically designed to bring together Labour's warring factions for the forthcoming General Election.

Soper took a leading role in that campaign and spoke on behalf of many candidates, including Barbara Castle in Blackburn and Ian Mikardo in Reading. Significantly, he also took part in a national party political broadcast alongside Gaitskell, Bevan and the party chairman Tom Driberg. Despite Gaitskell's attempts at party unity and his declaration of no tax rises, however, Labour lost further ground, securing 43.8

per cent of the vote and 258 seats. The party despaired and the leadership redoubled its efforts to break the increasing assumption that Labour must inevitably lose. In the face of the election defeat, and notably the loss of Labour seats around military bases, Soper himself did not budge on his twin priorities of nationalization and disarmament. Nonetheless, in the aftermath of Labour's third election defeat in a row, there were those who were beginning to question whether Soper's role in the party was more counterproductive than productive.

Nuclear disarmament

In 1957 Donald Soper and Michael Foot had become executive members of CND, whose annual march to Aldermaston provided a focus for public concern. CND sought to channel this pressure towards the Government and regularly submitted petitions to Downing Street and lobbied MPs. While Soper recognized that CND was not the sole weapon in the pacifist cause, he argued that it had altered the political climate. The presence of 50,000 protesters in Trafalgar Square during a demonstration in March 1961 meant that political leaders became more inclined to pursue disarmament, and it also influenced Labour's criticism of the Conservative Government's policy of overdependency on nuclear weapons.

Bevan remained sympathetic to the goals, if not the tactics, of CND and declared that a future Labour Government would end the testing of nuclear weapons, a position subsequently secured in the 1962 Test Ban Treaty. It was also CND's growing membership and political influence that helped win the vote for unilateral disarmament at Labour's 1960 party conference. However, 1960 was the peak of CND's influence on Labour policy and the unilateralist position was overturned at the 1961 conference following a concerted effort by the leadership.

The Christian Socialist Movement

The launch of another Soper project, the Christian Socialist Movement, also took place in 1960. CSM was the amalgamation of two groups, the Socialist Christian League and the Society of Socialist Clergy and Ministers. Bob Holman sees the launch of CSM as the relaunch of the Christian Socialist League of 1906. Over 600 people gathered at the launch event in Kingsway Hall, including Tom Driberg MP, Canon John Collins and R.H. Tawney.

The event opened with the congregation saying prayers for Nye Bevan, who by then lay terminally ill in hospital. When Bevan died later in the year, his widow Jennie Lee wrote to Michael Foot about her husband's memorial service. She said of Bevan, 'though not a Christian believer, neither was he a "cold-blooded rationalist"'.[10] She wanted a tribute with no hint of falseness and asked Donald Soper and Mervyn Stockwood to help in this.

Bevan's father had been a Baptist and his mother a Methodist, but during his boyhood the family had drifted away from the chapel. Bevan had attended a more liberal Congregational church for a while, but does not appear to have put down any roots. Nevertheless, his biographer Michael Foot identifies a Puritan streak in Bevan that seemed to have persisted from his Nonconformist roots. At Bevan's memorial service, as the light faded over a windswept Welsh mountainside, Soper addressed a crowd of 5,000 which included MPs, steelworkers and miners. He talked of Bevan as a man for others and declared that the way to thank him for all he had done was to finish the work he had started. Michael Foot later reflected on Soper's words: 'No-one else could have spoken as a socialist to colleagues, many of whom were not religious or agnostics, with such a command of appropriate language, sentiment and sympathy.'[11]

Standing up for principles

In the early 1960s Soper became increasingly antagonistic towards Hugh Gaitskell and his leadership of the Labour Party. Gaitskell had abandoned unilateralism and was also attempting to abandon the common ownership commitment of Clause 4. These were Soper's two great Socialist principles. The revisionists were influenced by Tony Crosland's 1956 book, *The Future of Socialism*, which argued that economic prosperity and social equality, not public ownership, were the keys to Socialism.

In 1961 the *Sunday Telegraph* reported the continuous civil war within Labour: '*Tribune* and Dr Donald Soper are keeping up their attack, which has been declared in Parliament, with Mr Anthony Greenwood and Mrs Barbara Castle pursuing their vendetta by contesting the leadership.'[12] Soper, however, was a little more gracious towards

Gaitskell following his sudden death in 1963, and warmer still after the election of Labour's new leader Harold Wilson. Wilson was regarded as more left wing and had described the attempted removal of Clause 4 as akin to taking Genesis out of the Bible.

Alderman and peer

Soper's own career in public office was by appointment rather than election. He started as an alderman in 1958 on the London County Council, later the Greater London Council. Soper only accepted the Labour whip on the proviso that on matters of conscience he would be free to speak and vote as he saw fit. These 'matters of conscience' included civil defence issues in the event of a nuclear strike and freedom to express his opinions in the press – all of which led to inevitable clashes with the Labour leadership. He resigned from the GLC in 1965 when he accepted a peerage in the House of Lords. This was a great disappointment for some Labour supporters, who regarded involvement in an unelected chamber as a betrayal of Socialism. Soper, on the other hand, simply regarded the Lords as another platform, like Tower Hill or Hyde Park Corner, where he could preach his faith in Socialism and in Christ.

Lord Soper remained a peer until his death in December 1998. He also remained active in a number of causes, including the campaign against the death penalty, the anti-apartheid movement and the campaign on immigration laws. In 1967 he became president of the League against Cruel Sports and he served on the board of Shelter for four years in the 1970s. He was President of the Christian Socialist Movement until his death, after which the CSM moved to abolish the office of president.

Influence on Labour

Reflecting on Soper's influence on the Labour Party, his biographer Brian Frost questions the description of him as Labour's 'National Chaplain'.[13] Frost instead suggests that Labour might have done better with a 'Niebuhrian' chaplain who understood better the political realities of compromise and power play that Soper so disliked. In America the Socialist theologian Reinhold Niebuhr (1892–1971) influenced a generation of US politicians towards a principled realpolitik. In *Moral Man and Immoral Society* (1932) Niebuhr outlined the need for Christian realism in an evil world. He rejected the optimism of Liberalism and the absolutist claims of both Marxist determinism and Christian pacifism. Instead he inspired the notion of US responsibility in the world, while warning against national pride. Unlike Soper, Niebuhr accepted the necessary evil of weapons as a means to protect one group from the evil intent of others. Niebuhr married Christian ethics and power in a way that Soper appeared unable or unwilling to do. The strength of Niebuhr's political theology was in its greyness, while the strength of Soper's was in its black-and-whiteness.

Soper's views on personal morality also appeared increasingly anachronistic in this post-war period. He would often argue that a good Socialist ought not to gamble, smoke or even drink. Labour's early history had conspired to associate these virtues with faithful Socialism and, despite the increasing liberalism of society, many found it hard to abandon these beliefs. Self-discipline and abstinence were dearly held values in the Nonconformist tradition that had influenced many of Labour's early leaders. Keir Hardie, Arthur Henderson, Ellen Wilkinson and George Lansbury had all been Temperance leaders, and Temperance almost became an article of Labour's faith at one time. Henderson, who dominated the party for so long, had also been a leader in the Trade Union and Labour Temperance Fellowship. Hugh Dalton once told how in 1927 Henderson almost resigned from the National Executive Committee over the issue of alcohol at Labour's party conference.[14]

This puritanical streak sat uneasily with the consumerism of the 1950s and the liberalism of the 1960s. In 1951 Britain had 2.5 million cars and 1 million televisions, but by 1964 there were 8 million cars and 13 million televisions. Commercial air travel was growing and by the end of the 1950s over 4 million people travelled abroad on holiday. It was also a decade of social change, with Mary Quant opening her first shop on the Kings Road, aimed directly at young people. The Church of England declared family planning acceptable in 1958, and 1961 saw the first oral contraception pills made available.

Tony Crosland's 1956 book on the future of Socialism had addressed these social changes in the light of Labour's puritanical legacy. He commented, 'Total abstinence and a good filing-system are not now the right signposts to the socialist utopia: or at least, if they are, some of us will fall by the wayside.'[15] Crosland maintained that Labour should embrace a new kind of Socialism by arguing for changes to ease people's psychological stress as well as their economic stress. This would include more open-air cafés, brighter streets at night and a reform of the law on homosexuality. It would require a culture shift by those who believed that economic management alone was the route to a Socialist utopia.

Tom Driberg

While many found these changes hard to take on board, others had already abandoned any notion of self-discipline and abstinence, perhaps none more so than the charismatic Labour MP Tom Driberg. Although Driberg was a colleague of Soper's in the CSM, he was as far from Soper's Puritan ethics as it was possible to be.

Thomas Edward Neil Driberg was born in 1905 and died in 1976. His obituary in *The Times* described him as 'a drinking man, a high-churchman and a homosexual' and 'the admiration and despair of his friends and acquaintances'.[16] Driberg was an enigmatic and extravagant character who enjoyed a lifestyle that raised eyebrows among his Socialist friends. What Keir Hardie or Arthur Henderson would have made of him provides pause for thought, but it is unlikely that they would have approved.

Was Driberg a spy?

Driberg's eclectic collection of friends in high places provided fuel for many rumours about his life, including the serious suggestion that he was a Russian spy. This accusation surfaced in Chapman Pincher's *Inside Story*, written after Driberg's death, which accused him of supporting Communist-front organizations and the withdrawal of troops from Northern Ireland. In Pincher's 1981 bestseller *Their Trade is Treachery*, he developed his character assassination of Driberg as a double agent who reported to MI5 and the KGB on his colleagues in Parliament. The claim that Driberg was a British agent reporting on the activities of the Communist Party was also included in Nigel West's 1981 book *MI5*. Whether Driberg was any kind of spy or not remains uncertain, however. The main basis for the rumours was his friendship with Captain Maxwell Knight of MI5, with whom Driberg socialized in London's top clubs.

His biographer Francis Wheen is extremely doubtful of the 'Driberg as spy' theory, although 'Driberg as gossip' is impossible to deny: 'He was a man who gossiped about everyone and everything.'[17] Wheen also argues that it was Driberg's passion for first-hand experience that both made him a top-class journalist and created his bizarre array of contacts. Add to this Driberg's complete lack of discretion, and here was a heady cocktail ripe for intrigue and conspiracy theories. Yet Wheen concludes on the spy allegation, 'Indiscretion is not synonymous with betrayal.'[18]

Nevertheless, reports about Driberg's security service connections did not go unheeded. The Communist Party of Great Britain revoked his party membership in 1941 without a word of explanation. Many years later the Bishop of Southwark, Mervyn Stockwood, declared that if he had known the things he now knew about Driberg (courtesy of Chapman Pincher), he would not have preached at Driberg's funeral. Yet many of Driberg's friends and parliamentary colleagues, including Michael Foot, simply could not believe he was a spy.

Early life and career

Driberg had grown up in a middle-class home in Crowborough, Sussex. Throughout his childhood he was involved in the custom of family prayers as well as attendance at the local Anglican church. In contrast to the Low Anglicanism of Crowborough, however, the High Anglicanism of Lancing College, where Driberg went at 13, proved to be much more to his taste. His other passions at Lancing included modern art, literature, Communism and homosexuality. This latter passion resulted in his early dismissal from the school because of inappropriate approaches towards another boy. Driberg's mother was told that his sudden departure was to allow extra time to prepare for an Oxford scholarship, which he duly secured before going to Christ Church in 1924.

Driberg's flamboyant character fitted well with the post-war era of individual expression at Oxford. His propensity for partying, however, was to stretch the liberal-minded college authorities to their limit. At the end of the summer term he arrived in the examination hall having not been to bed and still dressed in his white tie and tails from the previous night's ball. At the start of the exam he immediately fell asleep, and found himself expelled for the second time in his short career.

Despite this setback, Driberg knew he wanted to be a writer and he rented a flat in Soho as a base from which to pursue his objective. Before long he was working on the *Daily Express* and by 1928 he was writing a gossip column for *The Talk of London*. In 1934 his talents were requested for a new column in the *Express* written under the name of William Hickey, which would establish him as a nationally known figure. In the column Driberg often wrote about the hunger and unemployment of the 1930s alongside the activities of the rich and famous. In the late '30s he reported from Spain on the Civil War.

Political ups and downs

It was in 1942 that Driberg first stood for Parliament as an Independent MP. His strategy was to take advantage of the truce between Labour and the Conservatives to secure a seat in a by-election. As the war progressed, dissatisfaction with the Conservatives was running high and a number of Independents had already toppled Conservative MPs. So when the MP for Maldon died in May 1942, Driberg decided to stand. His campaign was a success partly because of his shameless exploitation of himself as the man behind the now-famous *Daily Express* column. Wheen comments on the new MP for Maldon, 'Parliament, like the Church, satisfied Tom's craving for exquisitely preposterous ritual.'[19]

At the end of the war Driberg needed to decide on his political allegiance, since few Independents would survive once the main parties became active again. Ellen Wilkinson encouraged him to choose Labour, and when the Maldon Labour Party asked him to be their candidate he secured party membership on the same day as his official adoption. Driberg won Maldon for Labour in 1945 with a 7,727 majority. Despite his initial enthusiasm for the Attlee Government, however, he later reflected that 'there was no fundamental or lasting change to the social structure of Britain'.[20]

If Driberg was critical of the Labour Party leadership, then the feeling was mutual. Thanks to his Independent background, his friendships with Tories and his flamboyant lifestyle, he was not trusted by many on the Labour benches. Nevertheless, as the man behind the *Express* column, his popularity was high among ordinary members and he was soon elected onto Labour's national executive, where he remained from 1949 until 1971. Driberg also continued his journalism despite his parliamentary commitments, travelling to Korea in 1950 to report on the war and incurring the wrath of the party when he failed to return for a series of votes following the 1950 election. As Labour only had a majority of five seats, MPs were being carried in on stretchers to make their votes, and Driberg's absence could literally have brought down the Government. His expulsion was only narrowly avoided following an abject apology and the recruitment of the respected Quaker Jimmy Hudson to speak on his behalf.

A newsworthy wedding

In 1951 he married Ena Binfield in what the *Sunday Express* described as the 'most interesting wedding of the season'.[21] Binfield was a nonpractising Jew, but Driberg persuaded her to join the Church of England for the marriage in St Mary's, Bourne Street. Aesthetically the wedding was very much to Driberg's taste, with a nuptial Mass and so much incense that the bride left the church choking. Nye Bevan growled that his 'Calvinistic blood was roused' by the elaborate display, while the Roman Catholic MP Hugh Delargy said the service made him feel like a Nonconformist.[22] Delargy had been recruited to the Christian Socialist fold by Driberg and was an early member of the Christian Socialist Movement.

Resignation

Shortly after the wedding, the 1951 election saw Driberg's majority in Maldon cut to 704. He announced that he would not fight Maldon again, since it was obvious that it would fall to the Conservatives in the next General Election. Driberg's home was on the left of the party and he was a leading figure in the Keep Left Group alongside Barbara Castle, Michael Foot, Harold Wilson and Nye Bevan. Like many on the left, Driberg was both captivated and distressed by the Cold War and the arms race throughout the 1950s. When Nye Bevan led his 1955 protest against Britain's development of nuclear weapons, Driberg went further with his own amendment calling the Government to take the moral lead and ban these weapons of mass destruction. Since this was against party policy, Driberg wrote a letter of resignation to Attlee declaring that in the absence of authoritative guidance from theologians and scientists, he found it impossible merely to abstain from a vote which had such fundamental importance to the future of mankind.[23]

Another MP who resigned in 1955 over Labour's support of the bomb was Sir Richard Acland. Acland was formerly a Liberal MP, but following the loss of his seat in 1945 he was re-elected as a Labour MP in 1947. During the war he was greatly influenced by reading the work of John Maynard Keynes[24] and developed a belief in universal communal ownership. After resigning the Liberal whip, his wartime group 'Common Wealth' grew rapidly and won three by-elections before the end of the war. In the Commons they attracted support from Labour's left, including Tom Driberg, Jennie Lee, Nye Bevan and Stafford Cripps. Acland's later career also saw him writing for the 1950 Group of Christian Socialists and as a founder of War On Want.

Christian Socialist discussions

When Driberg left Parliament in 1955, he decided to do something about the lack of 'guidance from the theologians' he had talked of in his letter to Attlee. He called together a group of Christian Socialist MPs and clergy who began meeting between 1956 and 1959. Their number included ministers of the Church Donald Soper, John Collins, Mervyn Stockwood and George McLeod, and MPs Hugh Delargy and F.T. Wiley. Driberg took the minutes at these meetings and in 1959 the group published their pamphlet entitled *Papers from The Lamb* – which, although seemingly a reference to Christ, was in fact the name of the Bloomsbury pub where the meetings took place. The publication of that booklet led to the launch of the Christian Socialist Movement in 1960.

Papers from The Lamb included essays on 'Common Ownership', 'Human and Racial Equality', 'Unity among Christians' and 'Christians and the Soviet Union'. It was a theological analysis on the political issues of the day, its chapters written after exhaustive discussion and redrafting by subcommittees. The authors required an understanding of both policy detail and theology, and each paper aimed to be accessible to a wide audience. It was an approach that took seriously the increasingly specialized knowledge in modern policy but also the belief that Christianity remained relevant to politics. In 'Common Ownership', nationalization was presented as only one example of the way industry can work. Its vision was of a new, socialized industry, a partnership between workers and management. In 'Human and Racial Equality', Britain's imperial domination was challenged with an admission of Christianity's role in subjecting native peoples. It concluded with a rejection of the white supremacy of South Africa's apartheid regime. Internationalism remained a dominant theme and there was also criticism of the Soviet denial of individual rights.

The papers addressed political issues, but also examined the question of relationships among Christians. In 'Unity among Christians', the World Council of Churches was recognized as imperfect but also as a key expression of Christian unity. The thorniest issue tackled was the idea that Christians could disagree on political issues. The concluding paper, on 'The Obligations of Prayer and Thought', condemned this notion as the clearest evidence yet of the invasion of individualism into the Church. A prophetic call was made to all Christians 'so to reason together, in a mood of Christian charity, that an informed and unanimous Christian mind, illuminated from many sources, can come into being'. This was, of course, easier said than done – when Donald Soper became chair of the CSM, for example, not all were pacifists as he was. The goal of a unanimous Christian mind was already proving hard to secure. Wheen comments that the booklet *Papers from The Lamb* is the closest Driberg ever came to defining his faith. Despite the fact that he was a journalist, he had never written about his beliefs, perhaps reflecting the mystery and awe in which he held them.

Disillusionment

Driberg's political career was relaunched when he became party chairman in 1957. In this role he helped to develop Labour's 1959 manifesto, 'Britain Belongs to You'. At the same time he was selected as the candidate for Barking and won by 12,000 votes, at a time when Labour lost its third election in a row. In the context of rising prosperity, Conservative leader Harold Macmillan had campaigned on the theme 'You've never had it so good, don't let Labour ruin it'. This theme resonated with an aspiring public and the Conservatives increased their Commons majority to 365 against Labour's 258.

Now returned to the back benches, Driberg fought Gaitskell's renewed attempts to reform the party. Driberg remained a respected figure on the left and when the national executive set up a committee to draft a new defence policy, Driberg was on it. Nevertheless, Gaitskell's supporters, including Denis Healey, drove through a pro-bomb, pro-NATO policy that reduced Driberg's role to one of simply repeating that nuclear weapons were evil and should be abandoned. After Gaitskell's sudden death in 1963 Driberg voted for Wilson, but by now he believed that idealism and radicalism had both gone out of politics. It had simply become a competition to see who could best manage the existing system. Although he was re-elected in 1964 when Wilson led Labour to victory, Driberg remained on the back benches – where, as Wheen says, he 'disagreed with the Government on almost every issue of conse-quence: Rhodesia, Vietnam, the Common Market, economic policy, industrial policy and immigration'.[25]

Facing political reality

Labour's successive losses in the 1950s produced the revisionist movement led by Hugh Gaitskell and Tony Crosland. Both Tom Driberg and Donald Soper were antagonistic to such attempts to revise the goals of Socialism. Their Socialism was about ideals and principles, and they found it difficult to amend these in the light of changes in public opinion or so-called public need. Such Socialist absolutism, however, had only limited usefulness to a party seeking to respond to the rapidly changing needs of the electorate.

This tension between ideals and reality has confronted all politicians, perhaps most especially those whose political convictions are ethically based. There is little doubt that Harold Wilson shared many of the ethical ideals of Soper and Driberg. However, as Wilson took Labour on to successive election victories, the party had to learn that realpolitik demanded real compromises. Under Wilson in the 1960s and '70s Labour returned to power to find that their challenge would not only be to run the country, but also to wrestle with the dilemma of how to marry progressive politics with political reality.

CHAPTER 9

Grey Power

HAROLD WILSON AND GEORGE THOMAS: 1964–79

*H*arold Wilson took Labour back to power after 13 years in opposition. *He won four out of five elections during the 1960s and 1970s, a record of which most politicians would be proud. Wilson finally laid to rest the demons of Labour's past and answered the question 'Must Labour lose?' with a resounding 'No!' In the progressive '60s, when tradition was out and modernization was in, there was even a widespread belief that Labour had moved from being the natural party of opposition to the natural party of government. Wilson captured the mood of the nation, yet for many in his party he was more mood than substance. People were not quite sure where he stood, and as for Christian commitment, his biographer Ben Pimlott comments, 'Labour colleagues, mainly atheist or agnostic, viewed Harold's piety with cynicism. Set against his cat-like manoeuvrings at Westminster, it looked like humbug.'*[1]

Herein lies the dilemma for conviction politicians – or is such a descrip-tion an oxymoron? Should they wear their ideals on their sleeves and then stick to them come hell or high water? Or is the ability to see – and even argue – both sides and to undertake 'cat-like manoeuvrings' one that every politician should covet? George Thomas MP was a pacifist but also a minister overseeing arms shipments to a divided Nigeria. Should he have resigned and acknowledged that pacifists cannot take such responsibility? Or was it right to stay and mitigate in whatever ways possible the problems that arose? This is the space between ideals and political reality, the space where conviction politicians work. For ethical Socialists the question is not whether politics should be infused with ethics, but how much ethics should be engaged.

Labour and the turbulent '60s

The 'swinging '60s' became the archetypal image of liberalism and toler-
ance. The Beatles, the Rolling Stones and the Chelsea Drug Store all
confirmed the view of *Time* magazine that London was swinging. Yet
London in the '60s was also heaving with tension. Racial tensions were
fuelled by politicians such as Enoch Powell and his talk of 'rivers of
blood'. Anti-Vietnam demonstrations erupted as images of napalmed
villages conflicted with all the talk of peace and love. In Northern
Ireland the civil rights movement was met with sectarian violence and
the deployment of British troops. There were mixed social messages too,
with Hugh Hefner's Playboy empire growing side by side with a
women's liberation movement demanding equality and respect. New
messages such as environmental concern came into focus through
Rachel Carson's *The Silent Spring* and the Torrey Canyon disaster.

Into this melting pot of cultural and political change came the
election of Harold Wilson and the Labour Party in 1964. In an age of
television and new ideas, people turned to Labour to manage the
dramatic social changes sweeping the country. The Wilson years were
the years that managed the advent of modernity and the liberalization
of Britain. These years saw the ending of executions, the freedom of
divorce without its cruel hypocrisies, the lifting of the criminal law from
practising homosexuals, and the introduction of the legal right for
women in need to secure an end to pregnancy. As Labour's official
history notes, 'Few of these measures were the product of official government bills but none of them would have happened without the
presence of men and women of good will in substantial numbers on
government benches.'[2]

Harold Wilson

Harold Wilson was born in 1916 in Cowersley, near Huddersfield. His
father Herbert was a chemist and the family lived in their own house in
a middle-class area. It was a home where religious belief was of primary
importance and although Herbert and his wife Ethel were Congregationalists, they worshipped at the local Milnsbridge Baptist Church.

Wilson later recalled that his upbringing was not one of religious fervour but of religious observance, where God was part of everyday life and was thanked for each meal. The church also provided a social framework, and Herbert ran the Operatic Society while Ethel was in charge of the Women's Guild. Sunday School and Scouts added to the plethora of influences, both social and spiritual, experienced by the young Harold.

Family life provided the framework not only for worship but also for political service. Herbert was once a Liberal, but had become a keen supporter of the Labour Party, inspired by the ethical Socialism of the former MP Philip Snowden. It was this 'ethical dimension' at the heart of the movement that later led Wilson to describe Labour as a moral crusade or nothing. His father's enthusiasm for political service had profoundly influenced Wilson's childhood, leading to his ambition to be an MP or even Prime Minister.

When the Wilson family moved to Bromborough, Harold met his future wife Gladys Baldwin. They both attended the local Congregationalist church and their Christian commitment was an essential part of their relationship. Gladys's faith was much more practical as a result of her father's inspiration and journey. He had started life as a mill worker, but through home learning and hard work had become a Congregationalist minister. Wilson's biographer Pimlott says, 'Where religion in the Wilson household had meant a framework for civic involvement and secular activities, in the Baldwin household it reflected deep moral heart-searching.'[3]

Student faith and politics

Wilson's religion as a framework for engagement with society was developed during his time at university, when he studied history at Jesus College, Oxford. He joined the University Congregational Society, enjoying the company of the evangelical group whom he described as the only group that was more than skin-deep. His university relationships and leisure activities were based around these religious discussion groups rather than the political ones. Wilson appreciated different styles of worship and after attending the Nonconformist Sunday morning services at Mansfield Chapel, he would go along to Evensong at Jesus College. This chapel attendance reflected a religious element to his character that was more than mere formality or family tradition. His colleague and friend at Oxford, Eric Sharpe, believes it influenced his political thinking and in later life, following his election to Labour's leadership, Wilson maintained, 'I have religious beliefs, yes, and they have very much affected my political views.'[4]

At Oxford Wilson also joined the League of Nations Union, which both formed and expressed his lifelong commitment to international-ism. He received an invitation from the Secretary of the University Labour Club too, but wrote that he found the club disappointing, with its members squabbling among themselves. It was only after leaving uni-versity, in 1938, that Wilson joined the party. He did enjoy hearing some famous speakers, however, including Stafford Cripps and G.D.H. Cole, and whenever their speeches were followed by a discussion time Wilson would usually ask questions. He was particularly interested in the rela-tionship between faith and politics, and in issues surrounding the Third World. At Oxford he learned to debate and joined a variety of discussion groups. He was confident on the subject of economics and once spoke on 'the last depression and the next', during which he referred to the 'mugs' on the Stock Exchange.

More than anything else, however, Wilson worked hard at university and later won a scholarship allowing him to undertake postgraduate studies and lecture part-time at New College. During this time he secured a job under William Beveridge, with whom he registered as a research student, to investigate 'the demand for labour in Britain'. The post proved providential and took him to Whitehall as a civil servant. His work with Beveridge continued throughout the war, so there was little time for political activity. Nevertheless, he became an active Fabian and in 1943 was co-opted onto the society's executive. He also began to look for a parliamentary seat.

Rapid promotion under Attlee

Wilson's first selection conference was in Peterborough, where he came second, but he was later selected for Ormskirk. Ormskirk was a mixed constituency with areas of high unemployment as well as more tradi-tional Liberal and Conservative areas. It was not a hopeful seat for Labour, but there were many surprising victories in 1945. Wilson won Ormskirk with 7,022 votes. His youthfulness and his background in

Whitehall meant that he was quickly noticed. The *News Chronicle* called him 'outstanding among the really new men on the Labour benches'.[5] Almost immediately Attlee appointed him as private parliamentary secretary to the Methodist George Tomlinson at the Ministry of Works. Chancellor Hugh Dalton also spoke well of him. Wilson did not let either of them down, performing well at the Ministry of Works where he was involved in post-war reconstruction.

His promotion was rapid and in 1947 he was appointed as the Secretary of Overseas Trade under Stafford Cripps at the Board of Trade. Cripps was to have a dramatic influence on him. Paul Foot says, 'Cripps' aloof command of detail, his scientific education and knowledge, his administrative genius, his belief in bureaucracy, his patriotism, his Christianity and even his vegetarianism combined to make what Harold Wilson regarded as the perfect politician.'[6] Cripps became Wilson's political mentor and this allegiance meant that Wilson was well placed to take over as President of the Board of Trade when Cripps went to the Treasury in 1948.

Another notable influence on Wilson was Nye Bevan. When Bevan resigned from Attlee's 1951 Cabinet over the imposition of NHS charges, Wilson resigned with him. It was Wilson's parliamentary secretary Barbara Castle who had introduced him to the circle of Bevanites on the left of the party, but Wilson never fully embraced a left-wing ideology and as a result many on the left resented his chairmanship of the Bevanite group. However, his association with the Bevanites did help to sustain a useful myth of left-wing credentials.

Increasing stature

After Labour's 1951 election defeat, Wilson made good use of his time out of office. He wrote a report on tackling world poverty following a commission from the left-wing publisher Victor Gollancz. His report was published under the title *War on Want* and its radical argument was for an international development agency financed through 10 per cent of the arms budget as well as 2 per cent of national income. The relief of world poverty, Wilson argued, needed more than free markets. The report helped Wilson gain wider recognition in the party and in 1952 he was elected to the national executive. He was a significant player in Labour's 1955 campaign, delivering one of the party's three televised political broadcasts in which he displayed household items that had risen in cost under the Conservatives. Labour was defeated again, however, and after Attlee's resignation Hugh Gaitskell became party leader.

Wilson was still only 39 and believed that Gaitskell would be leader for at least 10 years. He therefore set about ensuring that when the time came he would be best placed to challenge for the top job. Using his position on the national executive, he called for and then wrote an in-depth analysis of Labour's election defeat. It reported that party organization was woefully inadequate and that in some constituencies the only active workers during the campaign had been the candidate and the agent. It concluded that too much time was spent on converting floating voters and not enough on identifying and mobilizing Labour's core vote. It specifically recommended full-time agents for marginal seats. All these recommendations were to become features in Labour's subsequent campaigns.

Bridging the gap

In 1955 Gaitskell appointed Wilson as Shadow Chancellor, a position in which he once again performed well. By the time of the 1959 election Gaitskell, Wilson and Bevan were all working together, although beneath the surface rivalries remained. Nevertheless, despite their co-operation the Conservatives increased their majority and attempts were made to pin the blame on Wilson. Others, however, saw Gaitskell's last-minute promise not to raise taxes more as a sign of desperation than a thoughtful Labour policy.

Wilson, meanwhile, remained in the unusual position of not being identified wholly with either the right or left of the party. His strength was as a centrist, someone to bridge the gap between Labour's factions. Of course, this also meant that he had no natural block of support, only a grudging admiration for his skill. For many on both the left and the right he lacked ideological zeal and people were never too sure what he stood for. Pimlott agrees that 'Wilson's actual views were hard to pin down since his cleverness and knowledge made it possible for him to argue every position. He frequently shifted ground and critics wondered whether he had any.'[7] Such a description, however, begs a question as to whether this was a weakness or a political strength.

Leadership contest

During Gaitskell's attempts in 1960 to remove Clause 4, Wilson again appealed to what he believed was the mainstream view. He did so without actually attacking Gaitskell, saying, 'We are an ethical movement and one based on socialist principles and we shall neither win nor deserve to win elections if we merely stand forth as a technocratic alternative to the Conservatives.'[8] Gaitskell lost his attempts to abandon Clause 4 and Wilson now stood against him for the leadership after being provoked to do so by Anthony Greenwood.

Greenwood was a Bevanite and unilateralist co-campaigner with Donald Soper, George McLeod and others in the Christian Socialist League. The son of the Labour MP Arthur Greenwood, he had been in RAF intelligence before his by-election victory in 1946. Greenwood resigned from Gaitskell's shadow team over its support for the H-bomb and his candidature against him for the leadership was in part an attempt to get Wilson to stand. Wilson was so slow to do so, however, that in the end Greenwood had to be bullied to stand down. He later became a staunch ally of Wilson as Minister for Overseas Development in 1965 and Minister for Housing and Local Government in 1966. Like John Wheatley before him, Greenwood successfully saw the building of 400,000 new homes before the devaluation of the pound led to budget cuts. He remained in the Cabinet until 1969.

Gaitskell soundly defeated Wilson in the leadership contest by 166 votes to 81. The experience had invigorated Wilson nevertheless and, despite being moved to the post of Shadow Foreign Secretary, he began to develop new ideas on the future of the party. In 1962 he declared, 'The Labour Party is a moral crusade or it is nothing. We have to persuade the electors that we have the means and the men capable of transforming society into a socialist society.'[9] Wilson's language was designed to appeal to the left, who remained his most faithful supporters. It was their votes that ensured his victory following the sudden death of Gaitskell in 1963. The votes from the right were split between Jim Callaghan and deputy leader George Brown, and Wilson eventually beat Brown by 144 votes to 103.

Modernizer

Although Wilson had gained the position of leader because of his reputation as a left-winger, his Socialism was more about modernization
than nationalization. At the 1963 party conference he spoke of the
'white heat of the scientific revolution' and in doing so captured the
mood of both the party and the nation. The emphasis on modernity
was a tactic by which Wilson diverted attention from the continuing
divisions within the party. At 48 he represented a young, modern
approach and the 1964 manifesto, 'The New Britain', built upon this
theme. Launching the General Election campaign he was at his most
evangelical: 'We need men with fire in their bellies and humanity in
their hearts. The choice we offer ... is between standing still, clinging to
the tired philosophy of the day that is gone, or moving forward in partnership and unity to a just society, to a dynamic, expanding, confident
and above all purposive New Britain.'[10]

In the summer of 1963 the Conservatives were being ripped apart by
the 'Profumo Affair'. Secretary for War John Profumo had lied to the
Commons about his affair with Christine Keeler, who had links with a
Soviet diplomat. Prime Minister Macmillan was already unwell and
resigned that October in favour of the aristocratic Alec Douglas-Home.
Against Douglas-Home, Wilson epitomized the meritocracy and wider
opportunities of the 1960s and he exploited this advantage with his
populist touch. He knew how to use the television and in his first
months as leader made many broadcasts. He continued this populist,
up-with-the-minute approach as Prime Minister by appearing with the
Beatles on their return from conquering America, where their five
records were in the top five chart positions.

Money troubles

Wilson may have been a modern Prime Minister using modern images
to reach the nation, but ultimately it was a strategy that only half
worked. At the 1964 General Election Labour won 317 seats to the
Conservatives' 304 and the Liberals' 9 – which meant a majority of only
four. This margin would seriously undermine the Government's ability
to secure dramatic change and Wilson would need all his managerial
and manoeuvring skills for the crises that came thick and fast.

The first one came within 24 hours of Labour's arrival in government. An £800-million balance of payments deficit demanded an urgent decision on whether or not to devalue the pound. Wilson, Brown and Callaghan had not even caught up on sleep before they made the fateful decision not to devalue. Labour could have devalued and blamed the Conservatives, but Wilson was sensitive to the fact that Attlee's Government had devalued and he did not want to reinforce the image of economic weakness. The legacy of this decision, however, would limit Wilson's ability to govern for the next five years. He wrote in his memoirs, 'It was this inheritance which was to dominate almost every action of the government for five years of the five years, eight months we were in office.'[11]

On reflection, the decision not to devalue was the wrong one – although this is easier to see in hindsight and in the knowledge that devalued currencies can boost employment and exports. One result of not devaluing was that public expenditure cuts were needed to balance the books. Interest rate rises plus international loans were also required in order to defend the high level of the pound. The result was that Wilson's modernization plans became unworkable and he found his democratically elected Government being dictated to by the financial markets. Wilson's despair at this turn of events was evident:

We had now reached the situation where a newly-elected Government with a mandate from the people was being told, not so much by the Governor of the Bank of England but by international speculators, that the policies on which we had fought the election could not be implemented; that the Government was to be forced into the adoption of Tory policies to which it was fundamentally opposed. The Governor confirmed that that was, in fact, the case.[12]

The Government's whole social programme was conditional on economic growth that did not come. This was partly a result of international competition and industrial disputes, but it was also partly due to the fact that, despite the Cabinet's academic brilliance, none of them had any practical experience of management and wealth creation.

Making the best of it

In spite of the financial constraints, Wilson was determined to make some gestures that would indicate the values of his Government. Prescription charges were abolished at the first budget in November 1963 – although this decision would later be reversed. The budget also began a series of tax rises, a funding route which was still open to the Government. Between 1964 and 1970 taxes on personal incomes rose by 10–14 per cent and significant new taxes such as Capital Gains and Corporation Tax were introduced.

Meanwhile, in Foreign Affairs Wilson banned arms sales to South Africa and applied economic sanctions following Ian Smith's declaration of independence in Rhodesia. Under US pressure, however, Wilson had to accept the ongoing presence of the Polaris nuclear submarine base in Holy Loch and also gave British support for US policy in Vietnam. The accusation was levelled that America helped defend the pound while Britain helped defend US foreign policy.

Race relations

In his first Queen's Speech debate Wilson registered another issue in which his Government would be active: race relations. He accused the Conservative MP Peter Griffiths of running a racist election campaign and called for him to be treated as a 'parliamentary leper'. Race relations was a sensitive issue following the race riots of 1958 and growing calls for immigration controls. Wilson started with good intentions and looked to Archbishop Michael Ramsey, through the National Committee for Commonwealth Immigrants (NCCI), to help develop good race relations. New legislation would require to strike a balance between the needs of ethnic minorities and the growing calls for restrictions on immigration. The NCCI was critical of some aspects of the Race Relations Act (1965), however, and an uneasy relationship developed between Ramsey and Wilson over the next two years.

The problem came to a head in February 1968 when Home Secretary Jim Callaghan pushed through the Commonwealth Immigration ('Kenyan Asians') Bill in seven days to prevent Asians with British passports who had been expelled from Kenya from coming to Britain. Thirty-five Labour MPs voted against the Bill and Archbishop Ramsey said that 'the Bill had caused a good deal of dismay and distrust in Britain. Worse than that, it had created two levels of UK citizenship'.[13]

Nevertheless, the 1965 Act had for the first time outlawed racial discrimination and created an official mechanism whereby the needs of immigrant communities could be addressed via the Race Relations Board. The Race Relations Act (1968) also sought to strengthen ethnic minority rights and equality of treatment in areas of employment, housing and commercial and public services. These were difficult and bold moves in the context of a series of major speeches by Enoch Powell which only served to fuel tensions even further.

Ongoing challenges

Within a year of the 1964 election Labour's majority of four had been eroded through by-election losses. An early election seemed inevitable, but when Wilson ruled this option out in 1965, the Conservatives took the opportunity to replace Douglas-Home with Edward Heath, who fought Wilson in March 1966. Despite Labour's two difficult years, however, Wilson secured an outstanding election victory. This time the party's majority rose to 97 – the first time a sitting Labour Government had increased its majority. From 1966 to 1970 Wilson was released from the constraints of political instability, although there would be no let-up in the financial difficulties. By November 1967 the value of the pound had became unsustainable and it was reluctantly devalued by 14 per cent.

Another major challenge during this period was Labour's relationship with the trade unions. The seamen's strike of May 1966 welcomed Labour back to government and Wilson tackled the problem head on by attacking the 'tight-knit group of politically motivated men'[14] who were running the union. The strike, however, also had wider implications because it challenged efforts to control prices and incomes through the 1965 Prices and Incomes Board. The strike became part of an increasingly familiar pattern of walkouts and working to rule that was soon dubbed 'a British disease'. Although the TUC disapproved, they seemed unwilling or unable to act. Eight million working days were lost in 1970 alone. It was a thorny problem for a Government whose party was dominated and financially supported by the unions.

Wilson's response was to appoint the respected left-winger Barbara Castle as Minister of Employment and Productivity in 1969. She drew up her union reform white paper 'In Place of Strife', designed to provide freedoms but also requiring discipline from the trade unions. It included proposals to delay wildcat strikes and to ballot members on strike action. Wilson and Castle had underestimated the entrenched views of union leaders on legislative accountability, however, and with as many as one in three MPs backed by unions, it was impossible to get their proposals through. The face-saving formula which was eventually produced involved 'a solemn and binding agreement' to make every effort to overturn un-official strikes, but most people saw it as a victory for the trade unions.

Temporary return to opposition

More than any other issue, strike action resulted in Labour's surprise election defeat in 1970. Its share of the vote fell from 48 to 43 per cent, giving the party only 287 seats compared to the Conservatives' 330. Wilson remained as leader nonetheless. He had won two elections and could do it again. His first two Governments had been crippled by economic and industrial difficulties, but despite successive crises he had still delivered some radical social changes. This legislation reflected the increasingly liberal society Britain was becoming in the 1960s and '70s and included reforms to the laws on homosexuality, divorce and abortion, all either introduced or supported by the Wilson Government. Other small but significant actions included the abolition of the death penalty, the setting up of the Open University and the creation of select committees in the House of Commons.

In an age of increasing individual expression, Wilson had provided the greater freedoms that people demanded. This was consistent with Tony Crosland's advocacy of a Socialism set free from the Puritanism of the past and was a logical extension of Tawney's advocacy of economic equality into the fields of social and personal life. Despite Wilson's Christian ethos, he rejected a vision of society in which governments would prosecute people who could not or would not accept the morals of the majority. After Wilson became Prime Minister his wife Gladys explained this position in the following terms: 'What I mean is that I don't care for religious attitudes and ideas of morality which seem to depend on intolerance of one kind or another.'[15]

In opposition in the early 1970s Labour did not descend into the open civil war of the past. In the light of past difficulties, however, the new deputy leader Roy Jenkins called for Labour to be freed from trade union control. Also the British application for membership of the European Economic Community (EEC) proved divisive for Labour. In 1971 the party conference ordered MPs to vote against entry, but Jenkins led a rebellion of 67 pro-EEC MPs. When the Conservatives took Britain into the EEC in 1973, Wilson defused the row by promising a referendum when Labour returned to power. Meanwhile the Conservatives were making their own attempts at reining in the unions through their Industrial Relations Bill, introduced in 1970. They also had to deal with the oil crisis of 1973, imposed by Arab nations following the Israeli–Egyptian war.

An inconclusive win

The Conservatives called the 1974 General Election to coincide with the beginning of a second miners' strike. Heath had struggled with a miners' strike the previous year and this second strike provoked the Conservatives to fight the election on the theme 'Who Governs Britian?' The electorate's answer was, 'Not the Conservatives,' and Labour's theme 'Get Britain Back to Work' secured Wilson his third election victory.

Once again, however, the win was inconclusive, with 301 seats going to Labour over the Conservatives' 296 and the Liberals' 14. Despite this handicap Wilson established a minority Government and pushed ahead with reforms he believed the Liberals would support. The economy was in tatters, with unemployment at 600,000 and a balance of payments deficit of £3.3 billion. Nonetheless, an agreement was quickly secured to settle the miners' strike and within the first six months legislation was passed on fair rents and health and safety issues. The Government also suffered 17 Commons defeats in those first six months, however, and Wilson called a second election – at which Labour secured a majority of only three.

The year 1974 became a bleak one for Britain as direct rule replaced the Northern Ireland Assembly and the IRA began a bombing campaign on the British mainland. Five deaths in a Guildford pub and 21 deaths in a Birmingham pub provoked the Prevention of Terrorism Act. Perhaps the most notable event of Wilson's 1975–6 Government, however, was its promised referendum on EEC membership. Since the Cabinet was split on the issue, Wilson suspended the requirement for Cabinet unity in order to allow ministers to campaign on either side. The issue of membership was complex and not simply a case of the right being for and the left being against, but with the media broadly in favour, 67 per cent of the public voted to remain in membership while 33 per cent voted against.

Retirement

Within six months of the referendum Wilson fulfilled his pledge to retire at 60 and announced that he was standing down. His concluding period as Prime Minister was marked by a loan from the International Monetary Fund, which in return demanded cuts to the 1976/7 public expenditure plans. A white paper also announced further cuts of £1 billion in 1977/8 and £2.4 billion in 1978/9. Wilson's era as Prime Minister had begun with an attempt to defend Labour's reputation on the economy, but it ended with the case for the prosecution won. Wilson was not entirely to blame. The dominant Keynesian economic model of cutting taxes and boosting spending in order to drive the economy out of recession had simply not worked. Added to this were the deficits inherited from the Conservatives, global competition, industrial disputes and the inherent antagonism of money markets towards Socialism. These all played their part in undermining the Wilson years and the problems would be just as difficult to resolve for his successor. Six people stood for the leadership election and in the final ballot it was Jim Callaghan from the right of the party who triumphed over Michael Foot with 176 votes to 137.

George Thomas

One of the people who had stood with Wilson throughout his time in office was George Thomas MP. Thomas was a junior minister at the Home Office involved in the sensitive area of immigration. Many in the parliamentary party wanted to secure progressive legislation on race relations as well as the liberalization of the immigration laws. It proved to be a difficult balance to strike in an atmosphere of rising tensions. When Thomas was at the Home Office, Home Secretary Frank Soskice responded to the suggestion of liberal immigration controls by declaring,

'If we do not have strict immigration rules, our people will soon be all coffee-coloured.'[16]

Thomas himself had clear views on the importance of racial equality. When he visited Georgia in July 1959 as Vice President of the Methodist Conference, he found to his horror that he was due to preach in a church where black people were not allowed to worship. To protests that Thomas did not understand their problems, he quietly replied, 'I do not pretend to understand your problems; I am only a visitor. My trouble is that you do not understand *my* problem. I cannot preach in a church where blacks are refused admission.'[17]

Life in the Rhondda Valley

Thomas's Christianity had begun in 1925, the same year in which he joined the Labour Party. He was born in 1909 and brought up in the Rhondda Valley by his mother after his father left her during World War I. Thomas experienced the poverty and poor housing of life in a single-parent family. By day his mother washed other people's clothes and by night she stayed awake and mended them. Thomas once woke at two in the morning to find his mother busily sewing by the light of an oil lamp. She told him to go back to bed and as he lay there wondering why his mother had to work so hard, he promised that one day he would make sure she would not have to do so.

His mother was the most important influence on his life and it was she who introduced him to both the Chapel and the Labour Movement. Although her family had come from a long line of Liberals, she joined the Labour Party in 1915. At the time she was told that she had disgraced her father, but when she asked him directly if he was really disgraced by her decision, he replied, 'No Emma, the Liberals were the radicals when I was young. If I was your age, I'd probably be joining the Labour Party.'[18]

When Thomas was 10 he witnessed the grim reality of life in the Rhondda mines when he saw a procession of miners carrying one of their dead workmates. This experience was an incentive for him to pass a scholarship exam for Tonypandy Higher Grade School. In 1925 his mother remarried and they were able to move from their basement house to a new home where Thomas had his own bedroom.

At the age of 16 he was challenged by the local Methodist minister to give his life to Christ. As was the custom, Thomas stood up, said a prayer and then made his way to the front of the church. It was an experience that would change his life for ever. The minister of Tonypandy Central Hall, the Revd R.J. Barker, had a profound effect on Thomas's development. Barker was an ardent critic of Communism and taught the young Thomas the importance of the individual, their conscience, their rights and their responsibilities.

Teaching and politics

Throughout this period Thomas felt called to become a Methodist minister, but in the meantime decided to become a teacher. At 19 he went to Essex as an uncertified teacher and then to Southampton to train. His professor at Southampton was a committed Christian active in social work and he invited Thomas to assist in a school for handicapped children. When Thomas first went to the school and saw the disfigurement of the children, he felt physically sick and had to leave. He would rather never have gone back, but his professor persuaded him to return to the school and help out as he had promised. Having completed his training in Southampton, he went to teach in London where he worshipped at Westminster Central Hall and began to become more actively interested in politics, listening to debates in the Commons.

After a short time in London he was offered a job in Cardiff at the Marlborough Road School. There he joined the National Union of Teachers and later became the parliamentary secretary to the Cardiff Association of Teachers. His interest in politics was furthered by the mock parliament set up by the new minister of Tonypandy Central Hall. Up to 200 young men (women had not yet been invited) would debate issues such as the death penalty, the idea of a national health service and the right to work. Debates were vigorous and issues were addressed from a Christian perspective, which illustrated for Thomas the essential truth that not all Christians draw the same conclusions.

He was increasingly recognized for his leadership skills and in the 1930s he led the Tonypandy contingent of miners to London to protest for work. He later became secretary to the Workers' Temperance League within the Labour Party, and Dr Alfred Salter MP spoke at the League's conference and preached in Tonypandy Central Hall. Thomas's pacifist views were shaken as a result of World War II and the horror of the concentration camps. He decided not to declare himself a pacifist but to join one of the armed forces, although a medical examination would later declare him unfit for military service. In 1942 he was elected to the national executive of the NUT and in 1944 allowed his name to go forward as a parliamentary candidate.

Early parliamentary career

In the selection for Cardiff South he was beaten by Jim Callaghan, but was then selected for Cardiff Central. The basis of his campaign was simple: there should be no return to the poverty of the 1930s, and no mother should have to work as his mother had been forced to do. He also wanted to put Christian values into politics, but was dismayed when the local Catholic church posted a notice on its door saying that it was a mortal sin to vote for George Thomas. Nevertheless, in 1945, in what was one of the happiest campaigns of his life, Thomas was elected with a majority of 5,000.

In the 1945 Government it was George Thomas who would lead the hymn-singing as Attlee's reforms were pushed through the division lobbies. Although a loyal backbencher, he was once accused of disloyalty for abstaining in the vote on national service. Thomas turned to Willie Whiteley the chief whip, whom he knew as a fellow Methodist, and challenged him about following one's conscience even though it might sometimes be against one's party. The matter was allowed to rest.

In 1951 Thomas began his journey towards becoming the Commons Speaker when he was invited to sit on the Speaker's Panel. This gave him the opportunity to preside when the committee stage of a Bill was being taken through on the floor of the House. He remained sympathetic to peace issues although he had fought in the war, and when the US detonated the first hydrogen bomb in 1954 he attended the meeting that led to the formation of CND. In the 1955 leadership contest he voted for Bevan against Gaitskell and when the Welsh Grand Committee was established in 1958 his commitment to Welsh issues saw him elected as its first chairman.

The long years of opposition in the 1950s were compensated for by Thomas's active role in the Methodist Church. It was in his role as Vice President of the Methodist Conference that he had travelled to Georgia. He eventually did preach at the whites-only church on the Sunday morning, but only on the condition that he was allowed to preach at the black church on Sunday night. At the white church he was accused of being a one-world supporter, to which he responded, 'How many worlds do you believe in?' Meanwhile, at the black church he was described 'as having a white face but a heart as black as ours'.[19]

The Wilson years

In the 1963 leadership race Jim Callaghan, Thomas's neighbouring MP in Cardiff, lobbied hard for his vote, but Thomas had been committed to Harold Wilson for many years. When Wilson subsequently became Prime Minister he appointed Thomas to the Home Office and after the 1966 election he gave him the post of Minister of State at the Welsh Office. The decision to establish a Welsh Office in 1964 had provoked a tide of nationalism and the first Welsh Nationalist MP was elected in 1966.

In 1967 Thomas was moved to the Commonwealth Office where one of his successes was to defuse single-handedly a diplomatic crisis between Ghana and Britain. Efforts to resolve the problem had not been going well, but Thomas happened to mention to the President of Ghana that he was a Methodist. The President was also a Methodist, it turned out, and he immediately agreed to Thomas's request and the crisis was over. Another dilemma at the Commonwealth Office was the role of the Government in supplying arms which were used in Nigeria's civil war. Thomas's pacifism caused him to agonize over this issue and he seriously considered resigning. However, he concluded that someone else would simply continue the policy if he did resign, and to leave would only demonstrate that pacifists were unable to take on such responsibilities.

Thomas was appointed Secretary of State for Wales and a member of the Cabinet in 1969. This was a difficult job as it included the oversight of the investiture of the Prince of Wales in July 1969. On the one hand the royals were demanding more government money for the event, while on the other Labour activists were complaining that £200,000 was being spent which could be better used elsewhere. Welsh nationalism had always had a violent edge and throughout this period Thomas received almost weekly death threats. Such antagonism reached its worst point when his 88-year-old mother was woken at night by callers threatening her son's life. Despite this – or because of it – Thomas worked hard for Wales and during his time in office 195 new industries were established in Wales and unemployment fell to 33,000. When Labour lost the election in 1970 he continued as Shadow Secretary of State for Wales.

Mr Speaker

His mother's death in 1972 caused Thomas to question his Christian faith as well as the value of his political life. The departure of the woman who had done so much to form his belief in God and in politics knocked his faith in both. Following the 1974 election, however, he was offered the role of Deputy Speaker rather than a return to the Welsh Office, and in 1976 when the Speaker retired Thomas was unanimously supported as the new incumbent. It was a position that allowed him to focus once again on his faith and among other things he ruled that use of the expletive 'Christ' in the Commons chamber was blasphemy and unparliamentary. He also used the Speaker's house to host two prayer groups, one for MPs and one for their wives. Thomas confessed to fears that the American-inspired prayer network was actually a front for the CIA and its anti-Communist activities, but he was soon reassured that it was genuinely only about prayer. MPs from all parties attended and it reinforced the undercurrent of faith in the House of Commons.

Thomas also helped to facilitate the first Roman Catholic Mass to be held in Westminster since the Reformation. It was the idea of Labour MP Kevin McNamara, who wanted to commemorate the five-hundredth anniversary of the birth of Sir Thomas More. Not only did Thomas facilitate the Mass, presided over by Cardinal Hume, but he also facilitated the protest that the Revd Ian Paisley felt obliged to make. Thomas forewarned the worshippers that the protest would take place at the beginning of the service, after which Dr Paisley would leave. He later said of the service:

> It was more than 500 years since Catholics had been allowed to worship God according to their beliefs in that crypt and I found the service most moving. I believe that God used me on this occasion to provide another step forward for religious freedom in Britain: the bigotry of 500 years ago should not decide the way we behave today.[20]

In 1981 the Archbishop of Canterbury asked him to read the lesson at the marriage of the Prince and Princess of Wales at Westminster Abbey. Thomas's Methodism meant that he could represent the Free Churches, his role as Speaker meant that he could represent Parliament, and it was also appropriate that as a Welshman he should participate in the wedding of the Prince of Wales. Thomas's life – from his poverty-stricken background in a single-parent family to the peak of his career as Speaker at the House of Commons – provides a window onto the growing meritocracy that Britain was becoming. No longer was a child from such a background limited simply to going down the pits. Thomas showed that through hard work and increasingly available opportunity, every child could fulfil his or her potential.

Labour under Callaghan

Following Wilson's retirement in 1976, Callaghan won the party leadership to become Prime Minister. The economy would dominate and constrain his Government just as it had done with Wilson's, and within a year Callaghan was borrowing more money and announcing further spending cuts. Chancellor Denis Healey's budget tried to revive the economy with £1.3 billion of tax cuts, a package that demanded continued pay restraint by the TUC. However, by September 1976 the Government was forced to apply for $3.9 billion in IMF credits and was also required to sell shares in British Petroleum.

To stave off Conservative censure motions, Callaghan agreed a Lib-Lab pact with David Steel in March 1977. By 1978/9, however, the Government's pay restraint policy was being undermined from all sides and a series of industrial disputes led to the infamous 'winter of discontent'. In March 1979 the referendums on Welsh and Scottish devolution were rejected in Wales and proved inconclusive in Scotland. It was the straw that broke the camel's back. The Government lost a vote of no confidence for the first time since 1924 and an election was called for May 1979. The Conservative leader Margaret Thatcher campaigned on a programme of 'rolling back the state and releasing the market' and won with 339 seats to Labour's 269. Labour received only 39.9 per cent of the vote, its poorest performance since 1931. The party returned to opposition, this time for 18 very long years, many of them marred by internal strife.

CHAPTER 10

Terminal Illness

ERIC HEFFER AND TONY BENN: 1980–92

*I*n May 1979 Margaret Thatcher came to power with a radical agenda. It would involve the 'rolling back' of the state, the curbing of union power and a challenge to post-war assumptions on welfare and full employment. Thatcher rejected any state intervention to support ailing industry in favour of privatization or closure. These policies, combined with a global recession between 1979 and 1983, had a devastating effect on British manufacturing and employment. In May 1979 unemployment stood at 1.3 million, but by 1983 it had reached 3 million. Many of the unemployed had worked in the 5,000 factories that closed between 1979 and 1982.

The 1980s were to become an ideological battleground between the values of Socialism and the values of the new political right. Initially Labour tried to provide a radical left-wing alternative to Thatcherism, but the electorate rejected this in 1983. Instead the party had to reform its structure and policies to take heed of the new demands of the day. The ideological battle within Labour was as ferocious as any battle in the nation at large. The question was, did Socialism have a future and if so, what kind of Socialism would that be?

Two of the leading left-wingers were Tony Benn and Eric Heffer. Benn still held a powerful influence on the Nonconformist, ethical wing of the party. Heffer was an ex-Communist who had rediscovered the relevance of faith in political life. Both were at the epicentre of Labour's struggles in the 1980s and their individual fortunes were intimately connected to the future direction of the party.

185

Ideological conflicts

The question of religion and politics played an important part in the ideological conflicts of the 1980s. It was an age of individual enterprise and Thatcher questioned the very existence of community. The Archbishop's Commission report *Faith in the City* was one response to the riots and deprivation of Britain's inner cities. The Conservative Ian Gow MP denounced the report as Marxist and accused the Church of commenting on matters which should have been left to the judgement of politicians.[1] *Faith in the City* did admit some kind of Marxist influence by stating that 'against the background of the excessive individualism of much Christian thinking, we must place Marx's perception that evil is to be found, not just in the human heart but in the structures of economic and social relationships'.[2] However, the report then went on to say that this was not a Marxist concept but an Old Testament one.

The presence of the Church in communities which were suffering poverty and unemployment led an increasing number of clergy to condemn Government policies. This included the Bishop of Durham, David Jenkins, who spoke out on behalf of those who were losing their jobs. In his 1986 address entitled 'The Market', he described modern Conservatism as materialistic, secular, individualistic and the antithesis of the gospel. Prime Minister Thatcher chose to defend herself in an address to the Church of Scotland in 1988. She appealed to the example of John Wesley, 'who saved all he could to give all he could', and quoted the apostle Paul: 'If a man will not work, he shall not eat' (2 Thessalonians 3:10b). At the end of the decade the book *Christianity and Conservatism* sought to legitimize Thatcher's reforms by allowing individual Conservatives to tell their own stories.[3]

The formation of the SDP

Meanwhile, as Thatcher's reforms began to bite, the Labour Party was tearing itself apart. As the party swung to the left, just as in 1931 the internal battle resulted in a split that threatened its very existence. The left of the party had organized themselves well in the late 1970s and at the 1979 conference secured a vote to require all MPs to seek reselection during every Parliament. As MPs would have to be more accountable to largely left-wing activists, this would keep right-wingers in check. When Callaghan later resigned as leader the left was triumphant again as Michael Foot defeated Denis Healey for the leadership. However, it was the decision to elect future leaders via an electoral college and not by MPs alone that was the final straw for many on the right. In January 1981 Roy Jenkins, David Owen, Shirley Williams and Bill Rodgers announced the birth of the Council for Social Democracy. Jenkins described it as 'half in and half out of the party', but by March it had become the Social Democratic Party (SDP), a new party of the political centre.

The SDP was launched with just 12 Labour MPs and nine peers, but it would eventually attract 29 Labour MPs. Frustration with Labour was running deep and within 10 days the SDP had 40,000 members. Many Christians, including Shirley Williams, felt that the tradition of ethical Socialism was being squeezed out in favour of a rigid, scientific Socialism. The SDP even claimed to follow in Tawney's tradition of social democracy. As Ivor Crewe and Anthony King note, 'Firmly on the gradualist, reformist wing of the party, Rodgers saw himself as standing in the line of ideological descent running from R.H. Tawney through Evan Durbin and Hugh Gaitskell to Anthony Crosland.'[4] Anthony Wright, however, rejects this notion and argues that Tawney was firmly a democratic Socialist and, while he would have been dismayed at the present narrowness of the party, he would nevertheless have remained a party man.[5]

Meanwhile, 100 Labour MPs remained within the party despite misgivings about its current direction, and formed a solidarity group under Roy Hattersley to fight the leftward swing. The swing continued, nevertheless, and in 1981 the party conference once again accepted unilateral nuclear disarmament, just as it had done in 1960. As a founding member of CND, Labour's new leader Michael Foot was delighted at this decision. Yet Foot seemed less comfortable with his role as leader and the need to build an effective consensus from which to challenge Thatcherism. His Nonconformist roots and career in opposition (even when Labour was in power) had not prepared him well for leadership of the party.

The development of the SDP–Liberal Alliance became a real threat to Labour. By the end of 1981 support for the Alliance was up at 50 per cent, with Labour and the Conservatives on just 23 per cent each. The

Conservatives received an electoral boost from the Falklands War, but Labour was further damaged by the loss of the safe Bermondsey seat (the party had disassociated itself from the hard left, 'Militant' platform of the Labour candidate Peter Tatchell). Worse was to come in the 1983 election. Labour's manifesto, described by Gerald Kaufman as the longest suicide note in history, promised increased benefits, unilateral disarmament, the repeal of trade union legislation and a withdrawal from the EEC. Conservative Central Office was reported to have bought copies to use against Labour on the hustings. The Labour Party reached its nadir in June 1983 when the Conservatives secured a 144-seat majority and Labour's vote fell to 8.4 million, only 600,000 behind the SDP–Liberal Alliance.

Kinnock's attack on the hard left

Michael Foot resigned and Neil Kinnock was elected in his place after defeating Roy Hattersley, Peter Shore and Eric Heffer. Kinnock was from the left, but appointed Hattersley as his deputy in an effort to unite the party. He recognized that if Labour was to stop the SDP–Liberal Alliance and regain public confidence it would have to change. Within six months Kinnock's honeymoon period was over, however. Arthur Scargill, the president of the National Union of Miners, called a strike after a sudden pit closure. Scargill refused to ballot NUM members and adopted a policy of picketing miners who continued to work. By doing so he precipitated a strike that included attacks by miners on other miners as well as violent confrontations with the police. Margaret Thatcher had experienced the miners' strikes of 1972 and 1974, however, and this time the Government was thoroughly prepared. In the face of such a hostile and well organized Government, the NUM was defeated after a year.

Just before the 1985 party conference, the Militant-led Liverpool City Council brought Liverpool to administrative chaos through its policy of budget overspend. In a conference speech that defined his early leadership, Kinnock spoke against Militant and its activities in Liverpool. He accused the Militant leadership of playing politics with people's jobs, services and homes and adopting rigid dogma irrelevant to people's real needs. Despite some heckling, the majority of the conference delegates applauded this speech. The next day Kinnock attacked Scargill's leadership of the failed miners' strike. In two short days he had taken on and fatally damaged the hard left, helping to set the Labour Party on a new course.

The Militant-controlled Liverpool Council was at the core of many of the ideological wranglings going on within Labour at this time. Militant was a hard left Marxist group which adopted 'radical politics for radical problems'. The presence and organization of Militant Labour in Liverpool's poorest wards had led to electoral success and some local achievements. Nevertheless, Militant's brand of politics was never going to be acceptable to a national Government demanding reduced local rates. Kinnock's decision to tackle them was a difficult one, but he served notice to the party that its members must abide by the law, and those who were Militant members were expelled from the party.

Eric Heffer

There were some, however, who remained sympathetic to Militant. One such person was Liverpool MP Eric Heffer, who had walked from the platform during Neil Kinnock's conference speech. Heffer was an ex-Communist and his uncompromising politics emerged in part from his uncompromising Christian faith. He believed that Christ was on the side of the poor and that Christianity was a poor man's religion. The former Anglican Bishop of Liverpool, David Sheppard, said of him, 'He followed his faith with a fierce personal integrity that left no authority unquestioned. He was not a comfortable member of the Church or, I am sure, of a political party.'[6] Heffer had been a carpenter right up to his election as an MP and in that sense was very working class. This was one reason why he defended the Militant politicians of Liverpool. He felt that people had just not given them enough credit as 'working-class lads'. Their tactics had been unorthodox and flawed, but they had achieved some success in the midst of social deprivation.

Eric Heffer was born in Hertford in 1922 and was MP for Liverpool Walton from 1964 until his death in May 1991. The title of his autobiography, *Never a Yes Man: The Life and Politics of an Adopted Liverpudlian*,[7] identifies both his rebellious spirit and his commitment to Liverpool. Heffer wrote another book, published posthumously, entitled *Why I Am a Christian*.[8] This was an attempt to explain a faith that had pervaded his life but had never been worn on his sleeve. He wrote it to answer the

189

question of a journalist, who said to him, 'Yes, I know about your child-hood, you have told me, but what about your belief in God? Why do you believe, and why are you a Christian? Stop dodging and weaving, answer the question honestly.'[9]

Faith and family background

Why I Am a Christian conveys Heffer's belief that Socialism flows from Christianity, but he had not always felt like that. As a child Heffer had attended the local Church of England school and was a choirboy at the local church. Although he attended the Low Anglican Christ Church, he actually preferred the High Anglicanism of St Andrew's and would also visit the local Catholic church. It was the ritual and colourful vestments of these other churches which attracted him in contrast to the sombre dress worn by the clergy of Christ Church. Heffer was always outspoken and when he became a St Andrew's choirboy the other boys asked him to take their request for more money to the church authorities. Heffer duly presented their case, which included a threat that they might not sing at the Easter services if their demands were not met. The boys received their extra money, but the choirmaster soon got rid of Heffer on the pretext that his voice was breaking. Heffer's childhood faith was therefore part of the overall experience of attending a church school and involvement with the church choir and clubs.

Heffer's father was a bootmaker and his mother a cook, and the family never went hungry, although his brother died from TB, a condition exacerbated by their damp cottage. At home together, his family would often talk politics and most days there would be conversations around the dinner table. In particular the Spanish Civil War captivated their attention and Heffer recalls an occasion when his father grabbed some copies of a Fascist newsletter being sold by a young man and threw them into the river.

From Labour to Communism

At the age of 14 Heffer became an apprentice carpenter, but after a couple of years he realized that he was being used as a full craftsman while still being paid as an apprentice. His objection resulted in him being thrown out by the firm and he only secured another job after help from the union. At around this time Heffer says he was looking for a purpose in life and initially he found it in the Labour Party and the trade union movement.

The 1936 hunger marchers arrived in Hertford on their way to London and Heffer went along to a public meeting. This made a big impact on him and his political education continued through the various people he met and heard. An elderly chairman of the Hertford and Ware Branch of the Amalgamated Society of Woodworkers talked about what Labour stood for and how the unions had created the party. Heffer also heard the preaching of Father Conrad Noel from Thaxted who argued that Christ was a revolutionary, which was why the Roman and Jewish establishment crucified him.

The teachings of Noel and other Christian Socialists developed Heffer's understanding of Christianity, but when he was 17 he left the Labour Party to join the Communist Party, a decision that ensured the rejection of his faith, or at least its denial, for more than 25 years. He reflected later that the Communist Party had seemed attractive to young men living under the National Government led by Neville Chamberlain. Chamberlain seemed more interested in appeasing Fascism than fighting it and Heffer also felt that Labour dragged its feet in terms of supporting the International Brigade in Spain. Indeed, people such as Stafford Cripps and Nye Bevan had been temporarily driven from the party because of their commitment to fighting Fascism.

New horizons

During World War II Heffer served in the Royal Air Force, repairing and refitting aircraft. Aged 21, he was transferred to a maintenance unit in Liverpool where he met his future wife Doris at the Young Communist League. Although he was still a Communist at this stage, he offered his services to the Labour Party at the 1945 election and, dressed in his uniform, spoke for the local candidate on the eve of the poll. Heffer criticized Churchill for claiming that the Conservatives had won the war and asked rhetorically, 'If that is so, what have we servicemen and women and civilians been doing?'

In 1945 he married Doris and after two years in Hertford they settled in Liverpool with Doris's Catholic aunt and uncle. At that time Liverpool was a city deeply divided along sectarian lines. The Catholics lived in the area around Scotland Road, while Everton and Walton were mainly Protestant areas. Heffer's position as a Protestant with Catholic in-laws gave him a unique perspective and helped him to build bridges between the workers in both communities. For Heffer these working-class communities were interwoven with Socialist and Christian values. The people accepted that they were each other's brothers and sisters and they were prepared to sacrifice themselves for each other.

Despite Heffer's commitment to Communism, the Communist Party itself did not consider his politics sound enough and expelled him. After the initial shock Heffer reflected that this was in fact the best thing that could have happened. He began to read more widely and understood that critics of Communism were not simply part of a grand capitalist conspiracy, but had some valid points to make. He also realized that he had abandoned his Christian faith for a Communist faith and he now felt free to explore new aspects of Socialism and Christianity.

Outspoken MP and spokesman for the left

In 1957 Heffer rejoined the Labour Party and also became president of the Liverpool Trades Council. By 1960 he had been elected to Liverpool City Council as a councillor for the Pirrie ward, which was part of the Walton parliamentary constituency that he won at the General Election of 1964. At Westminster Heffer's qualities were quickly appreciated and in 1967 Harold Wilson offered him the role of parliamentary secretary to Tony Benn. Heffer was still uncompromisingly outspoken, however, and he refused the position, saying that he lacked confidence in the Government and believed that Jim Callaghan should be sacked from the Treasury.

He missed out on parliamentary promotion, therefore, but a year later he had a spiritual experience that changed his life. In 1968 he joined a Labour Friends of Israel delegation to the Holy Land. Heffer later described what happened as he walked along the Via Dolorosa, the route that Christ had taken to Calvary: 'It seemed to me as if everything I had ever believed in my childhood was coming alive. Jesus was cruci-fied because he took the side of the poor. His message is as valid today as it was then. My old beliefs overwhelmed me and I once again accepted Christianity. I have never since had any great doubts about it.'[10]

In Parliament Heffer continued his activity on the left, mainly through the Tribune Group. He was very active in Wilson's 1966–70

Government, participating in 44 debates as well as asking over 100 questions. He introduced Bills to abolish live hare coursing and to end the 'lump system' of labour-only subcontracting on building sites. Yet despite some modest progress, Heffer remained concerned over the Government's support for the USA in Vietnam and over its prices and incomes policy, which failed to tackle the incomes of the rich.

The most irritating issue for Heffer, however, was his front-bench role as an opposition spokesman on the Conservatives' Industrial Relations Bill in 1970. He spoke alongside Barbara Castle on the Bill, but was incensed when the Government guillotined the debate. With other members of the Tribune Group, he protested by assembling in front of the mace when the vote was called. They refused to move, which resulted in the suspension of the sitting for 15 minutes. The press called on Wilson to sack Heffer from the front bench, but he refused to do so and in the 1974 Government promoted Heffer to Minister of State at the Department of Industry under Secretary of State Tony Benn.

There was a tense relationship between the Department of Industry and No 10, however, and Heffer believed that 'Harold became convinced that we were a bunch of loony leftists'.[11] Heffer was angered by such accusations, as he was merely intervening in an attempt to save jobs and fulfil Labour's manifesto. He reasoned that if private industry could be given grants, why could workers' co-operatives not receive them too? For Heffer the referendum on the EEC was the last straw. Wilson allowed Cabinet freedom to campaign around the country but not to speak in the House. Heffer defied this ruling by speaking out against EEC membership in the Commons, and the following day he was sacked.

His popularity in the wider party remained strong despite this, and he was elected to the NEC, replacing the right-winger Denis Healey. Both from this position and as a backbencher Heffer continued to act as a spokesman for the left throughout all Kinnock's efforts to reform the party. Following Labour's third election defeat in 1987, Kinnock launched various wide-ranging policy reviews which extended the party leadership's control over policy-making. This provoked both Heffer and Benn to make a last-ditch effort to secure the leadership for the left, but Heffer's challenge to Hattersley for the deputy leadership was defeated.

Tony Benn

Heffer's main colleague on the left was Tony Benn. Benn had also been a supporter of Militant and had left the conference chamber in response to Kinnock's 1985 speech. Outside he tried to comfort a crying female delegate, but then he too began to cry, having been overcome by the whole incident. Throughout the 1980s Benn became identified with the hard left of the party, despite having been in the Cabinet during the '70s. Davies says of him, 'Unlike those of most socialists, Tony Benn's ideas became more left-wing and not less. The response of his colleagues was summed up by Harold Wilson's aside that, "he immatures with age".' [12]

Throughout the 1980s Benn was subject to a great deal of mainly negative media attention, often focused on his tea-drinking habits, teetotalism or working-class pretensions. His full name was Anthony Neil Wedgwood Benn and he was an hereditary peer, but he rejected both his name and his peerage in favour of plain Tony Benn and a seat in the Commons. He had a profound interest in and understanding of Labour history and he did more than any other politician to communicate the shared roots of Christianity and Labour. His 1979 bestseller *Arguments for Socialism* sold over 75,000 copies, and traced the roots of the British Labour Movement back through English history to the time of Christ and the Old Testament. He commented, 'Critics often seek to dismiss socialism as being necessarily atheistic. But this is not true as far as British socialism is concerned. For the Bible has always been and remains a major element in our national political – as well as our religious – education.' [13]

It was Benn's own historical research that introduced him to the seventeenth-century Levellers and their claims for universal suffrage, equality between the sexes and the sovereignty of the people. The spiritual values of the Levellers had been defined by the Bible's radical teaching to love God and love one's neighbour. Through this teaching the Bible endorses the equality of humanity and the priesthood of all believers. Benn's conclusion was that equality is central to Socialism, universal priesthood is central to Nonconformity, and both are central to the British Labour Movement. 'No wonder that many bishops and clergy in England before the Reformation feared that the Bible – if available to be read widely – might undermine the priestly hold over the minds of their flock.'[14] As a dedicated Nonconformist, Benn's favourite painting in the Commons is one of peasants in the fields reading Wycliffe's Bible, an act that was deemed illegal.

Heritage

Tony Benn comes from a long tradition of religious and political dissenters. His mother Margaret was from a Scottish Nonconformist family and his father Wedgwood was a Liberal MP for Leith. By 1927, however, Wedgwood Benn felt unable to continue with the Liberal Party because of what he saw as Lloyd George's lack of principle. Instead of simply crossing the floor, Wedgwood felt obliged to resign his seat and MP's salary and seek election to another seat as a Labour candidate. It was a brave decision at the age of 49 with two young children, but Leith already had its own Labour candidate and Wedgwood's future could clearly not be there. He was later selected as the Labour candidate for North Aberdeen, where he won a by-election in 1928.

Tony Benn's parents were not only politically active, but were also biblical scholars. Young Tony would often be told by his father to 'dare to be a Daniel, dare to stand alone, dare to have a purpose firm, dare to let it be known'.[15] It was a prophetic calling he would later take to his political career. Looking back on his life in 1989, Benn reflected, 'I was brought up on the Old Testament, the conflict between the kings who exercised power and the prophets who preached righteousness. Faith must be a challenge to power.'[16]

The road to Parliament

Ever since he was a child Tony Benn had wanted to be an MP. When he was in London to celebrate his seventeenth birthday on 3 April 1942, he went to Smith Square and joined the Labour Party. There followed some memorable and formative years. In 1943 he enlisted in the RAF and sailed to South Africa, where he witnessed the terrible treatment suffered by black South Africans. That same year his older brother Michael, who was a pilot in the war but had decided to train for the Christian ministry, was killed in his Mosquito plane. It was a shock from which Benn never fully recovered. At the 1945 election Benn was too young to vote but campaigned for the Labour candidate in Westminster. In 1947 he sailed to America as president of the Oxford Union and while he was there he spent time in the home of the theologian Reinhold Niebuhr, a contact of his mother who was now a leader in the Congregational Church. He also met Caroline, an American student at Oxford, and they were married in Cincinnati in 1949.

In 1950 Benn was working for the BBC and debarred from political activity, but he was in contact with Roy Jenkins and Tony Crosland. When Stafford Cripps resigned through ill health, Jenkins and Crosland lobbied Cripps' close friend the Revd Mervyn Stockwood to lend his support to Benn's candidature. After Benn was selected for Bristol South East, Cripps wrote with approval in the *Bristol Evening World* that Benn was a Socialist and Christian like himself. Benn's father also described his son as an active member of the Church, although this was a little embarrassing to Benn, who did not want to 'sell' his faith. Nevertheless, Benn's speeches at this time contained far more Christian references than they had done before or would do later. He often talked of the connections between trade unionism and Nonconformity, and between religious and political dissent, as well as about the importance of morality in politics and not just economics. As his biographer Jad Adams notes, however, 'he was moving away from organized religion, retaining a fundamental belief in Christian principles without embracing the structure of Church dogma'.[17]

At the Bristol by-election Benn won with 19,367 votes and at the age of 25 became the youngest Benn to be elected in three family generations of MPs. This political heritage would, however, come back to haunt him later in his attempts to renounce his father's peerage. The title would be inherited automatically on his father's death and would thus deny Tony his seat in the Commons.

Commons campaigner

Benn's early contributions in the Commons were on race relations and he spoke against the increasing incidences of racist attacks on immigrants. He was also remarkably progressive on marriage reform, arguing that instead of making divorce easier, marriage should be made harder, with requirements for a longer notice period and premarital education. Later in the 1950s he became a regular contributor to Labour Party broadcasts and the BBC's *Any Questions*. He was elected to Labour's national executive in 1959. That year he was also made Shadow Transport Minister and many of his ideas became law, including the compulsory wearing of seat belts, harsher penalties for drink-driving, MOT tests and road safety programmes.

When his father suddenly died in 1960, it provoked a crisis. Benn automatically became Lord Stansgate and lost his Commons seat and salary. Although he had cross-party support for his attempts to stay in the Commons, he had to argue his case before an unsympathetic Committee of Privileges. A by-election was called in Bristol South East and although Benn won by a majority of 13,044 it was the Tory candidate who took the seat in the Commons. It would require another two years and a new Peerage Bill to allow Benn to fight his seat again and return to the Commons in October 1963.

In Wilson's 1964 Government Benn was appointed Postmaster General and was responsible for introducing first- and second-class stamps. He also proposed the splitting of the Post Office into separate organizations for telecommunications and mail. As Minister for Technology in 1966 he oversaw the completion of Concorde, but despite such achievements Benn became increasingly dissatisfied with his ministerial duties, feeling that his radical conscience was being smothered. When Fenner Brockway criticized the Government, Benn wrote in his diary, 'He really made us feel very uncomfortable, the way prophets must have made the kings of Israel feel uncomfortable.'[18]

Challenging the leadership

Following the 1970 election defeat Benn made his first attempt for the party leadership and gained 46 votes to Foot's 96 and Jenkin's 140. It would be the first of many attempts to gain the leadership of the party. Being in opposition meant that Benn had more freedom to align himself with radical causes close to his heart. In 1970 Germaine Greer had written *The Female Eunuch* and by 1971 a large and vocal women's liberation movement was demanding equal education, jobs, pay and benefits. Benn was the first male politician to support this movement, despite it being systematically caricatured in the press. In a speech to the Yorkshire Labour Women's Rally he declared, 'Every struggle for rights by an oppressed group is exposed to ridicule by those who are frightened of the power it generates.'[19]

Benn reached his highest office in 1974 when Wilson appointed him Secretary of State for Industry, with Eric Heffer as Minister of State. It was during this time that his relationship with Wilson deteriorated, however. By the time of the 1975 EEC referendum, Benn had changed his original position on Europe and was one of five dissenting ministers. After the referendum he was demoted to Secretary of State for Energy where one of his first responsibilities was to start the flow of North Sea oil. In the wake of the oil crisis of 1973, this was a hopeful sign for Britain and the country would soon become a net exporter of oil.

Benn remained in the Energy post until the 1979 election, when he held his Bristol seat with a dramatically reduced majority. Boundary changes meant that Bristol South East was to be split, however, and Benn was forced to fight for the traditional Tory seat of Bristol East in 1983. Despite a massive effort by loyalists, he lost by 1,790 votes and his 30-year relationship with the city of Bristol came to an end. Within the year he had been selected for the Chesterfield by-election, where he gained a 6,264 majority and returned to the Commons.

Leader of the left

During the early 1980s Benn led the Labour Party's leftward march. He believed that Margaret Thatcher's radical Conservative agenda ought to be countered with an equally radical one from Labour. He was vocal in his support for the 1981 party conference decision on unilateral disarmament in the light of new, more deadly US and Soviet missile systems, and he also took advantage of the SDP split by challenging Denis Healey for Labour's deputy leadership. He only narrowly lost by 49.6 per cent to Healey's 50.4 per cent, but if he had won, many more on the right might have left the party.

By continuing to pursue his radical agenda Benn began to lose his traditional support as the mood in the party swung back towards unity and concentrated on the fight with the Conservatives. In fact, both Kinnock and Foot had been disillusioned with the Bennite challenge to Healey. Benn's radical alternative to Thatcher put him at odds with the reforming leadership of Neil Kinnock. Although Kinnock was from the left of the party himself, his leadership campaign identified two enemies to the party's progress: the Social Democrats who had defected, and the hard left who remained.

Despite Kinnock's reforms between 1983 and 1987, however, the Conservatives won again. Labour's failure provoked Benn to challenge Kinnock for the leadership once more. He did so against the advice of his closest allies and was heavily defeated by 88.6 to 11.3 per cent. It was an overwhelming defeat, but Benn's response was to keep the faith. 'I dare say,' he said, 'that the General Secretary of the Scribes and Pharisees announced in Jerusalem in AD 32, "What's the point in following a leader who gets crucified?" '[20]

Speaking out for principles

Nonetheless, that leadership defeat was a decisive moment not only in Benn's eclipse but in Kinnock's ascendancy. Andrew Thorpe comments, 'By 1989 ... Kinnock's hegemony within the party was virtually complete. It was buttressed by Labour's improving electoral performance.'[21] By the end of the 1980s it was clear that Benn represented the dissenting, idealistic and unelectable party that Neil Kinnock had been elected to reform. Kinnock had now reformed it and there was no place for Benn other than where he felt most comfortable, as a prophet crying in the wilderness.

Benn continued to be outspoken in a religious kind of way well into the 1990s. When New Labour's leadership tried to replace Clause 4 in the party's constitution, he commented, 'Anyone who really thinks that Clause 4 and common ownership was invented by Karl Marx ... might go back to the Acts of the Apostles for the idea of all things in common.'[22] Chris Bryant says of Benn that despite his claim to be a 'Christian without God' (when he was asked at a party conference event if he accepted 'Jesus as Lord', Benn replied, 'Since I don't believe in lords in any shape, it is a bit difficult to acknowledge Jesus as one'[23]), he was nevertheless one of two influential politicians in the 1980s who inspired Christian Socialism.

Without doubt, Benn wants to hold on to the Christian heritage of both the Labour Movement and the nation. In 1995 he addressed the Sheffield Academic Press on the very evangelical-sounding theme of 'The Power of the Bible Today'. He also argues persuasively that 'the moral force of Bible teaching, and the teachings of Jesus are not necessarily weakened by being secularized. Indeed, it can be argued that humanism may entrench them more strongly, for those who cannot accept the Christian faith.'[24]

Other influential Christians

Frank Field

Not all Christians in the party were antagonistic to Kinnock's reforms, however, and many worked for them. The other MP regarded by Bryant as being influential to Christian Socialism through the 1980s was Frank Field. He was at the other end of the political spectrum from Benn and maintained a right-wing Socialist critique of Labour policy. He upset many by publicly admiring aspects of Thatcherism, especially her acknowledgement of the role of self-interest in human behaviour.

Despite this, Field has an admirable record in poverty campaigning and before entering Parliament he was director of the Child Poverty Action Group and founder of the Low Pay Unit. He consistently argues that the individual is pre-eminent in tackling poverty and has criticized the left's obsession with blaming the state as the sole creator of poverty. He is particularly critical of Richard Titmuss, whose ideas on welfare dominated the post-war period but depended on a wholly unrealistic view of human altrusim. Put simply, Field talks of the need for a fresh emphasis on human responsibility. Field's views saw him swing from a position of unpopularity and near-deselection in the 1980s to rehabilitation as the Minister for Welfare Reform in the 1990s.[25] The rehabilitation proved to be short-lived, however, as his single-mindedness about welfare reform was not compatible with wider Government policy.

Derek Foster

Another Christian serving on the reformers' side was Derek Foster MP. Foster played a significant role in Neil Kinnock's Commons team as his parliamentary secretary from 1983 through to 1985 when Kinnock publicly tackled the hard left. This was a turbulent period and Foster shared the pressures of the leadership. He retains a great admiration for Kinnock as the man who started the reforms and almost saw them through to the end – 'a bit like taking us to the Promised Land but not being able to enter'.[26] Foster believes that without Kinnock's leadership the party would either have disappeared totally or would have become a rather insignificant force.

He is well placed to comment on Kinnock's attitude to faith, too: 'Kinnock would call himself an agnostic rather than an atheist,' he says.[27] Kinnock's religion was a cultural legacy, and he enjoyed singing hymns and reading the Bible and never criticized Foster's own open Christian faith. 'Neil and Glenys came from the Nonconformist Welsh chapels and certainly Neil's oratorical skills came from a long tradition of Welsh Nonconformist oratory.'[28] Foster himself would not have been an MP had it not been for his faith. His mother and grandmother were both Salvationists and he was confirmed in the Salvation Army at the age of 14. The Salvation Army gave him a background in community work, and politics seemed a natural development when he became a councillor in 1972.

He was elected as MP for Bishop Auckland in 1979 when Thatcher first came to power. As a member of the Trade and Industry Select Committee from 1980 to 1982, Foster watched in despair as Government policies wiped out 25 per cent of the manufacturing jobs in the Northeast. He tells of one community of 14,000 people where 2,600 of them lost their jobs between 1979 and 1981. In the Commons he joined the All Party Christian Fellowship, but commented that it was mainly Tories who attended and because he believed it was Conservative policy that was destroying industry and jobs he found it very difficult to pray with Conservative MPs. In 1983, as a Shadow Social Security spokesman, he was at least able to speak for some of the casualties of Conservative policies and defend their social security rights. After his time as Kinnock's parliamentary secretary he was appointed as Labour's chief whip in 1985. It was a demanding role as he encouraged and helped to build the party into an effective opposition. Throughout his parliamentary activities, Foster tried to apply Christian values in his dealings with other people and would always attempt to identify individuals' strengths and release them to perform in those areas.

Brenda Dean

One influential activist outside the Commons during this period was Brenda Dean, who as a union leader struggled against the effects of Government policy. Her values came first from her childhood attendance at a Church of England Sunday School, although the family eventually moved away from the Church of England as they thought it too snobby. Instead Dean went with another family to the Salvation Army Citadel. She found this very uplifting and was inspired by the way their faith flowed through their lives and was not a separate part of it. As a young adult Dean flirted with Christian Science, which even today she finds helpful – for example, its teaching that if you think ill of someone else it will not affect that person but will affect you instead. Faced with a challenge, be that a debate in the Lords[29] or another engagement or confrontation, she will always prepare with prayer, asking for peace and strength.

As general secretary of the SOGAT Union (Society of Graphic and Allied Trades) Dean was caught up in one of the most controversial and symbolic industrial disputes of the 1980s. The treatment of the workers gave her plenty of reasons both to pray for strength and to think ill of the media magnate and owner of News International Rupert Murdoch. Murdoch was preparing a new printworks at Wapping and in September 1985 he delivered an ultimatum to the printworkers to sign new contracts or face banishment from the new plant. Redundancy would mean workers with 20 years' service receiving just £4,000 and only a few hundred of the 5,500 workforce were to be transferred. The new contracts were designed to break up the unions and included the threat of instant dismissal with no right of appeal for anyone involved in strike or industrial action. In a meeting with SOGAT members, Dean explained that the contracts would also mean that individual workers would be personally liable for any damages resulting from a strike.

In the face of this, at an emergency meeting in January 1986 Dean requested that members give the SOGAT executive the authority to call a strike. She concluded, 'We have dignity as human beings and Murdoch is going to have to recognize that.'[30] The unions offered Murdoch a series of concessions and suggestions on flexible working patterns. Murdoch said it was too late, however, and on 24 January 1986 the strike began and was to last for over a year. Murdoch had prepared well and it would only take a small staff to keep the papers running at Wapping. The strike dragged on into the spring and early summer. On May Day 1986, 10,000 people marched to Wapping in a demonstration of support against the management. There were 30 arrests. On 3 May, 15,000 protesters marched to Wapping, and after a smoke bomb was thrown the scene descended into violence with 100 demonstrators and 20 police injured.

A number of new offers were made to the workers through the summer, but all of them were rejected as inadequate and none of them guaranteed what the workers wanted – their jobs and union recognition. In an effort to break the strike, News International bypassed the unions to make compensation offers directly to the workers. Only a third of those eligible to do so accepted them. The first anniversary of the strike in January 1987 saw 20,000 people march to Wapping, but again the demonstration was marred by violence. By early February, in the face of the continuing violence and the intransigence of the management, the SOGAT executive decided to end the strike.

While the workers received some compensation, the struggle for their jobs and for union recognition had ended in defeat. Yet they remained unbroken, and the experience of the strike had reinforced their sense of unity. Jean Sargeant later wrote, 'With all our shortcomings and human failings, we had been fighting for something bigger than ourselves which had lent our struggle a dignity and value that lifted us up as individuals … As St Paul says, "We are members one of another", a saying which for me summarizes Labour ethics – I felt it as a reality during the strike.'[31] Brenda Dean commented recently, 'The treatment of the workers by Rupert Murdoch and the failure of Government to support individuals against the high-handedness of employers was a sad epitaph of the '80s. Yet the workers retained their dignity as human beings and in the context of being shown little respect by management, held onto their self-respect.'

Difficult years

This, then, was the context of the 1980s, when Margaret Thatcher's new right philosophy was in full swing. Labour's failure to reform industrial relations in the 1970s provided a momentum for the more radical reforms of Thatcher in the 1980s. If success is to be judged on the basis of securing political office, the '80s were unhappy years for the Labour Party. Nevertheless, while Neil Kinnock did not become Britain's Prime Minister and resigned in 1992 after Labour's fourth election defeat, he did save the party from electoral oblivion. In that sense Kinnock's legacy to Labour was as crucial as that of any previous leader. Kinnock brought Labour back to electoral success, if not ultimately to General Election success. This was realized most clearly in the European elections, where Labour moved up from 17 seats in 1980 to 45 in 1989.

By 1990 Labour had a 28-point lead in the opinion polls, but then the Conservatives dumped Margaret Thatcher in favour of the more conciliatory John Major. They also wisely dropped the Poll Tax, which was universally disliked and inextricably linked to Thatcher. Although Labour's 1992 manifesto was measured and its campaign professionally run, the swing to Labour of just 2.1 per cent only served to reduce the Conservative majority to 21 seats. Following Labour's fourth defeat, Kinnock and his deputy Roy Hattersley both resigned. It was time for a new leadership to take over.

CHAPTER 11

Recovery or Remission?

JOHN SMITH AND TONY BLAIR: 1992 ONWARDS

*L*abour continued to change throughout the 1990s from a semi-reformed *party of opposition to a radically reforming party of government. This process was driven by the resolve to win and the quality of the leadership. When Neil Kinnock announced his resignation in 1992 it was to John Smith, the Shadow Chancellor, that the party now turned. Smith was a natural successor, having guided the party's economic policy since 1987. His leadership victory with 91 per cent of the vote demonstrated the party's overwhelming support for him. Smith was from the right of the party, but even those on the left such as Tony Benn believed he was the right person for the job.*

Smith's early death rocked the party and robbed the nation of a potentially great Prime Minister. Labour tentatively turned to another leader-in-waiting – Tony Blair. Despite his early promotion, Blair hit the ground running, pushing through deeper reforms to take Labour to its greatest election victory in history. The forward momentum did not stop there and, just as reform had come to Labour, Labour now set out to reform the country. Blair's obsession to get the job done – in schools, hospitals and employment, the people's concerns – was an obsession and a challenge to which the party rose.

At the end of both the millennium and Labour's first 100 years, people of faith again led the party. Both John Smith and Tony Blair were keen neither to hide their faith nor to wear it aggressively on their sleeves, but they were deeply influenced by their Christian beliefs. A week is a long time in politics, but so too were the 18 years of opposition and reform that Labour had endured. The party had changed, had always been changing, and now as it worked to change the country, people of faith were at the forefront of its struggle.

The world in the early 1990s

The world in the early 1990s was dramatically different from the world of the early 1980s. The Cold War was over and Eastern Europe struggled to rebuild its faith in politics. A people's revolution had breached the Berlin Wall and Communism had collapsed in Poland, East Germany, Hungary, Czechoslovakia, Bulgaria and Romania. The sheer speed of the collapse left many bewildered, however, and some would not go quietly. In the Soviet Union, a hard-line coup against President Gorbachev was defeated because the people demonstrated in protest. The failed coup was a watershed event and by the end of the year every former Soviet Republic had peacefully declared its independence.

The forces unleashed in Yugoslavia had a much more devastating effect. The Federation had struggled to maintain Tito's iron rule since 1980. Now it descended into civil war as Slobodan Milosevic rejected the independence of Croatia, Slovenia and Bosnia. Croatia and Slovenia secured independence, but Bosnia's mixed population fought each other. Europe once again witnessed genocide as Bosnian Serbs, supported by the army, killed, raped and destroyed Muslim and Croat communities.

In America the political right had dominated the 1980s, but in 1992 Bill Clinton became the first Democrat President since Jimmy Carter. The Clinton campaign had watched Kinnock's defeat in Britain with dismay, feeling they were now alone in promoting progressive politics against the forces of the right. The Republicans had taken a few leaves from the Conservatives' book, and Clinton suffered smears about tax bombshells and Kremlin connections. When such accusations were aired in the Clinton v. Bush televised debates, 200,000 media outlets received instant rebuttals and attacks from Democrat headquarters. The efficiency of Clinton's campaign and its ability to define its message rather than simply be caricatured by its opponents finally won through.

John Smith

Following Clinton's election victory, Philip Gould and Patricia Hewitt wrote a paper entitled 'Lessons from America' which argued that the Labour Party had not modernized enough under Kinnock. They claimed that Labour needed to move towards a new populism and be associated with improving the lives of ordinary working people – to make links with the future not the past.[1] Others, however, believed that Labour's reforms had already gone too far. Paul Anderson wrote in *Tribune*, 'The whole approach adopted by Labour from 1987 to 1992, designed precisely to address a lack of trust in the party and its perceived obsolescence, failed miserably to achieve its objectives.'[2]

These were the controversies that greeted John Smith's leadership, but Smith's personal and political stability helped the party resist the temptation towards factionalism. He not only united Labour in its resolve to fight another day, but also continued the reforms that would equip it for the fight. For Smith politics was about service and he viewed the leadership of the party as simply another opportunity to serve. More than anything it was the idea of service that would become the epitaph for his political life. That political life was tragically cut short. Two years into his leadership John Smith suffered a heart attack from which he did not recover, and he was robbed of his ambition to see a new Labour Government serving the people. On the night before his death he said to the British people, 'Please give us the opportunity to serve our country. That is all we ask.'[3]

Christian Socialism

Of all recent Labour leaders, John Smith was the most open about his Christian faith. He attended Cluny Parish Church in Edinburgh and his Christianity was prominent during his campaign for the leadership. He told BBC Radio 4's *Sunday* programme, 'I am an active and professing member of the Church of Scotland … It gives meaning to my political activities, because you have a sense of obligation to others.'[4] To *Scotland on Sunday* he said, 'Just as the Christian stands by the fundamental tenets of Christianity, so the socialist should stand by the tenets of socialism. For me, socialism is largely Christian ethical values. Politics is a moral activity. Values should shine through at all times. You could either call it evangelism or salesmanship. I want the spirit of the evangel but the success of the good salesman.'[5]

When the Labour Party voted for Smith, therefore, they were voting for someone whose Christian Socialism permeated both his personal and political life. Smith played a vital role in helping to rehabilitate the role of Christian Socialism within the party. When he addressed the Christian Socialist Movement at their annual Tawney Lecture, the media focus that followed highlighted the faith of other leading Labour figures, including Chris Smith, Jack Straw, Hilary Armstrong and Keith Vaz. It was Smith's example that created a space in which others could talk more openly about how faith motivated their politics.

Early faith and politics

John Smith was born on 13 September 1938 in Dalmally in the west of Scotland. His first two years were spent on the windswept island of Islay where his father was a teacher, but when he was appointed to Ardishaig Primary School the family moved back to the mainland. This childhood in Argyllshire had a profound effect on the person and politician Smith became. The harshness of the landscape and the neighbourliness of the people reinforced in him the ideas of community and equality. His father was a strict but popular teacher – but he was most strict with his son John. Smith said in 1992, 'It was always, "Why weren't you top of the class?" In the end it was easier just to be top of the class.'[6]

It was through his family that Smith was introduced to both religion and politics. The family was not too 'religious' about churchgoing, however, and the fact that the family cat was called Billy Graham displays a certain irreverent if evangelical edge. The family's politics, on the other hand, were definitely Labour, a notable distinction in the Conservative area of Argyll. Both faith and politics were to grow in the young Smith and when he moved to secondary school at Lochgilphead he was involved with Scripture Union, an organization which worked to help young people develop their faith. At 16 Smith joined the Dunoon branch of the Argyll Constituency Labour Party and later he joined the Glasgow University Labour Club, becoming its president in 1959–60. At Glasgow Smith studied history and law, and also began to develop his debating career. (It was more the case that his legal career benefited from his political experience than that his political oratory was the result of skills gained during legal training.)

His reputation in the Labour Club brought him to the attention of the East Fife branch of the party and in 1961, at the tender age of 22, he was asked to stand at a by-election. With no prospect of beating the Conservative, Smith nevertheless wanted to come second and push the

Liberals into third place. In the campaign and television debate that followed he demonstrated an ability that not only secured him second place but also recognition as a future MP. He fought East Fife again in 1964 but not in 1966, instead pursuing his career as an advocate in the Scottish legal system and marrying Elizabeth Shanks, a friend from university. Elizabeth was also from a family with a religious and political background, and her uncle Robert Shanks had been a Liberal councillor in Glasgow before World War I.

It was not until 1970 that Smith once again stood for election, this time for North Lanarkshire. The retiring MP Peggy Herbison had been Minister for Pensions in Harold Wilson's 1964–70 Government. Roy Hattersley, her parliamentary secretary from 1964 to 1967, described her as 'an austere, non-drinking, non-swearing, non-plotting Scottish lady'.[7] Herbison later became the first female Lord High Commissioner to the General Assembly of the Church of Scotland. She had held North Lanarkshire since 1945 and was keen to influence the choice of her successor. She felt the culture of the constituency demanded someone who was equally austere, religious and right wing, and her political agent Dick Stewart said he knew just the man. Smith was duly elected in June 1970 with a majority of 5,000.

In Westminster

During his first year at Westminster Smith demonstrated an independent resolve in his voting intentions despite pressure from the party. A three-line whip required all MPs to vote against entry into the EEC, but Smith joined the small pro-Europe rebellion. It was a move that had no obvious strategic benefit and risked losing him favour with Wilson. Following the 1974 election he risked annoying Wilson again by refusing the post of Solicitor General for Scotland, feeling that the position would too clearly define him and limit opportunities for wider experience. He was later chosen to be the parliamentary secretary of Willie Ross, the Secretary of State for Scotland.

Smith also showed an independent spirit by voting against the prevailing party policy on abortion. Throughout his career he consistently voted with the anti-abortion lobby, or at the very least abstained. He did this right up to the 1990 Human Embryology Bill, when he accepted the compromise 24-week time limit for abortions. This was controversial behaviour that had not gone unnoticed by the party. Smith was reluctant to talk about the issue. His motives were deeply personal and did not stem simply from his Christian faith. While he clearly felt able to vote on principle on some issues, however, on other issues he remained noncommittal. On the subject of disarmament and defence spending he once said, 'There are hawks who think that no cuts should be made and doves who want to make cuts for the sake of cuts. I do not know what species of bird is halfway between a hawk and a dove, but I fancy the posture of that bird.'[8]

Following the 1974 General Election Smith became a Junior Minister for Energy under Tony Benn. Although Benn and Smith came from opposite wings of the party, they nevertheless got on well. In Benn's diaries, while there were criticisms of other ministers there was nothing negative about John Smith. When Wilson retired in 1976, Smith campaigned for Callaghan and it was under his leadership that the question of Scottish devolution came to a head. Labour had a thin majority and the Liberals, along with the Welsh and Scottish nationalists, all needed to be given reasons not to bring the Government down. This was the rather inglorious motivation for Labour's first attempt at devolution. Smith was called upon to assist Bruce Millan, the Scottish Secretary, in taking the Scotland and Wales Bills through the Commons. The progress of the Bills was torturously slow and only passed after the Liberal leader David Steel was assured that the assemblies would be elected under proportional representation. Smith's reward for his work on the devolution issue was to be made a Privy Councillor, and he became the Rt Hon. John Smith.

Smith and Kinnock

Following Labour's defeat in 1979 Smith again supported the right-wing candidate Denis Healey against Michael Foot for the leadership. In the early 1980s he fought against every leftward move in the party, but also spent more time in his legal practice and with his young family. He remained completely faithful to the party during its traumatic split with the SDP. His character was one of dependable solidarity and he was offended when anyone suggested that he would consider leaving. Despite the electoral disaster of 1983, Smith was returned in his new seat of Monklands East with a majority of 9,799. He backed Roy

Hattersley in the leadership campaign that followed, but it was Neil Kinnock's vitality and oration that captivated the wider party.

Kinnock's pragmatism from the left and Smith's pragmatism from the right served to draw them both together as leaders. In different ways they shared the same passion to rescue Labour from itself, to secure power and to change Britain. Kinnock appointed Smith as Shadow Employment Secretary and later moved him to Trade and Industry. It was there that Smith would excel in his critique of Michael Heseltine and Leon Brittan over the Government's 1986 Westland helicopter sale. Both Heseltine and Brittan eventually resigned over Thatcher's handling of the affair. Following the 1987 election Smith was called upon to produce a paper on personal taxation, an issue on which Labour had done badly in the election.

Smith's stoical Scottish reserve, thoughtful manner and conservative image were in sharp contrast to Kinnock's fiery Welsh nature and ideological passion – an ideal match. The future looked positive. In 1988, however, Smith experienced the first of the serious heart attacks that would eventually claim his life. He took three months off to recuperate and started to climb the Scottish Munros in an effort to adopt a healthier lifestyle. During his absence, it was fellow Scottish MP Gordon Brown who effectively fulfilled his role of Shadow Chancellor.

The role of Smith's shadow budget in Labour's 1992 election defeat remains controversial. Smith's team openly declared Labour's spending plans beforehand. The plans included tax breaks for most, but a few sections of the population were to be taxed more. Smith cited a desire for fairness in defence of his policies, but his enemies described the budget as 'envy dressed up as policy'.[9] Be that as it may, the shadow budget – however fair and reasonable – had given the Conservatives a target and they ruthlessly attacked Labour as a tax-raising party. Smith's attempted transparency had backfired, and in the final analysis the public still did not trust Labour. Labour had run a professional campaign with coherent policies, but had still failed to secure that elusive ingredient of trust.

A reforming leader

Nonetheless, when Smith became leader he inherited a party in a condition that many previous leaders would have envied. Despite its recent

General Election defeat, there was a pervasive belief that Labour would win the next time. Smith's leadership campaign, 'New Paths to Victory', promised continued reform and in the two short years before his death he would provide two important legacies for the party. The first was the introduction of 'one member one vote' for parliamentary selections and the second was the recovery of moral language in the policies and language of the party.

The 'one member one vote' proposal to remove the union block vote was a controversial one. It had been rejected by the party conference in 1992, but in 1993 Smith was determined to raise the issue again. He believed the image of Labour as a party controlled by the unions was one that needed to be broken. In his characteristically inclusive style he tried to bring all sides on board, but when key union leaders would not budge he pushed ahead anyway. He was even willing to stake his leadership on it and made it clear that he would resign if the vote went against him. Following a last-minute speech by John Prescott, however, the 1993 conference supported the proposal and Smith's leadership was secure.

The second legacy that Smith gave to Labour was the renewed use of moral language. Smith believed that some policies were wrong because they were morally wrong and some were right because they were morally right. It was a high-risk strategy and John Major would become disastrously unstuck with a similar 'Back to Basics' slogan. For Smith, however, it was more than just a strategy – it was the practical expression of his belief that politics was ultimately about values. From early 1993 he adopted this distinctive tone and language, so much so that Rory Bremner, the television impressionist, began to portray him as making speeches from a pulpit. It was a deliberate attempt on Smith's part to take the moral high ground and he highlighted the word that would become the defining issue in the Conservative Party's demise: 'sleaze'.

In March 1993 Smith did take to the pulpit at Bloomsbury Baptist Church in London for the annual R.H. Tawney Lecture staged by the Christian Socialist Movement. He was quick to point out that Christianity made no exclusive claim to ethics, and nor did Christians have to be Socialists, but he did embrace the ethical vision of R.H. Tawney. In the course of the lecture, Smith said, 'R.H. Tawney was throughout the whole of his long and productive life an uncompromising ethical socialist. He founded his political outlook on the moral principles of his Christian commitment. From that strong redoubt he assailed the deficiencies of both communism and capitalism and espoused the cause of a democratic socialism. This sought to enhance individual freedom in a framework of collective common purpose and opportunity, in which fellowship was the bond of a community of equality. He saw British socialism as ethical, individualistic, parliamentary and pragmatic.'[10] It was an important speech for Smith, laying out the ethical foundations that would inform the secular foundations of his future administration.

A great loss

Throughout 1993 and the beginning of 1994 Smith continued his moderate reforms of Labour and moral assaults on the Conservatives. The party had regained its feet under his steady leadership and had started to walk more confidently towards the coming General Election. Then, on the morning of 12 May 1994, Smith suffered a second major heart attack, from which he did not recover. He was suddenly taken from a party and, indeed, a nation that had invested its hope in him. The expression of grief was universal, not only in the party but throughout Britain and beyond. Many described him as the best Prime Minister that Britain had never had.

At his funeral the Archbishop of Canterbury spoke movingly of John Smith whose name was the name of everyman. 'This is fitting,' he said, 'because everyman is what John Smith the political leader stood for and worked for. It is a name loved and known by God: I have called you by name and you are mine.'[11] Smith's political colleague Helen Liddell was less eloquent but equally profound, commenting that he was 'a dedicated Christian, but never a Holy Willie, his beliefs guided his politics'.[12] In the foreword to Smith's biography his wife Elizabeth declared,

> John was not ambitious for himself. He saw politics as a service to others, and when Neil Kinnock stood down, he saw leading the Party as just another opportunity to serve. He remained an intensely practical politician. When he was asked – as all three leaders were – what his 'big idea' was and how he was going to get it across, preferably in three words, his reply was simply: 'A Labour Government.'[13]

The Smith family had spent many holidays on the island of Iona, the ancient burial ground of Scottish kings. In a tribute to the respect with which Smith was held, the residents of Iona agreed to Elizabeth Smith's request that John's body be laid to rest there.

Tony Blair

John Smith had been taken too early and everyone felt betrayed – yet his legacy of reform and the moral dimension he had brought to the party would not die with him. Smith had a dramatic impact on his successor, Tony Blair. Not only did his early death result in Blair, at the age of 41, becoming the youngest ever leader of the Labour Party and the youngest British Prime Minister this century, but Smith's legacy of party reform and a moral vision was one that Blair would embrace and develop. Smith's language of moral values had already become a feature in Blair's political vision by 1993. Smith also encouraged him to become more public about his faith, not least by influencing his decision to join the Christian Socialist Movement in 1992.

A clear expression of Blair's moral vision came to the fore when as Shadow Home Secretary he spoke of the murder of James Bulger. In describing a society where two 10-year-olds could kill a two-year-old, he said, 'A solution to this disintegration doesn't simply lie in legislation. It must come from the rediscovery of a sense of direction as a country and most of all from being unafraid to start talking once again about the values and principles we believe in and what they mean for us, not just as individuals but as a community. We cannot exist in a moral vacuum. If we do not learn and then teach the value of what is right and what is wrong, then the result is simply moral chaos which engulfs us all.'[14] While Blair's moral vision emerged more clearly in his time as Shadow Home Secretary and would develop further, it was nevertheless one that had been developing all through his life.

Education

Blair was born in Edinburgh on 6 May 1953. His father Leo was an examiner for the Inland Revenue, but only as a stopgap while he pursued his efforts to achieve a doctorate and become a lecturer. In 1955 he secured a post teaching law at Adelaide University, and then moved to Durham University in 1958. Leo also practised as a barrister, but it was his enthusiasm for local Conservative politics that betrayed his ultimate ambition to become an MP. The family's prosperity meant that Tony and his elder brother William could go to the private Chorister School at Durham Cathedral. When Tony was 10, however, his father suffered a serious stroke which nearly killed him and reduced the family's income. The school's headmaster, Canon John Grove, remembers praying with the young Tony Blair at this time, but also recalls more generally that he was good at Scripture and was a serious believer.

At the age of 12 Blair stood as the Conservative candidate in the school's mock election of 1966. His father's political influence did not go deep, however, and by the time he was 18 he had absorbed a different kind of political outlook. It had been gleaned from his experience of family, school and the people of County Durham – an outlook not yet analysed but involving an intuitive sense of mutual care and the value of community. In 1966 Blair also won a scholarship to Fettes College in Edinburgh and his privileged education continued. He hated the Fettes regime, though, and ran away before finally settling into a more progressive house attached to the school. Nonetheless, Blair remained rebellious and in contrast to his childhood reputation as being good at Scripture, he now became known for his drama, drinking and smoking. After Fettes he went to Oxford University in 1972 to study law, but also became a singer in the rock band Ugly Rumours. Oxford was also the place where he developed many of his spiritual and political convictions.

Peter Thomson

Blair was particularly influenced by an unorthodox and left-wing group of St John's students who met to discuss religion and politics. It was here that he met Peter Thomson, an Australian, larger-than-life, mature (at 36), radical priest and tennis coach. Blair later described Thomson as the person who most influenced him, while Thomson described Blair at the time as a 'lost soul'. Thomson was a worldly-wise guru and purveyor of late-night coffee and cigarettes to a coterie of young undergraduates trying to make sense of the world. His own journey had introduced him to people and ideas that would immediately resonate with Blair. If Thomson's theology had been mystical and otherworldly, his impact would have been rather less, but instead it was practical and radical and suggested answers to the questions that Blair had been asking.

One result of these late-night conversations was that Blair's faith came alive again and took on a new relevance. He started to attend the college chapel and at the end of his second year was confirmed in the Church of England. Thomson's lost soul had found a home and he even believed that one day Blair might go into the Church. It was certainly true that Blair now wanted to achieve something meaningful in his life, and not simply settle for a conventional career.

John Macmurray

One of Thomson's heroes was the Scottish philosopher and theologian John Macmurray (1891–1976). It was Macmurray's writings that would provoke Blair's thinking on his central political idea of community. Macmurray believed that only through community could an individual realize his or her full potential. He rejected the belief that the pursuit of individual self-interest would lead to the benefit of the whole community and argued instead that only by pursuing the interest of the whole community would the whole community benefit, including the individual. As John Rentoul notes, 'The effect of Macmurray's rethinking was to invert Adam Smith's dictum, "Social and self-love are the same". Smith said that if we follow our self-interest, we benefit the whole community. Macmurray said that by pursuing the community's best interests we benefit the individuals within it, including ourselves.'[15]

Such thinking was later seen in Blair's 1993 foreword to *Reclaiming the Ground*, a book on Christianity and Socialism: 'In reality the Christian message is that self is best realized through communion with others. The act of Holy Communion is symbolic of this message. It acknowledges that we do not grow up in total independence, but inter-dependently, and that we benefit from that understanding.'[16] It was also present in a political speech he made in the same year: 'We do not lose our identity in our relations with others; in part at least, we achieve our identity by those relations.'[17]

Many of Macmurray's ideas, however, had no immediate application to modern politics and some, such as his suggestion that governments are run by megalomaniacs,[18] would lead Blair to describe his general concepts as helpful, while avoiding the detail. One other element in

Macmurray's thinking that did dramatically resonate with Blair was the idea of action. Macmurray inverted the Greek-based dictum of Descartes' 'I think, therefore I am' – which saw thinking as the highest activity – to his own more Hebrew-based version, 'I do, therefore I am.' This advocacy of value-based action helped to connect the vision and pragmatism of Blair and resonated with his desire to change the world.

London lawyers

Blair graduated from university in 1975, and in the same year he joined the Labour Party. He also joined the Society of Labour Lawyers after moving to London to do his one-year course at the Bar. The following year he had to secure a pupilage in legal chambers and it was while applying for a scholarship that he first met Cherie Booth. She came from a Catholic Socialist background and not only shared Blair's interest in law but was also fascinated by politics. Their relationship developed further when they both became pupils to Alexander Irvine. Irvine had already accepted the academically outstanding Cherie Booth, but was struck by Blair's enthusiasm and decided to take two pupils on in the same year. The pair's relationship became rather more than strictly professional and they were eventually married in 1980. One aspect of the 'deal' was that Blair would give up smoking, and he had his last cigarette just 30 minutes before the wedding ceremony.

Election to Parliament

After the pupilage Blair secured a permanent place in Irvine's chambers, where he worked in employment law and acted for a number of unions as well as the Labour Party. He began to look for a parliamentary seat, trying unsuccessfully for Middlesbrough in 1980 and Teeside Thornaby in 1981. It was his selection for Beaconsfield in 1982, however, that was to secure his reputation and propel him to Parliament. The by-election was fought against the backdrop of the Falklands War and the rise of the SDP, and despite Blair's hard work Labour's percentage of the vote fell from 20 to 10 per cent. Nevertheless, Blair was warmly praised, with Michael Foot declaring on *Newsnight*, 'We're very proud of everything he's been saying here and whatever the result, we believe he's going to have a very big future in British politics.'[19]

Armed with this endorsement, Blair sought selection for the new seat of Sedgefield in County Durham. Many believed that Les Huckfield, a Labour MP with a hard-left reputation, would secure the nomination, but others wanted to avoid such a factional candidate. There was also a feeling that Huckfield was being forced on Sedgefield and the independence of its members was to prove a crucial point in Blair's favour. He scraped onto the shortlist after the members were made aware of Michael Foot's endorsement from the Beaconsfield campaign, courtesy of Blair's supporters in the nominating Trimdon Branch of the Sedgefield constituency. The following day Blair went to pray in Durham Cathedral. Unknown to him, John Burton, the secretary of the Trimdon Branch, had also gone to church to pray. The prayers may not have secured the victory, but they did reflect a sense that both Blair and Burton remained dependent on something beyond themselves. Later the seven shortlisted hopefuls spoke and took questions and, after a series of votes, Blair was victorious over Huckfield in the fifth round.

His selection came only 20 days before the 1983 election, when he secured a majority of 8,281 for Labour in Sedgefield. Blair expressed his sense of obligation to those who had nominated him, saying, 'There was one thing that I really wanted to do, and I have been given the chance by you to do it. I only hope your faith in me will be repaid.'[20] At Westminster Blair was the youngest MP at just 30 years old. His maiden speech addressed an issue to which he would return time and again – the need for Government to support the aspirations of ordinary people to work, to get married and to raise a family. 'British democracy,' he said, 'rests ultimately on the shared perception by all the people that they participate in the benefits of the common weal.'[21]

Rising star

In the leadership contest that followed the 1983 election, Blair campaigned for Kinnock and became a faithful member of his team for the next nine years. He strongly supported the appointment of Peter Mandelson to Labour's communications team and Mandelson became a close friend and adviser. Blair had already made the point at Beaconsfield that Labour had to develop its expertise in communication and image projection. Between 1983 and 1987 he shared his Westminster office with Gordon Brown and it was Brown who introduced him to the Tribune Group of MPs, formerly on the left but now the centre left of the parliamentary party.

The party's annual Shadow Cabinet elections were the means by which MPs gained recognition among their colleagues as well as acquired positions as shadow spokespeople. By the 1987 General Election Blair had already established a good reputation in Parliament and in Sedgefield, where his majority increased to 13,058. That year he also stood for the Shadow Cabinet for the first time, coming seventeenth in the contest for 15 places. By 1988, however, his reputation was further enhanced and he secured ninth place, becoming Shadow Energy Secretary with a brief to tackle the Tories' plans for electricity privatization. In addition Blair developed a positive television image and media presence and was often called upon to represent the party.

By the late 1980s both Blair and Brown were firmly on the modernizing wing of Labour, coaxing and cajoling Kinnock to go further and faster on party reform. By 1990, Kinnock had recognized Blair's future potential and joked about him as the next leader of the party. The Conservative Lord Whitelaw also identified Blair as the person the Conservatives had to watch and beat.

When John Smith and Margaret Beckett were elected leader and deputy leader in July 1992, Gordon Brown and Tony Blair secured first and second places in the Shadow Cabinet elections, becoming Shadow Chancellor and Shadow Home Secretary respectively. It was here that Blair developed a new angle for Labour on crime – 'Tough on crime, tough on the causes of crime.' The expression demonstrated Blair's mastery of the media and his ability to encapsulate a policy in a few words that nevertheless had huge ramifications. The more 'right-wing' toughness on crime was combined with a more 'left-wing' approach to tackling the deprivation often associated with it. Blair thus brought the individual and community dimensions together in one memorable phrase.

Moral values

He also developed the language of moral values as a compass for policy development. Blair argued that '60's liberalism had gone too far and he developed a theme based around rights and responsibilities. Individual responsibility was to become a helpful counterbalance to his central idea of community. The idea of responsibility would later resonate across a range of Government policies, especially in the area of welfare reform. Many of Blair's themes – 'rights and responsibilities', 'a commitment to community' and 'equality for all' – emerged from or were enhanced by his faith. Blair's belief in human equality before God informs his belief in equality before the law – hence, for example, his support for the equalization of the age of consent. 'Central to Christianity,' he said once, 'is the belief in equality; not that we are uniform in character or position, but on the contrary that despite our differences we are entitled to be treated equally, without regard to our wealth, race, gender or standing in society.'[22]

Despite his faith being a compass for values and policy, Blair nonetheless remains reluctant to publicize it. He is quick to point out, as John Smith was before him, that Christianity has no monopoly on ethics, nor should all Christians necessarily be Socialists. According to those close to him, however, maintaining his faith and attending Communion are central disciplines and resources in his busy life. In 1991, for example, while on a visit to New York and after a late night of socializing, colleagues were surprised to see him up at the crack of dawn and setting off to find a church. Any reticence Blair displays in publicizing his faith reflects his abhorrence of religion as a vehicle for electioneering and, as a politician, his sensitivity about the plurality of Britain's religious culture. Nevertheless, there is little doubt that it continued to inform his thinking and policies and contributed to his success as Shadow Home Secretary. Blair was now being widely talked of as the next leader of the Labour Party, but no one believed it would come so soon.

New leader

When John Smith died on 12 May 1994, Blair was in Aberdeen campaigning for the European elections. There was immediate speculation and lobbying of possible successors, but both Smith's funeral and the European elections delayed any decisions. By 1 June Gordon Brown had pulled out of the race in favour of Blair, and John Prescott and Margaret Beckett had declared themselves as rivals. In his leadership campaign Blair outlined his themes in an early internal memo. These included putting values at the heart of policy, an emphasis on the family, bold but open leadership, change and renewal for the nation. There would be new policy directions in welfare to provide opportunities not dependency, as well as investment in skills, devolved power and Britain leading in Europe.[23] As a summary of all these diverse initiatives, Blair talked about modernizing the Labour Party in order to renew the nation.

Despite the immense pressure of the campaign, or perhaps because of it, one story emerged that once again indicated the importance of worship in the would-be leader's hectic life. After a busy hustings meeting late on a Sunday afternoon, Blair insisted on leaving immediately in order to find a church and receive Communion. His campaign team piled into the car and as they drove off in no particular direction they looked intently along the skyline for the tell-tale sign of a steeple. Even when they spotted one it took several minutes of U-turns and sorties down country lanes to arrive in front of it, flustered but on time for the evening service. As the campaign team kicked their heels in the churchyard outside, Blair no doubt gave the anxiety and pressure of the election over to God, just as he had done all those years before in Durham Cathedral.

On 21 July 1994 Blair won the leadership of the Labour Party with 57 per cent of the total vote and a majority in all three voting categories – 60.5 per cent from MPs and MEPs, 58.2 per cent from party members and 52.3 per cent from the unions. He had only three short years to change Labour from what he regarded as its semi-reformed state into a party that could once again secure the trust of the electorate. Blair immediately began the process of redefining the Labour Party. The day after the election he said that trade unions would receive 'fairness not favours' from a future Labour Government, another classic Blairism that would create mountains of media comment. In his promotion of the family on a Sunday morning television programme, he was forced by the logic of his position to agree that 'single parents who have chosen to have children without forming a stable relationship are wrong'.[24] Blair tackled this controversial issue head-on, despite the heavy criticism which had been directed at Conservative ministers after similar pronouncements.

Clause 4

The Labour Party under Blair was receiving popularity ratings of 61 per cent by the end of 1994. This period also saw an unprecedented rise in the party's membership, reflecting despair at the Conservative Government as well as the attraction of Blair's leadership. His biggest battle, however, was still to come and would be over the reform of Arthur Henderson's Clause 4 in the party's constitution. John Smith had intended to reform Clause 4 and his policy adviser David Ward said that 'it would have been a rewrite and purely secular version of his Tawney Lecture in March 1993'.[25] Blair also wanted to rewrite Clause 4 – as a sign that Labour had changed and out of his conviction that it needed to say what it meant and mean what it said. The old Clause 4, despite people's emotional attachment to it, simply did not do that.

The battle to change Clause 4 was a critical one and was an issue that had caused the downfall of many previous leaders. It had become a totemic symbol around which the forces of the right and left had traditionally fought. After a year of debate on the proposal to change the clause, the party membership voted on 29 April 1995, with Blair winning the vote by 65 per cent. Within two years of gaining the leadership, he had achieved what many previous leaders had tried and failed to do. A personal reward for Blair was the privilege of shaping the new Clause 4 to include his ideals of community over narrow individualism and the pursuit of justice for all parts of that community. The new Clause 4 reads:

> *The Labour Party is a democratic socialist party. It believes that by the strength of our common endeavour we achieve more than we achieve alone, so as to create for each of us the means to realize our true potential and for all of us a community in which power, wealth and opportunity are in the hands of the many not the few, where the rights we enjoy reflect the duties we owe, and where we live together freely in a spirit of solidarity, tolerance and respect.*

Election victory

In May 1997, following three years as leader, Tony Blair led Labour to its biggest election victory in its entire history. Labour secured 418 seats, 253 more than the Conservatives and 178 more than all the other parties put together. The Labour Party had come a long way and now it was breaking the mould of British politics. There were now, for example, 119 women MPs, of whom 101 were Labour. The sheer size of the parliamentary Labour Party demanded that it met outside Parliament, in Church House, the home of the Church of England's General Synod. This was a fitting venue from which Blair could urge his new MPs to be servants, not masters, a direct rejection of a previous sentiment from a victorious leader.

The British public had endorsed Blair's modernizing project and had once again put its trust in Labour after 18 years. As he had done after his first election in Sedgefield, Blair would work to ensure that this regained trust would not be betrayed. Within days of the election, Chancellor Gordon Brown had announced the independence of the Bank of England and Foreign Secretary Robin Cook spoke of a new ethical dimension to foreign policy.

The reforming vigour with which Blair had led in opposition would now be pursued in Government. In the three years before the millennium the Labour Party would introduce, among many other innovations, a national minimum wage, a parliament for Scotland, an assembly for Wales, and measures to help people move from welfare into work. For Christians and others the commitment to abolish child poverty in a generation and the aim to halve global poverty by 2015 were particularly welcome. Finally, as Labour's first 100 years drew to a close, the party enacted a measure that had been on its agenda since its birth – the reform of the House of Lords. When Keir Hardie had first talked of it he had been laughed out of court; now he had the last laugh. There was perhaps no better way to end the century than with the abolition of 800 years of power and privilege. It registered another of Tony Blair's central themes: government for the many, not for the few.

CHAPTER 12

Conclusion

GOD'S POLITICIANS

*A*lmost everyone in Britain has been impacted in some way by 100 years *of Labour. The people featured in this book, and others working with them, have changed the lives of millions of ordinary people. Rachel McCallum (1908–99) was one of those ordinary people. She never got involved in politics, but benefited from those who did. The biggest benefit came in 1939 when she moved with her husband to their first council home. Her son recalls that the house was like heaven compared to what had gone before. It boasted an inside toilet, running hot-and-cold water, separate bedrooms for parents and children, and electric lights. It was a veritable mansion compared to the homes of Rachel's childhood where open sewers and outside 'dry' toilets were the norm.*

Rachel's grandsons

Rachel's family had moved from Ireland in 1905 in search of work in the mines and iron-smelting works of Scotland. She had four sisters and three brothers, although one brother – Hugh – remained in Ireland as an estate gardener. He later volunteered for military service in World War I and lost his life in France. Rachel's father, John, got a job as a blacksmith in the mines and was to work hard all his life without the security of the National Health Service or the welfare state. It was for families like these that the Labour Party was created, and Rachel's life would be easier because of the changes Labour would bring.

In the early years of the twentieth century Rachel grew up in the family's two-roomed cottage, where the food for seven children was cooked on an open fire. There was no running water or drainage and only latterly was there a paraffin lamp to give them light. The road outside was made of rubble and the outside wash-houses adjoined outside toilets, behind which lay rat-infested rubbish heaps. At 14 Rachel left school to work in the wool factory, a five-mile walk each way for a day that lasted from 8 a.m. to 6 p.m. She worked for 15 years in the factory before marrying Peter Meney, a bus driver and one-time brickmaker. They made their first home together in a room and kitchen rented from a private landlord. In 1929 their first child was born, and two others followed. The move to their first council house in 1939 provided the clearest social change for the family. This luxury home became a base from which Rachel and Peter worked back-to-back shifts in the ICI armaments factory, supporting the war effort and sharing the childcare. Their garden was transformed into a vegetable plot, with a greenhouse for tomatoes and chickens for eggs.

After World War II their son William left school to become a bricklayer, seeing this as his contribution to the task of rebuilding the nation. As a child William had suffered from scarlet fever and experienced the limited medical care of the local fever hospital. After the war he remembers being visited by the new NHS doctor and visiting the newly opened NHS clinic. Despite these improvements, William planned to emigrate to Australia. Australia House, however, insisted that he first do his national service and he joined the Royal Medical Corps, whose caring role helped express his Christian convictions.

After completing his national service William met and married a local Salvation Army girl, Sarah Dale, and instead of heading for Sydney they settled in Scotland. Their first home was another two-roomed dwelling, with an outside toilet and a cooker and sink in the living room. Like William's parents in 1939, in 1965 William and Sarah also secured a council home – in which they still live today. An inside toilet and hot-and-cold water were now the norm, and their two sons grew up in a safe environment, with free health and dental care and education right up to college level. Rachel's grandsons experienced a world of opportunities entirely transformed from the one into which she had been born and in which her father had lived.

This story can be told in such detail because it is my story. I am the son of William and the grandson of Rachel. My family's history represents just one dimension of the multifaceted history of 100 years of

Labour. Rachel McCallum died at the age of 92 while this book was being written and joined her husband in a place even better than that first council home. She spent her last years in sheltered housing, with central heating, assistance with meals and daily care. Until the end she was a beneficiary of the NHS and the welfare state that had served her family for over 50 years.

Politics and religion

Ironically, both Rachel and Peter were anti-politics and anti-politicians, believing that such worldly matters demeaned their Christian lives. They acknowledged that Christians should pray for politicians, but maintained that they should never become involved in the world's affairs, never publicly argue a case and never vote. Party politics was a difficult area and political debate rarely provided the black-and-white solutions that many sought. Politics was about temporal concerns and compromise, while religion aimed for the eternal and absolute.

Like my grandparents, many other Christians are tempted to believe the ancient heresy which views the spiritual world as inherently good and the physical world as inherently bad. Under this belief system nonengagement becomes a virtue instead of the vice that it really is. It is my conviction that while Christianity and politics are a difficult mix, mixing faith and politics is exactly what Christians are called to do. We should reject the subdivision of life into separate boxes marked 'politics' and 'religion', and we should reject the thinking of those who accused the *Faith in the City* report of commenting on matters exclusively within the judgement and responsibility of politicians. One MP said at the time, 'Many of us would be happier if the report had directed its attention to saving souls rather than making political judgements on how housing might be improved.'[1] Some of us reject this thinking not least because we have lived in the houses provided by these very political judgements.

This dualism between the spiritual and physical worlds has been a temptation for Christians since the Gnostic heresies of the Early Church. The teaching of the prophets in the Old Testament and of Christ in the New Testament, however, is of an *inseparable* physical and spiritual world. When the Israelites were tempted to reduce their relationship with God to the private sphere, God sent his prophets to challenge their thinking. Isaiah said:

> *Is not this the kind of fasting I have chosen:*
> *to loose the chains of injustice*
> *and untie the cords of the yoke,*
> *to set the oppressed free*
> *and break every yoke?*
> *Is it not to share your food with the hungry*
> *and to provide the poor wanderer with shelter –*
> *when you see the naked, to clothe him,*
> *and not to turn away from your own flesh and blood?*
> (ISAIAH 58:6–7)

The message and mission of Christ sums it up – 'to love God and to love your neighbour as yourself'.

The ancient Greek Aristotle said, 'Politics is the people ordering their lives together for the common good,' and in one sense everything is political – family politics, office politics, church politics or party politics. While party politics may be frustrating and difficult, it is the stuff of life itself and the alternative to politics is the law of the jungle. True Christian faith is worked out in everyday life and should not be an escape from it. Jesus Christ is the most 'down-to-earth' God and remains our pre-eminent example for engagement in the world. Christianity remains the most 'worldly' religion because Jesus created the world and then came down to live in it, taking on flesh and being tempted in every way just as we are. Christians must strive to marry their ideals of faith to the everyday demands of living in society, including the complexities of party politics. At the very least they should exercise their right to vote in an informed way. While I accept my grandparents' decision not to vote, therefore, I profoundly disagree with it.

However, my grandparents did vote once, despite their convictions. As they became increasingly frail they wanted to secure a move from their council house to a sheltered home. They successfully lobbied a local councillor and then voted for that councillor at the subsequent elections. For once in their lives they voted, and the principle of noninvolvement was temporarily abandoned. As I reflect on this event now, it fills me with a kind of despair. Is this what politics is for? To secure for oneself an advantage and then retreat into splendid isolation until another personal problem or goal requires a political solution?

In contrast to this approach, I believe Christ's command to love God and our neighbour means we must engage politically for the benefit of all, not simply for our own family or other interest group. The Christian contribution to political life is simply not good news if it is only good news for us. It must also be good news for others, for people of other faiths and for people of no faith. Politics should not be where we conduct our religious, class or culture wars. Political action to secure political privilege is ultimately selfish and anti-Christian. Instead politics is where we pursue justice and resolve our wars by constructing a just and equitable society, one that helps us love or at least live with our neighbour, wherever or whoever they may be.

100 years of Labour

Anniversaries are good times for reflection. One hundred years of Labour gives Christians an opportunity to reflect on the achievements of the countless people who have served the party throughout these years. This book has looked at only some of them, but it has proved in my own mind – and hopefully in yours – that Labour's 100 years have been full of connections between Christianity and Socialism. The political system of Socialism and the religious claims of Christianity are, of course, very different, yet they travel similar paths and share many assumptions and goals. In the Early Church no one claimed any possession for themselves but shared everything, which resulted in there being no needy person among them. Whether one interprets these teachings as a model for modern society or merely as ideals, they find powerful echoes in the principles of Socialism. The Bible's teaching provides strong support for a society based on shared resources and equality.

This anniversary also provides an opportunity to ask the big questions of politics and to consider what we want our political structures to achieve. For me the overarching issue is what kind of society we want to create for our children or other people's children. Do we want a society where everyone gets educated and has opportunities to fulfil their God-given potential? Do we want a society free from violence and crime yet tolerant of differences, whatever creed, colour or lifestyle? Do we want a society where the sick are helped regardless of their ability to pay? And do we want a society which recognizes that the powerless will always require defending and the poor will always need help? This was the kind of society that Keir Hardie wanted, and Labour was created to achieve it. How well we have achieved it reflects how far we have travelled and how much further we have to go.

The stories in this book are of people who became involved with Labour because of their faith. While this did not make Labour a Christian party, there is little doubt that it was influenced in countless ways by those who joined, served, argued and represented it throughout its first 100 years. What, then, was the particular contribution of 'God's politicians', and what distinctive elements did they bring to Labour? Scanning all these very different lives, I can see three central and recurring themes emerging – a commitment to service, a sense of urgency and a belief in equality. These themes underpinned and informed the diverse and unique contributions of individual lives, which combined with others to create the Christian contribution to 100 years of Labour. My belief today is that if these themes are practised and recaptured for the future they can once again shape the party and all society for the better.

A commitment to service

The first theme, a commitment to service, emerges out of a basic Christian belief. Christians recognize selfishness because it is the centrality of the self that is challenged and dethroned when Jesus Christ is followed. Christ's teaching that only those who are willing to take up a cross can be his disciples is not a call to the faint-hearted or the half-committed. To carry a cross was the walk of a condemned person and this image of dying to self and rising in service to Christ is central to Christian baptism. Combined with the commandment to love God and one's neighbour, it is this teaching that drives many into the caring professions, into charities and into politics.

Christians do not denigrate the need to look after oneself, since this is the natural and wisest thing to do, but they are compelled to look beyond self and their own lives to those who are less fortunate. They do this in obedience to Christ but also in order to encounter Christ in the poorest and least advantaged people. Christ teaches in Matthew 25, 'I was hungry and you gave me something to eat, I was thirsty and you gave me something to drink, I was a stranger and you invited me in, I needed clothes and you clothed me, I was sick and you looked after me, I was in prison and you came to visit me' (vv. 35–6). Today in some of the country's poorest communities and in some of the world's poorest nations it is often Christians who provide an unpublicized and ongoing service to their fellow humans.

This Christian commitment to service has been a part of the Church's service to the world for over 2,000 years. For Christians in Britain throughout the last 100 years, however, the Labour Party has provided a unique opportunity to combine human service with political solutions, to combine charity with justice. Not only have Christians fed the hungry but they have argued for rises in starvation wages; not only have they visited the sick but they have created a service providing preventative health care and free medicine. It was this commitment to serve one's fellow workers that motivated people like Arthur Henderson, Margaret Bondfield and Brenda Dean to serve first in their unions and later in the Labour Party. This commitment to service on behalf of others must remain central to Labour politics if Labour is to remain central to local and national life. Locally, Labour politicians must be where people are and where their concerns are greatest. At a national level, our health and welfare services must always have a human touch and serving others must be the reason for all that we do.

A sense of urgency

The second characteristic which I believe God's politicians brought to the party was a sense of urgency. Christians in Labour, unlike those in other parties, were not content to defend the status quo and this was never their intention when joining the party. It was a sense of urgency that broke the complacent monopoly of the Liberal and Tory structure and put the priorities of ordinary people at the top of the agenda. For these people every unnecessary death through ill health or poor conditions was offensive to God and was a motivation to pursue immediate change. Gradual reform was not attractive to Keir Hardie, a self-confessed 'man in a hurry', or to Stafford Cripps, whose impatience for change provoked the wrath of many.

Like Old Testament prophets, these trailblazers railed against the injustice experienced by the poor and the indulgences assumed by the rich. They did not understand the complacency and conservatism of those who saw destitution and death and merely reacted with reflection and moderation. Their urgency led them to make offensive remarks, such as Hardie's attack on royalty or Wheatley's description of government ministers as 'murderers'. This was in keeping with the prophetic tradition that portrayed God as rejecting the worship of the establishment for the sake of justice for the people:

> *I hate, I despise your religious feasts;*
> *I cannot stand your assemblies.*
> *Even though you bring me burnt offerings…*
> *I will not accept them…*
> *Away with the noise of your songs!*
> *I will not listen to the music of your harps.*
> *But let justice roll on like a river,*
> *righteousness like a never-failing stream!*
> (AMOS 5:21–24)

The urgency of Labour's Christians was the very opposite of the Marxist accusation that religion is the opium of the people. Instead of having a soporific effect, the hope of heaven gave to these politicians the motivation to work for God's rule on earth. Instead of being a sedative, faith was the adrenaline that drove them to refuse the status quo. People such as George Lansbury fought against all odds to keep the concerns of the poor and unemployed high on the political agenda; Ellen Wilkinson in the 1930s and Derek Foster in the 1980s fought and spoke fearlessly against mighty political oppositions. This urgency can also be seen today in Prime Minister Tony Blair's commitment to get things done and his reluctance to accept failure in education or health care. Christians within Labour have always challenged the notion of a 'caretaker' government and instead have worked for progressive government and changes in the way things are done. For God's politicians, power is for a purpose and that purpose is change for the common good.

An emphasis on equality

The third characteristic that Christians have brought to the Labour Party is an emphasis on equality. This can be seen in the educational and empowering work of R.H. Tawney and Will Crooks, or in the economic assumptions of John Smith. Christians have promoted policies based on the belief that all are of equal worth and deserve equal treatment. This is true not only for those born in Britain but for those born throughout the world. The Jubilee 2000 campaign for the cancellation of Third World debt is a unique, if rarely practised, Old Testament solution to inequality.

The creation story of Genesis communicates the radical belief that all are made in the image of God and thus all are of equal worth. St Paul reinforces this for those who are in Christ: 'There is neither Jew nor Greek, slave nor free, male nor female, for you are all one in Christ Jesus' (Galatians 3:28). The prophet Malachi at the end of the Old Testament and St James at the end of the New Testament condemned those who cheated hired labourers of their wages (see Malachi 3:5; James 5:4). For God's politicians this was not simply biblical theory, but was to be reflected in the real world of policy and law. The Labour Party's continual appeal for workers' rights has been consistent with the great values of Scripture. In contrast, the ruthlessness with which mine owners cut wages in the General Strike of 1926 was not.

God's politicians brought to the party these great egalitarian convictions which were strongly at odds with a system of government that perpetuated class distinctions and hierarchy. For those who regarded the privileges of the upper classes as unassailable, such radical thinking was, of course, a threat. Bob Holman puts it well: 'Jesus did not anger the Jewish and Roman authorities because he sang hymns or said prayers, not even because he fed the poor. They arrested him and condemned him to death on a cross because he challenged the status quo, because he was a threat to their position.'[2]

God's politicians argued for equality of treatment towards those whom others would treat as second-class citizens. The representative nature of MPs added to this practice of equality. In an increasingly secular and multifaith society, God's politicians represented and worked on behalf of those of other faiths and of none. They worked for those who were poor and for those who were rich, for those who flattered politicians and those who loathed them. They worked for those who were innocent victims of misfortune and for those who brought calamity on themselves. God's politicians believed that all people are made in the image of God and as a result all people are equal.

This commitment to others, regardless of who they are, is central to a Christian notion of public service. For me this truth is exemplified in the words of the German pastor and victim of the Nazis, Martin Niemöller:

> First they came for the Jews and I did not speak out – because I was not a Jew. Then they came for the communists and I did not speak out – because I was not a communist. Then they came for the trade unionists and I did not speak out – because I was not a trade unionist. Then they came for me – and there was no one left to speak out for me.

Niemöller could equally well have mentioned homosexuals, the mentally ill, gypsies or the poor – all were victims of the Nazis. Christian Socialists will have nothing to do with such prejudices, but rather seek to provide justice for all.

These, then, are the stories, the ideals and the legacy of Christians in Labour's first 100 years. It is a proud history and, while it is not flawless, Britain is better as a result of their service. If improvements are to continue, both in Britain and throughout the world, then Christians must continue to serve, to be urgent in the task of seeking justice and pursuing equality. This will not be easy and we are right to acknowledge our weakness, but in Christ our weakness can be strength, and through prayer and perseverance we can build a society infused with the values of the rule of God.

Notes

Acknowledgements and Introduction

1　George Eliot, *Middlemarch* (Penguin Classics, 1994 edition), p. 896.
2　Ibid.
3　Harry Moncrieff, *Roots of Labour* (Linden Hall and Industrial Pioneer, 1990), p. 145.
4　J.K. Hardie, *Socialism and Christianity* (ILP No 4 – reprint of Chapter 4, *From Serfdom to Socialism*, George Allen & Unwin, 1907).
5　Kenneth O. Morgan, *Keir Hardie – Radical and Socialist* (Weidenfeld and Nicolson, 1975), p. 49.
6　Will Crooks, *From Workhouse to Westminster* (George Haw, 1908), p. 259.
7　George Lansbury, *My England* (Selwyn & Bount Ltd, 1934), p. 37.
8　Bob Holman, *Good Old George – The Life of George Lansbury* (Lion, 1990), p. 73.
9　From R.H. Tawney's diary, quoted in Anthony Wright, *R.H. Tawney* (Manchester University Press, 1987).
10　Will Hutton, 'The Jubilee Line that Works', *Observer* (3 October 1999).

Chapter 1

1　Harry Moncrieff, *Roots of Labour*, p. 3.
2　See Ross McKibbin, *The Ideologies of Class: Social Relations in Britain 1880–1950* (Clarendon Press, 1990), Chapter 1 'Why was there no Marxism in Great Britain?' (originally published by *English Historial Review*, April 1984), p. 14; and J.H.Y. Briggs, *History of Christianity* (Lion, 1977), p. 514.
3　Eric Delderfield, *The Great Victorians and their Achievements: A Summary of the Golden Age* (Delderfield, 1993), p. 54.
4　John Stevenson, *British Society 1914–45* (Penguin, 1984), p. 30.
5　Ibid., p. 22.
6　Moncrieff, *Roots of Labour*, p. 117.
7　Quoted ibid., p. 132.
8　Joseph Clayton, *Socialism for Bishops – Why Do Bishops and Curates Ignore Socialism?* (No 18, 1909), p. 1.
9　R.H. Tawney, *Religion and the Rise of Capitalism* (Pelican Books, 1969 edition), p. 275.
10　See ibid., Chapter 4.

11 Quoted ibid., p. 195.
12 George Edwards, *From Crow Scaring to Westminster* (The Labour Publishing Co. Ltd, printed by Unwin Brothers Ltd, The Gresham Press, 1922), p. 23; and Noel G. Edwards, *Ploughboy's Progress: The Life of Sir George Edwards* (Centre of East Anglian Studies, University of East Anglia, 1998), p. 22.
13 Bob Scarth, *We'll All Be Union Men: The Story of Joseph Arch and His Union* (Industrial Pioneer Publications, 1998), p. 2.
14 Ibid.
15 Ibid.
16 Ibid., p. 6.
17 Ibid., p. 10.
18 Fenner Brockway, *Bermondsey Story: The Life of Alfred Salter* (Allen & Unwin, 1951), p. 24, cited in Bob Holman, *Towards Equality* (SPCK, 1997), p. 98.
19 See Chapter 5 in Richard Foster, *Streams of Living Water* (HarperCollins, 1999).
20 A. Skevington Wood, *The Burning Heart* (Paternoster Press, 1978), p. 142.
21 To the House of Commons, 22 June 1813, in *Parliamentary Debates XXVI*, column 853.
22 From Shaftesbury's diary, 1844, quote provided by Alison Inglis Jones at the Shaftesbury Society.
23 Quoted in Briggs, *History of Christianity*, p. 519.
24 John C. Cort, *Christian Socialism: An Informal History* (Orbis, 1988), p. 141.
25 Ibid., p. 151, quoting J.M. Ludlow's unpublished autobiography.
26 Quoted in F.G. Bettany, *Stewart Headlam*, 67, cited by Alan M. Suggate, *William Temple and Christian Social Ethics Today* (T. & T. Clark Ltd, 1987), p. 20.
27 Chris Bryant, *Possible Dreams: A Personal History of the British Christian Socialists* (Hodder & Stoughton, 1996), p. 82.
28 Ibid., quoting T. Hancock, *The Pulpit and the Press* (Brown, 1904), pp. 248–9.
29 Philip Snowden, *The Christ that is to be* (ILP, 1904), p. 13.
30 Clayton, *Socialism for Bishops*, p. 18.
31 Ibid., p. 19.
32 R.J. Campbell, *Christianity and Social Order* (Chapman and Hall, 1907), p. 36, cited in Bryant, *Possible Dreams*, p. 129.
33 Briggs, *History of Christianity*, p. 518.
34 Stephen Mayor, *The Churches and the Labour Movement* (Independent Press, 1967), p. 68.
35 Gilbert Clive Binyon, *The Christian Socialist Movement in England* (SPCK, 1931), p. 182.
36 Daniel Weinbren, *Generating Socialism: Recollections of Life in the Labour Party* (Sutton Publishing, 1997), p. 30.
37 Ibid., p. 33.
38 Ron Todd in the Foreword to Don Simpson, *Manning – The People's Cardinal* (Industrial Pioneer Publications, 1992).
39 Quoted ibid., p. 17.
40 See Chapter 4 of this book, and comments on John Wheatley.
41 Joyce Caggiano, *Religious Socialism* (The Religions and Socialism Committee, Autumn 1999), pp. 4–5.
42 Tony Wright and Matt Carter, *The People's Party* (Thames and Hudson, 1997), p. 12.
43 Moncrieff, *Roots of Labour*, p. 4.

Chapter 2

1 E. Hughes (ed.), *Keir Hardie's Speeches and Writings* (Forward Ltd, 1928).
2 The Labour Party, *Centennial Report* (1999), p. 8.
3 Sidney Webb, 'Historic', in G.B. Shaw (ed.), *Fabian Essays in Socialism* (1889), cited in Wright and Carter, *The People's Party*, p. 17.
4 Philip Gould, *The Unfinished Revolution* (Little, Brown and Company, 1998), pp. 24–5.
5 Hilary Armstrong, 'The Logic of Community', in Christopher Bryant (ed.), *Reclaiming the Ground: Christianity and Socialism* (Hodder & Stoughton, Spire, 1993), p. 94.
6 A.J. Davies, *To Build a New Jerusalem – The British Labour Movement from the 1880s to the 1990s* (Penguin, 1992), p. 16.
7 Kenneth O. Morgan, *Keir Hardie – Radical and Socialist*, p. 288.
8 Quoted by Bob Holman, 'Keir Hardie in 1901', *Third Way* (November 1992), p. 24.
9 Hardie to Engels, 21 May 1889 (Institute of Social History, Amsterdam, Marx/Engels Archive, L2158), cited in Morgan, *Keir Hardie*, p. 40.
10 Moncrieff, *Roots of Labour*, p. 149.
11 Davies, *To Build a New Jerusalem*, p. 23.
12 *Hansard* (19 February 1903).
13 Quoted in Moncrieff, *Roots of Labour*, p. 145.
14 O. Chadwick, *The Victorian Church, Part II* (A. & C. Black, 1970), p. 264.
15 Davies, *To Build a New Jerusalem*, p. 30.
16 Frank Bealey and Henry Pelling, *Labour and Politics, 1900–1906: A History of the Labour Representation Committee* (Macmillan & Co., 1958), pp. 30–31.
17 Morgan, *Keir Hardie*, p. 149.
18 *Hansard* (23 April 1901).
19 Weinbren, *Generating Socialism*, p. 30.
20 Elizabeth Bradbaun, *Margaret McMillan: Portrait of a Pioneer* (Routledge, 1989).
21 Margaret McMillan, *1860–1931: Reminiscences* (The Rachel McMillan College Association, 1977).
22 Mayor, *The Churches and the Labour Movement*, p. 320.
23 Moncrieff, *Roots of Labour*, p. 10.
24 Ibid., p. 20.
25 Ibid., p. 22.
26 Ibid., p. 19.
27 Ibid., p. 37.
28 Ibid., p. 13.
29 J.R. Clynes, *Memoirs, Volume I, 1869–1924* (Hutchinson & Co., 1937).
30 Moncrieff, *Roots of Labour*, p. 46.

Chapter 3

1 Norman and Jeanne MacKenzie (eds), *The Diary of Beatrice Webb, Volume III* (Virago, 1984), entry for 23 June 1918.
2 Morgan, *Keir Hardie*, p. 250.
3 See Lavinia Byrne, *The Hidden Voice, Christian Women and Social Change* (SPCK, 1995), p. 3.
4 Martin Gilbert, *History of the 20th Century* (HarperCollins, 1997), p. 313.

5   Quoted ibid., p. 5.
6   Quoted in Adrian Hastings, *A History of English Christianity 1920–1990* (SCM Press, 1991), p. 19.
7   Ibid., p. 45.
8   Davies, *To Build a New Jerusalem*, p. 83.
9   See J.M. Winter, *Socialism and the Challenge of War: Ideas and Politics in Britain, 1912–18* (Routledge and Kegan Paul, 1974).
10 *Conference Report* (1912), pp. 92–4.
11 Henderson to Middleton, 9 August 1906 (Labour Party Archive), cited in F.M. Leventhal, *Arthur Henderson* (Manchester University Press, 1989), pp. 33–4.
12 'Papers on Elections, Registration and Organization' (The Labour Party, 1908), cited ibid., p. 34.
13 Ibid., pp. 77–8.
14 Chris Wrigley, *Arthur Henderson* (GPC, 1990), p. 2.
15 Leventhal, *Arthur Henderson*, pp. 3–4.
16 Skevington Wood, *The Burning Heart*, p. 111.
17 Kenneth D. Brown, *Evangelical Faith and Public Zeal* (SPCK, 1995), p. 139.
18 W.T. Stead, 'Character Sketches: The Labour Party and the Books that Helped Make It', in *Review of Reviews* (1906), p. 568.
19 Wrigley, *Arthur Henderson*, p. 41, quoting from *Labour and Religion by Ten Labour Members* (1910).
20 Mary Agnes Hamilton, *Arthur Henderson* (William Heinemann Ltd, 1938), p. 27.
21 Leventhal, *Arthur Henderson*, p. 29.
22 Ross McKibbin, *The Evolution of the Labour Party 1910–1924* (Oxford University Press, 1974), p. 3.
23 David Marquand, *Ramsay MacDonald* (Jonathan Cape, 1977), p. 55.
24 Arthur Henderson, *A People's Peace* (London, 1917), reprinted in the *Daily News* (28 September 1917), quoted in Leventhal, *Arthur Henderson*, p. 51.
25 Leventhal, ibid., p. 74.
26 See McKibbin, *The Evolution of the Labour Party*.
27 See Leventhal, *Arthur Henderson*, pp. 77–8.
28 Cited ibid., pp. 76–7.

Chapter 4

1   Clynes, *Memoirs*, pp. 343–4, cited in Davies, *To Build a New Jerusalem*, p. 88.
2   Margaret Morris, *The General Strike* (Pelican), p. 323.
3   Davies, *To Build a New Jerusalem*, p. 86.
4   Ian S. Wood, *John Wheatley* (Manchester University Press, 1990), p. 4.
5   *Glasgow Observer* (24 February 1906), cited in Bob Purdie, *Outside the Chapel Door: The Glasgow Catholic Socialist Society 1906–22* (unpublished thesis submitted for Ruskin History Diploma, Spring 1976), p. 9.
6   Ibid., cited in Wood, *John Wheatley*, p. 18.
7   *Forward* (10 November 1906), cited in Bryant, *Possible Dreams*, p. 156.
8   John Wheatley, *Mines, Miners and Misery* (Glasgow, 1909), p. 22, cited in Wood, *John Wheatley*, p. 26.
9   *Glasgow Observer* (31 October 1908), cited in Purdie, *Outside the Chapel Door*, p. 2.

10 *Glasgow Observer* (19 October 1907), cited in Wood, *John Wheatley*, p. 24.
11 *Forward* (6 July 1912), cited in Bryant, *Possible Dreams*, p. 155.
12 *Forward* (21 May 1910), cited in Bob Purdie, *Frank McCabe: An Irish Socialist Pioneer in Scotland*, (unpublished paper, 1982), p. 4.
13 Bob Purdie, ibid., p. 1.
14 G. Gunnin, *John Wheatley: Catholic Socialism and Irish Labour in the West of Scotland 1906–24* (Garland Publishing, 1987), pp. 337–8.
15 *The Nation* (1 March 1924).
16 See Colin Cross, *Philip Snowden* (Barrie and Rockcliff, 1966), p. 4.
17 Philip Snowden, *An Autobiography (with Portraits)* (1934), p. 32, cited in Christian John Heycocks, *Labour Leaders and Christianity 1880–1920* (University of Wales, Bangor, unpublished Labour History MA thesis, 1995).
18 Philip Snowden, in *The Labour Prophet* (April 1898), pp. 169–70, cited in Bryant, *Possible Dreams*, p. 134.
19 See Chapter 5.
20 Keith Laybourn and David James (eds), *Philip Snowden – The First Labour Chancellor of the Exchequer* (Bradford Libraries, 1987), p. 1.
21 Hastings, *A History of English Christianity*, p. 189.
22 D.R. Davies, *In Search of Myself* (1961).
23 Morris, *The General Strike*, pp 322–3.
24 R.T. Davidson to E.S. Talbot, 25 May 1926 (Archbishop Davidson Papers, Lambeth Palace), cited ibid., p. 327.
25 See Hastings, *A History of English Christianity*, p. 164.
26 Morris, *The General Strike*, p. 328.

Chapter 5

1 Cited in Tony Benn, *The Moral Basis of the Radical Left* (CSM pamphlet, 1988), p. 1.
2 Keith Laybourn, *A Century of Labour* (Sutton Publishing, 2000), p. 42.
3 R.H. Tawney, *Equality* (George Allen & Unwin Ltd, 4th impression, 1979), p. 173.
4 Ibid., p. 164.
5 'British Socialism Today', in *The Radical Tradition*, p. 178, cited in Wright, *R.H. Tawney*, p. 58.
6 Tawney, *Equality*, pp. 208–9.
7 T. Parsons, 'Richard Henry Tawney (1880–1962): In Memoriam', in *American Sociological Review* (27 December 1962), cited in Ross Terrill, *R.H. Tawney and His Times – Socialism as Fellowship* (André Deutsch, 1973), p. 3.
8 Hastings, *A History of English Christianity*, p. 185.
9 *The Times* (28 November 1960), cited in Terrill, *R.H. Tawney and His Times*, p. 3.
10 For background on Gore see Alan Wilkinson, *Christian Socialism: Scott Holland to Tony Blair* (SCM Press, 1998), Chapter 3.
11 'Poverty as an Industrial Problem' (1913), in J.M. Winter (ed.), *The American Labour Movement and Other Essays* (Harvester, 1979), p. 111, cited in Wright, *R.H. Tawney*, pp. 9–11.
12 Wright, ibid., p. 14.
13 Ibid., p. 14.
14 Ibid., p. 15.
15 Tawney, *Religion and the Rise of Capitalism*, p. 278.

16 Wright, *R.H. Tawney*, p. 22.
17 Quoted in Wilkinson, *Christian Socialism*, p. 98.
18 See Tawney, *Religion and the Rise of Capitalism*, pp. 198–210.
19 *Christianity and Industrial Problems* (Church of England, 1918), p. 116, cited in Morris, *The General Strike*, p. 319.
20 Tawney, *Equality*, p. 57.
21 Suggate, *William Temple and Christian Social Ethics Today*, p. 25.
22 M. Cole (ed.), *Beatrice Webb's Diaries 1924–1932* (Longman, 1956), p. 2, cited in Terrill, *R.H. Tawney and His Times*, p. 63.
23 Terrill, ibid., p. 63.
24 Adam Fox, *Dean Inge*, p. 203, cited in Hastings, *A History of English Christianity*, p. 177.
25 Hugh Gaitskell, Tawney Memorial Service, 8 February 1962, cited in Wright, *R.H. Tawney*, p. 130.
26 Michael Foot, *Loyalists and Loners* (Collins, 1986), p. 96, cited ibid.
27 Wright, ibid., p. 25.
28 Annie Lockwood, *A Celebration of Pioneering Labour Women* (North Tyneside Fabians, 1995), p. 42.
29 Ibid., p. 27.
30 Ibid., p. 29.
31 Ibid., p. 34.
32 Davies, *To Build a New Jerusalem*, p. 92.
33 Wright and Carter, *The People's Party*, p. 50.
34 Lockwood, *A Celebration of Pioneering Labour Women*, p. 40.

Chapter 6

1   Davies, *To Build a New Jerusalem*, p. 117.
2   R. Postgate, *The Life of George Lansbury* (Longman, Green & Co., 1951), p. 56.
3   *The Times* (20 February 1959), cited in Bob Holman, *Good Old George – The Life of George Lansbury*, p. 183.
4   *The Times* (20 February 1959), cited ibid., p. 179.
5   A.J.P. Taylor, *English History 1914–1945* (Penguin, 1987), cited ibid., p. 135.
6   George Lansbury, *My Life* (Constable & Co., 1928), p. 75.
7   George Lansbury, *Looking Backwards and Forwards* (Blackie & Son Ltd. 1935), p. 54.
8   See Chapter 2, p. 44.
9   William Temple, 'The Church and the Labour Party', *Economic Review* (April 1908), cited in Bryant, *Possible Dreams*, p. 129.
10 Holman, *Good Old George*, p. 72.
11 For a full summary of these arguments, see ibid., pp. 96–7.
12 Edgar Lansbury, *George Lansbury: My Father* (Sampson Low, Marston & Co., 1934), p. 120.
13 St John B. Groser, *Politics and Persons* (SCM Press, 1949), pp. 22–3.
14 Postgate, *The Life of George Lansbury*, p. 104.
15 Ibid., p. 117.
16 Lansbury, *My Life*, p. 118.
17 For further details see Noreen Branson, *Poplarism 1919–1925: George Lansbury and the Councillors' Revolt* (Lawrence and Wishart, 1979).

18 Sidney Webb, 'The First Labour Government', *Political Quarterly* (vol. xxxii, 1961), pp. 13–14.
19 Lansbury, *My Life*, p. 272.
20 Holman, *Good Old George*, p. 123.
21 Cited ibid., p. 125.
22 James Douglas in the *Sunday Express* (5 July 1931), cited in Edgar Lansbury, *George Lansbury*, pp. 13–14.
23 Lansbury, writing in the *Herald* (23 October 1931), cited in Holman, *Good Old George*, p. 29.
24 Postgate, *The Life of George Lansbury*, p. 277.
25 Wright and Carter, *The People's Party*, p. 55.
26 Ibid.
27 See Peter Weiler, *Ernest Bevin* (Manchester University Press, 1993), p. 4.
28 Francis Williams, *Ernest Bevin* (Hutchinson, 1952), p. 20.
29 Kenneth O. Morgan, *Labour People: Leaders and Lieutenants, Hardie to Kinnock* (Oxford University Press, 1987), p. 101.
30 Betty D. Vernon, *Ellen Wilkinson: 1891–1947* (Croom Helm, 1982), p. 137.
31 Ibid., p. 236.
32 Morgan, *Labour People*, p. 103.
33 See Chapter 4, p. 71.
34 Vernon, *Ellen Wilkinson*, p. 141.
35 Durham in *The Times* (26 October 1936), Sheffield in the *Sheffield Independent* (17 October 1936), cited ibid., p. 144.
36 *Hansard* (11 November 1936), cited ibid., p. 145.
37 Vernon, ibid., p. 146.
38 Morgan, *Labour People*, pp. 103–4.
39 E. Wilkinson, *The Town That Was Murdered – The Life Story of Jarrow* (Left Book Club, 1939), pp. 11, 28, 31, 32, 45, cited in Heycocks, *Labour Leaders and Christianity*, p. 37.
40 *Methodist Recorder* (16 March 1939), cited in Vernon, *Ellen Wilkinson*, p. 19.
41 *Methodist Magazine* (April 1947), cited ibid., pp. 237–8.

Chapter 7

1 Davies, *To Build a New Jerusalem*, p. 160.
2 George Thomas, *George Thomas, Mr Speaker: The Memoirs of The Viscount Tonypandy* (Century, 1985), p. 55.
3 Chris Bryant, *Stafford Cripps: The First Modern Chancellor* (Hodder & Stoughton, 1997), p. 400.
4 Stafford Cripps, *Democracy Alive: A Selection from recent speeches* (Sidgwick & Jackson, 1946), pp. 21–3, cited ibid., pp. 350–51.
5 Martin Gilbert, *Descent into Barbarism 1933–51* (HarperCollins, 1999), p. 336.
6 Davies, *To Build a New Jerusalem*, p. 156.
7 Wright and Carter, *The People's Party*, p. 70.
8 Bryant, *Stafford Cripps*, p. 57.
9 Colin Cooke, *The Life of Richard Stafford Cripps* (Hodder & Stoughton, 1957), p. 103, cited ibid., p. 78.
10 Bryant, ibid., pp. 78–9.
11 Clement Attlee, *As It Happened* (Heinemann, 1954), p. 76.

12 Bryant, *Stafford Cripps*, p. 95.

13 Michael Foot, *Aneurin Bevan: Volume 1, 1897–1945* (Paladin Granada, 1975), p. 158.

14 Ibid., p. 289.

15 Norman and Jeanne MacKenzie (eds), *The Diary of Beatrice Webb, Volume IV* (Virago, 1985), entry for 21 January 1939.

16 *Sunday Referee* (4 June 1939), cited in Bryant, *Stafford Cripps*, p. 182.

17 Bryant, ibid., p. 270.

18 Cripps, *Democracy Alive*, pp. 21–3, cited ibid., pp. 350–51.

19 Stafford Cripps, *God in our Work: Religious Addresses* (Thomas Nelson & Sons, 1949), pp. 2, 5, cited ibid., p. 367.

20 Ruth Edwards, *Victor Gollancz: A Biography* (Victor Gollancz, 1987), pp. 538–9, cited ibid., p. 464.

21 Bryant, ibid., pp. 481–2.

22 Leah Manning, *A Life for Education: An Autobiography* (Victor Gollancz, 1970), p. 175.

23 Thomas, *George Thomas, Mr Speaker*, p. 56.

24 Ron Bill and Stan Newens, *Leah Manning* (Leah Manning Trust, 1991), p. 78.

25 Ibid., pp. 15–16.

26 See Chapter 1, p. 17.

27 Manning, *A Life for Education*, p. 37.

28 Ibid., p. 39.

29 Ibid., p. 78.

30 Ibid., pp. 79–80.

31 Cited in Gilbert, *Descent into Barbarism*, p. 136.

32 Manning, *A Life for Education*, p. 125.

33 *Labour Organizer* (August 1945), p. 11, cited in Bryant, *Stafford Cripps*, p. 354.

34 Manning, *A Life for Education*, p. 81.

35 Dudley Seers, *The Levelling of Incomes since 1938* (Blackwell, 1951), p. 72, cited in Davies, *To Build a New Jerusalem*, pp. 167–8.

Chapter 8

1 Gilbert, *Descent into Barbarism*, p. 732.

2 Ibid., p. 780.

3 *Daily Herald* (1 November 1939), cited in Brian Frost, *Goodwill on Fire: Donald Soper's Life and Mission* (Hodder & Stoughton, 1996), p. 48.

4 Ronald Ferguson, *George McLeod: Founder of the Iona Community* (Fount, 1990), p. 249.

5 Ibid., p. 261.

6 Donald Soper, *Christian Politics* (Epworth Press, 1977), p. 12.

7 *Christian World* (1 October 1953), cited in Frost, *Goodwill on Fire*, p. 71.

8 *Spectator* (8 July 1956), cited ibid., p. 74.

9 Cited in Wright and Carter, *The People's Party*, p. 93.

10 Jennie Lee, *My Life with Nye* (Jonathan Cape, 1980), pp. 254–5, cited ibid., p. 78.

11 Michael Foot interview (5 August 1993), cited ibid., p. 78.

12 *Sunday Telegraph* (5 November 1961), cited ibid., p. 80.

13 Hastings, *A History of English Christianity*, p. 423, cited ibid., p. 253.

14 Hugh Dalton, *Call Back Yesterday, 1887–1931* (Muller, 1953), p. 172, cited in Vernon, *Ellen Wilkinson*, p. 26.

15 Wright and Carter, *The People's Party*, p. 88.

16 Francis Wheen, *Tom Driberg: His Life and Indiscretions* (Chatto & Windus, 1990), pp. 1–2.

17 Ibid., p. 166.

18 Ibid., p. 167.

19 Ibid., p. 178.

20 Ibid., p. 210.

21 Ibid., p. 244.

22 Ibid., pp. 250–51.

23 Driberg to Attlee (28 February 1955), cited ibid., p. 319.

24 John Maynard Keynes (1883–1946) argued in his writings on economic theory that investment in public works would result in employment growth and consumer power, leading on to wider economic growth.

25 Wheen, *Tom Driberg*, p. 353.

Chapter 9

1   Ben Pimlott, *Harold Wilson* (HarperCollins, 1992), p. 41.

2   Centenary Celebration, *100 Years of the Labour Party* (The Labour Party, 1999), p. 18.

3   Pimlott, *Harold Wilson*, p. 11.

4   Kenneth Harris, *Conversations* (Hodder & Stoughton, 1967), p. 266.

5   Pimlott, *Harold Wilson*, p. 93.

6   Paul Foot, *The Politics of Harold Wilson* (Penguin, 1968), p. 55.

7   Pimlott, *Harold Wilson*, p. 177.

8   *Observer* (8 November 1959), cited ibid., p 229.

9   *Daily Herald* (2 June 1962), cited ibid.

10 Quoted in Clive Ponting, *Breach of Promise: Labour in Power 1964–1970* (Hamish Hamilton, 1989), p. 15.

11 Cited in Wright and Carter, *The People's Party*, p. 107.

12 Harold Wilson, *The Labour Governments 1964–1970: A Personal Record* (Weidenfeld and Nicolson, and Michael Joseph, 1971), p. 37.

13 Michael Ramsey in the House of Lords, 29 February 1968, cited by Kenneth Leech, *The Gospel, the Catholic Church and the World: The Social Theology of Michael Ramsey (1904–1988)* (The Jubilee Group, 1990), p. 17.

14 Wright and Carter, *The People's Party*, p. 113.

15 *Observer* (17 January 1965).

16 Thomas, *George Thomas, Mr Speaker*, p. 91.

17 Ibid., p. 80.

18 Ibid., p. 24.

19 Ibid., p. 81.

20 Ibid., p. 216.

Chapter 10

1   See *Hansard* (13 February 1989).

2   *Faith in the City* (Church of England, 1985), Chapter 3, paragraph 3.4.

3   See Michael Alison and David L. Edwards (eds), *Christianity and Conservatism* (Hodder & Stoughton, 1990).

4   Ivor Crewe and Anthony King, *SDP: The Birth, Life and Death of the Social Democratic Party* (Oxford University Press, 1995), p. 34.

5   See Wright, *R.H. Tawney*, p. 131.

6   David Sheppard in his Foreword to Eric Heffer, *Why I Am a Christian* (Hodder & Stoughton, Spire, 1991).

7   Eric Heffer, *Never a Yes Man: The Life and Politics of an Adopted Liverpudlian* (Verso, 1991).

8   See note 5 above for publication details.

9   Heffer, *Why I Am a Christian*, p. 18.

10 Heffer, *Never a Yes Man*, p. 127.

11 Ibid., p. 153.

12 Davies, *To Build a New Jerusalem*, p. 262.

13 Tony Benn, with Chris Mullin (ed.), *Arguments for Socialism* (Jonathan Cape, 1979), p. 24.

14 Ibid., p. 26.

15 Tony Benn, 'The Power of the Bible Today', The Twelfth Annual Sheffield Academic Press Lecture (University of Sheffield, 17 March 1995), *Occasional Papers* (Sheffield Academic Press), p. 2.

16 Tony Benn, *It's My Belief* (ITV network programme, 21 July 1989).

17 Jad Adams, *Tony Benn* (Macmillan, 1992), pp. 67–8.

18 Tony Benn, *Office without Power: Diaries 1968–72* (Hutchinson, 1988), entry for 2 November 1968.

19 'The Role of Women in Society', speech at the Yorkshire Labour Women's Rally (Rotherham, 5 June 1970), cited in Adams, *Tony Benn*, p. 316.

20 Adams, ibid., p. 455.

21 Andrew Thorpe, *A History of the British Labour Party* (Macmillan, 1997), p. 225.

22 Benn, 'The Power of the Bible Today', p. 7.

23 Bryant, *Possible Dreams*, p. 287.

24 Benn, *Arguments for Socialism*, p. 28.

25 For more on Field, see Wilkinson, *Christian Socialism*, pp. 228ff.

26 Interview with author, February 1997.

27 Interview with author, March 2000.

28 Ibid.

29 Brenda Dean was made a life peer in 1993 in recognition of her lifelong commitment and service to trade unionism. From 1985 to 1991 she was general secretary to her own SOGAT union, having been a member since the age of 16.

30 From the Foreword by Tony Benn in Jean Sargeant, *Liberation Christianity on the Wapping Picket Line* (The Jubilee Group, 1992), p. 2.

31 Sargeant, ibid, p. 23.

Chapter 11

1   See Philip Gould, *The Unfinished Revolution*, p. 175.

2   *Tribune* (26 June 1992), cited ibid., p. 159.

3   Gordon Brown, 'John Smith's Socialism: His Writings and Speeches', in Gordon Brown and James Naughtie, *John Smith: Life and Soul of the Party* (Mainstream Publishing, 1994), p. 61.

4   Cited in Andy McSmith, *John Smith: A Life 1938–1994* (Mandarin, 1994), p. 320.
5   11 July 1992, cited ibid., p. 320.
6   Isobel Hilton, 'Profile of John Smith', *Independent* (16 July 1992).
7   Andy McSmith, *John Smith: Playing the Long Game* (Verso, 1993), p. 32.
8   Ibid., p. 47.
9   James Naughtie, 'A Political Life Observed', in Brown and Naughtie, *John Smith*, p. 47.
10   See Bryant (ed.), *Reclaiming the Ground*, p. 127.
11   Cited in Brown and Naughtie, *John Smith*, p. 109.
12   Helen Liddell, 'He was witty, he was bright and could spot fools at ten paces!', *Daily Record* (13 May 1994), cited ibid., p. 172.
13   Elizabeth Smith, Introduction to Brown and Naughtie, ibid., p. 13.
14   Speech in Wellingborough (19 February 1993), cited in John Rentoul, *Tony Blair* (Warner Books, 1996), p. 291.
15   Rentoul, ibid., p. 43.
16   Tony Blair, Foreword, Bryant (ed.), *Reclaiming the Ground*, pp. 10–11.
17   Speech in Wellingborough, 19 February 1993.
18   See John Macmurray, *Persons in Relation* (Humanities Press International, 1961), p. 200.
19   Rentoul, *Tony Blair*, p. 101.
20   Ibid., p. 137.
21   *Hansard* (6 July 1983).
22   Foreword, Bryant (ed.), *Reclaiming the Ground*, p. 10.
23   See Gould, *The Unfinished Revolution*, pp. 202–4.
24   Rentoul, *Tony Blair*, p. 406.
25   Ibid., p. 414.

Chapter 12

1   *Hansard* (13 February 1989).
2   Bob Holman, *Towards Equality*, p. 136.

Bibliography

Adams, Jad, *Tony Benn* (Macmillan, 1992)

Adelman, Paul, *The Rise of the Labour Party 1880–1945* (Longman, 1972)

Alison, Michael and Edwards, David L. (eds), *Christianity and Conservatism* (Hodder & Stoughton, 1990)

Attlee, Clement, *As It Happened* (Heinemann, 1954)

Attlee, Clement, 'Sir Stafford Cripps Memorial Lecture' (The Stafford Cripps Memorial Trust, 1957)

Bealey, Frank and Pelling, Henry, *Labour and Politics, 1900–1906: A History of the Labour Representation Committee* (Macmillan & Co., 1958)

Bebbington, D.W., *The Nonconformist Conscience: Chapel and Politics 1879–1914* (Allen & Unwin, 1982)

Benn, Tony with Mullin, Chris (ed.), *Arguments for Socialism* (Jonathan Cape, 1979)

Benn, Tony, *The Moral Basis of the Radical Left* (CSM Pamphlet, 1988)

Benn, Tony, *Office without Power: Diaries, 1968–72* (Hutchinson, 1988)

Benn, Tony, *Against the Tide: Diaries, 1973–76* (Hutchinson, 1989)

Benn, Tony with Winstone, Ruth (ed.), *Conflicts of Interest: Diaries, 1977–80* (Hutchinson, 1990)

Benn, Tony, *The End of an Era: Diaries, 1980–90* (Hutchinson, 1992)

Benn, Tony, 'The Power of the Bible Today' (The Twelfth Annual Sheffield Academic Press Lecture, delivered at the University of Sheffield, 17 March 1995, *Occasional Papers*, Sheffield Academic Press)

Beveridge, Baron William Henry, *The Pillars of Security and other wartime essays and addresses* (George Allen & Unwin, 1943)

Bill, Ron and Newens, Stan, *Leah Manning* (Leah Manning Trust, 1991)

Binyon, Gilbert Clive, *The Christian Socialist Movement in England* (SPCK, 1931)

Blair, Tony, *New Britain: My Vision of a Young Country* (Fourth Estate, 1996)

Bradbaun, Elizabeth, *Margaret McMillan: Portrait of a Pioneer* (Routledge, 1989)

Branson, Noreen, *Poplarism 1919–1925: George Lansbury and the Councillors' Revolt* (Lawrence and Wishart, 1979)

Briggs, Asa and Macartney, Anne, *Toynbee Hall: The First Hundred Years* (Routledge and Kegan Paul, 1984)

Briggs, J.H.Y., *History of Christianity* (Lion, 1977)

Brockway, Fenner, *Bermondsey Story: The Life of Alfred Salter* (Allen & Unwin, 1951)

Brown, George, *In My Way: The Political Memoirs of Lord George Brown* (Victor Gollancz, 1971)

Brown, Gordon and Naughtie, James, *John Smith: Life and Soul of the Party* (Mainstream Publishing, 1994)

Brown, Kenneth D. (ed.), *The First Labour Party 1906–1914* (Croom Helm, 1985)

Brown, Kenneth D., *Evangelical Faith and Public Zeal* (SPCK, 1995)

Bryant, Chris (ed.), *Reclaiming the Ground: Christianity and Socialism* (Hodder & Stoughton, Spire, 1993)

Bryant, Chris, *Possible Dreams: A Personal History of the British Christian Socialists* (Hodder & Stoughton, 1996)

Bryant, Chris, *Stafford Cripps: The First Modern Chancellor* (Hodder & Stoughton, 1997)

Buchanan, T. and Conway M. (eds), *Political Catholicism in Europe 1918–1965* (Oxford University Press, 1996)

Butler, D.E., *The British General Election of 1955* (Macmillan, 1955)

Byrne, Lavinia, *The Hidden Voice, Christian Women and Social Change* (SPCK, 1995)

Caggiano, Joyce, *Religious Socialism* (The Religions and Socialism Committee, Autumn 1999)

Campbell, R.J., *Christianity and Social Order* (Chapman and Hall, 1907)

Castle, Barbara, *The Castle Diaries: 1964–1976* (Papermac, 1990)

Ceadel, Martin, *Pacifism in Britain 1914–1945: The Defining of a Faith* (Clarendon Press, 1980)

Chadwick, O., *The Victorian Church Part II* (A. & C. Black, 1970)

Churchill, Winston, *The Second World War* (Chiswick Press, 1948–53)

Clayton, Joseph, *Socialism for Bishops – Why Do Bishops and Curates Ignore Socialism?* (No 18, 1909)

Clifford, John, *Socialism and the Teaching of Christ* (Fabian Society Tract No 78, 1897)

Clifford, John, *Socialism and the Churches* (Fabian Society Tract No 139, 1908)

Clynes, J.R., *Memoirs, Volume 1, 1869–1924* (Hutchinson & Co., 1937)

Coates, David, *The Labour Party and the Struggle for Socialism* (Cambridge University Press, 1975)

Cole, G.D.H., *James Keir Hardie* (Victor Gollancz, Fabian Society, 1941)

Cole, G.D.H., *A History of the Labour Party from 1914* (Routledge and Kegan Paul, 1948)

Collins, Diana, *Partners in Protest: Life with Canon Collins* (Victor Gollancz, 1992)

Coman, Peter, *Catholics and the Welfare State* (Longman, 1977)

Conway, Katharine St John and Glaiser, J. Bruce, *The Religion of Socialism – Two Aspects* (The Manchester Labour Press Society, 1890?)

Cooke, Colin, *The Life of Richard Stafford Cripps* (Hodder & Stoughton, 1957)

Cort, John C., *Christian Socialism: An Informal History* (Orbis Books, 1988)

Crewe, Ivor and King, Anthony, *SDP: The Birth, Life and Death of the Social Democratic Party* (Oxford University Press, 1995)

Cripps, Alfred, *A Retrospect, looking back over a life of more than 80 years* (Heinemann, 1936)

Cripps, Frederick H., *Life's a Gamble: An Autobiography* (Odhams Press, 1957)

Cripps, Richard Stafford, *Can Socialism Come by Constitutional Means?* (Socialist League, 1933)

Cripps, Richard Stafford, *Towards Christian Democracy* (George Allen & Unwin, 1945)

Cripps, Richard Stafford, *Democracy Alive: A Selection from Recent Speeches* (Sidgwick & Jackson, 1946)

Cripps, Richard Stafford, Foreword to *In This Faith We Live* (Parliamentary Socialist Christian Group, April 1948)

Cripps, Richard Stafford, *God In Our Work: Religious Addresses* (Thomas Nelson & Sons, 1949)

Cripps, Richard Stafford, *The Spiritual Crisis: A Sermon preached in St Paul's Cathedral* (A.R. Mowbray & Co., 1950)

Crosland, Anthony, *The Future of Socialism* (Jonathan Cape, 1956)

Cross, Colin, *Philip Snowden* (Barrie and Rockliff, 1966)

Crossman, Richard, *The Backbench Diaries of Richard Crossman* (Hamish Hamilton and Jonathan Cape, 1981)

Dalton, Hugh, *The Fateful Years: Memoirs, 1931–45* (Frederick Muller, 1957)

Davies, A.J., *To Build a New Jerusalem – The British Labour Movement from the 1880s to the 1990s* (Penguin, 1992)

Deakin, Nicholas with Cohen, Brian and McNeal, Julia, *Colour, Citizenship and British Society* (Panther Modern Society, 1970), Foreword by E.J.B. Rose, editor of the original report, *Colour and Citizenship: An Institute of Race Relations Report* (Oxford University Press, 1969)

Dearmer, Percy, *Socialism and Christianity* (Fabian Society Tract No 133, 1907)

Delderfield, Eric, *The Great Victorians and their Achievements: A Summary of the Golden Age* (Delderfield, 1993)

Dennis, Norman and Halsey, A.H., *English Ethical Socialism: Thomas More to R.H. Tawney* (Clarendon Press, 1988)

Dixon, Bernard (ed.), *Journeys in Belief* (George Allen & Unwin, 1968)

Driberg, Tom, *Ruling Passions* (Cape, 1977)

Ecclestone, G.S., *The Church of England and Politics* (CIO Publishing, 1981)

Edwards, George, *From Crow Scaring to Westminster* (The Labour Publishing Co. Ltd, printed by Unwin Brothers Ltd, The Gresham Press, 1922)

Edwards, Noel G., *Ploughboy's Progress: The Life of Sir George Edwards* (Centre of East Anglian Studies, University of East Anglia, 1998)

Edwards, Ruth, *Victor Gollancz: A Biography* (Victor Gollancz, 1987)

Estorick, Eric, *Stafford Cripps* (Heinemann, 1949)

Evans, Stanley G., *Christian Socialism: A Study Outline and Bibliography* (CSM Pamphlet 2, 1962)

Ferguson, Ronald, *George McLeod: Founder of the Iona Community* (Fount, 1990)

Foot, Michael, *Aneurin Bevan: Volume 1, 1897–1945* (Paladin Granada, 1975)

Foot, Michael, *Aneurin Bevan: Volume 2, 1945–1960* (Paladin Granada, 1975)

Foot, Michael, *Loyalists and Loners* (Collins, 1986)

Foot, Paul, *The Politics of Harold Wilson* (Penguin, 1968)

Foster, D.B., *Socialism and the Christ: My Two Great Discoveries in a Long and Painful Search for Truth* (Leeds, 1921)

Foster, Richard, *Streams of Living Water* (HarperCollins, 1999)

Frost, Brian, *Goodwill on Fire: Donald Soper's Life and Mission* (Hodder & Stoughton, 1996)

Gilbert, Martin, *History of the 20th Century* (HarperCollins, 1997)

Gilbert, Martin, *Descent into Barbarism 1933–51* (HarperCollins, 1999)

Gilbert, Martin, *Challenge to Civilization 1952–1999* (HarperCollins, 1999)

Gould, Philip, *The Unfinished Revolution* (Little, Brown and Company, 1998)

Graves, P.M., *Labour Women: Women in British Working Class Politics 1918–1939* (Cambridge University Press, 1994)

Groser, St John B., *Politics and Persons* (SCM Press, 1949)

Groser, St John B., *Does Socialism Need Religion?* (Fabian Society Pamphlet, 1961)

Gunnin, G., *John Wheatley: Catholic Socialism and Irish Labour in the West of Scotland 1906–24* (Garland Publishing, 1987)

Hamilton, Mary Agnes, *Arthur Henderson* (William Heinemann Ltd, 1938)

Hancock, T., *The Pulpit and the Press* (Brown, 1904)

Hardie, J. Keir, *Socialism and Christianity* (ILP No 4 – reprint of Chapter 4, *From Serfdom to Socialism*, George Allen & Unwin, 1907)

Harmer, Harry, *The Longman Companion to the Labour Party 1900–1998* (Longman, 1999)

Harris, Kenneth, *Conversations* (Hodder & Stoughton, 1967)

Harris, Robert, *The Making of Neil Kinnock* (Faber & Faber, 1984)

Hastings, Adrian, *A History of English Christianity 1920–1990* (SCM Press, 1991)

Hastings, Max, *Bomber Command* (Michael Joseph, 1979)

Haw, G. (ed.), *Christianity and the Working Classes* (Macmillan and Co., 1906)

Headlam, Stewart, *Christian Socialism* (Fabian Society Tract No 42, 1899)

Heffer, Eric, *The Class Struggle in Parliament: A Socialist View of Industrial Relations* (Victor Gollancz, 1973)

Heffer, Eric, *Never a Yes Man: The Life and Politics of an Adopted Liverpudlian* (Verso, 1991)

Heffer, Eric, *Why I Am a Christian* (Hodder & Stoughton, Spire, 1991)

Heycocks, Christian John, *Labour Leaders and Christianity 1880–1920* (University of Wales, Bangor, unpublished Labour History MA thesis, 1995)

Holman, Bob, *Good Old George – The Life of George Lansbury* (Lion, 1990)

Holman, Bob, *Towards Equality* (SPCK, 1997)

Howell, David, *British Social Democracy* (Croom Helm, 1980)

Iremonger, F.A., *William Temple* (Oxford University Press, 1948)

Jeffreys, Keith (ed.), *Labour and the Wartime Coalition: from the diary of James Chuter Ede, 1941–1945* (Historians Press, 1987)

Jenkins, Roy, *Nine Men of Power* (Hamish Hamilton, 1974)

Jenkins, Roy, *A Life at the Centre* (Pan, in association with Macmillan, 1992)

Jupp, James, *The Radical Left in Britain 1931–1941* (Frank Cass, 1982)

Koss, Stephen, *Nonconformity in Modern British Politics* (B.T. Batsford, 1975)

The Labour Party, *Centennial Report* (1999)

Lansbury, Edgar, *George Lansbury: My Father* (Sampson Low, Marston & Co., 1934)

Lansbury, George, *Your Part in Poverty* (George Allen & Unwin, 1917)

Lansbury, George, *These Things Shall Be* (Swarthmore Press, 1920)

Lansbury, George, *My Life* (Constable & Co., 1928)

Lansbury, George, *Looking Backwards and Forwards* (Blackie & Son Ltd, 1935)

Lansbury, George, *My Quest for Peace* (Michael Joseph, 1938)

Laybourn, Keith, *Philip Snowden: A Biography* (Temple Smith, 1988)

Laybourn, Keith, *A Century of Labour* (Sutton Publishing, 2000)

Laybourn, Keith and James, David (eds), *Philip Snowden – The First Labour Chancellor of the Exchequer* (Bradford Libraries, 1987)

Leech, Kenneth, *Struggle in Babylon: Racism in the Cities and Churches of Britain* (Sheldon Press, 1988)

Leech, Kenneth, *The Gospel, the Catholic Church and the World: The Social Theology of Michael Ramsey (1904–1988)* (The Jubilee Group, 1990)

Leventhal, F.M., *Arthur Henderson* (Manchester University Press, 1989)

Lockhart, J.G., *Cosmo Gordon Lang* (Hodder & Stoughton, 1949)

Lockwood, Annie, *A Celebration of Pioneering Labour Women: Grace Colman, MP for Tynemouth Constituency 1945–51; Rt Hon. Margaret Bondfield, MP for Wallsend Constituency 1926–31* (North Tyneside Fabians, 1995)

MacKenzie, Norman and Jeanne (eds), *The Diary of Beatrice Webb, Volume III, 1905–1924: The Power to Alter Things* (Virago, 1984)

MacKenzie, Norman and Jeanne (eds), *The Diary of Beatrice Webb, Volume IV, 1924–1943: The Wheel of Life* (Virago, 1985)

Macmurray, John, *Persons in Relation* (Humanities Press International, 1961)

Manning, Leah, *A Life for Education: An Autobiography* (Victor Gollancz, 1970)

Marquand, David, *Ramsay MacDonald* (Jonathan Cape, 1977)

Mayor, Stephen, *The Churches and the Labour Movement* (Independent Press, 1967)

McKibbin, Ross, *The Evolution of the Labour Party 1910–1924* (Oxford University Press, 1974)

McKibbin, Ross, *The Ideologies of Class: Social Relations in Britain 1880–1950* (Clarendon Press, 1990)

McKie, David and Cook, Chris (eds), *The Decade of Disillusion* (Macmillan, 1972)

McMillan, Margaret, *1860–1931: Reminiscences* (The Rachel McMillan College Association, 1977)

McSmith, Andy, *John Smith: Playing the Long Game* (Verso, 1993)

McSmith, Andy, *John Smith: A Life 1938–1994* (Mandarin, 1994)

Mikardo, Ian, *Back-bencher* (Weidenfeld and Nicolson, 1988)

Mitchell, Austin (ed.), *Election '45: Reflections on the Revolution in Britain* (Fabian Society, 1995)

Mitchison, Naomi, *You May Well Ask* (Flamingo, 1986)

Moncrieff, Harry, *Roots of Labour* (Linden Hall and Industrial Pioneer, 1990)

Moran, Lord, *Churchill* (Constable, 1966)

Morgan, Kenneth O., *Keir Hardie – Radical and Socialist* (Weidenfeld and Nicolson, 1975)

Morgan, Kenneth O., *Labour People: Leaders and Lieutenants, Hardie to Kinnock* (Oxford University Press, 1987)

Morrison, Herbert, *An Autobiography* (Odhams Press, 1960)

Morris, Margaret, *The General Strike* (Pelican edition, originally published by Penguin, 1976)

Mowat, Charles Loch, *Britain Between The Wars* (Methuen, 1956)

Moyser, George (ed.), *Church and Politics Today: The Role of the Church of England in Contemporary Politics* (T. & T. Clark Ltd, 1985)

Norriss, Mrs St Clare, *Watchman Awake! Save the Children!* (1911)

Ormrod, David (ed.), *Fellowship, Freedom and Equality – Lectures in memory of R.H. Tawney* (Christian Socialist Movement, 1990)

Pelling, H., *The Origins of the Labour Party 1880–1900* (Clarendon Press, 1965)

Pimlott, Ben, *Labour and the Left in the 1930s* (Cambridge University Press, 1977)

Pimlott, Ben, *Harold Wilson* (HarperCollins, 1992)

Pincher, Chapman, *Inside Story* (Sidgwick & Jackson, 1978)

Pincher, Chapman, *Their Trade is Treachery* (Sidgwick & Jackson, 1981)

Ponting, Clive, *Breach of Promise: Labour in Power 1964–1970* (Hamish Hamilton, 1989)

Postgate, R., *The Life of George Lansbury* (Longmans, Green & Co., 1951)

Priestley, J.B., *English Journey* (Penguin, 1977)

Priestman, Alfred Tuke, *Socialism: An Essentially Christian Movement* (West, Newman and Co., VII, 1901, Socialist Quaker Society Tract No 2, reprinted from the *Friends Quarterly Examiner*)

Purcell, William, *Portrait of Soper: A Biography of the Reverend Lord Soper of Kingsway* (Mowbrays, 1972)

Purdie, Bob, *Outside the Chapel Door: The Glasgow Catholic Socialist Society 1906–22* (unpublished thesis submitted for Ruskin History Diploma, Spring 1976); *Frank McCabe: An Irish Socialist Pioneer in Scotland* (unpublished paper, 1982)

Reeves, Marjorie (ed.), *Christian Thinking and Social Order: Conviction Politics from the 1930s to the Present Day* (Cassell, 1999)

Rentoul, John, *Tony Blair* (Warner Books, 1996)

Sandel, Michael J., *Liberalism and the Limits of Justice* (Cambridge University Press, 1982)

Sargeant, Jean, *Liberation Christianity on the Wapping Picket Line*, with a Foreword by Tony Benn (The Jubilee Group, 1992)

Saville, John, *The Labour Movement in Britain* (Faber & Faber, 1988)

Scarth, Bob, *We'll All Be Union Men: The Story of Joseph Arch and His Union* (Industrial Pioneer Publications, 1998)

Seers, Dudley, *The Levelling of Incomes since 1938* (Blackwell, 1951)

Simpson, Don, *Manning – The People's Cardinal* (Industrial Pioneer Publications, 1992)

Skevington Wood, A., *The Burning Heart* (Paternoster Press, 1978)

Snowden, Philip, *The Christ that is to be* (ILP, 1904)

Snowden, Philip, *An Autobiography, Volume II, 1919–1934* (Ivor Nicolsen and Watson, 1934)

Socialist Sunday Schools: A Manual (National Council of British Socialist Sunday Schools, 1923)

Sopel, Jon, *Tony Blair: The Moderniser* (Michael Joseph, 1995)

Soper, Donald, *The Advocacy of the Gospel* (Hodder & Stoughton, 1961)

Soper, Donald, *Christian Socialism: Questions and Answers* (CSM Pamphlet 1, 1962)

Soper, Donald, *Christian Politics* (Epworth Press, 1977)

Soper, Donald, *Calling For Action: An Autobiographical Enquiry* (Robson Books, 1984)

Stead, W.T., 'Character Sketches: The Labour Party and the Books that Helped Make It', *Review of Reviews* (1906)

Stevenson, John, *British Society 1914–45* (Penguin, 1984)

Stewart, Michael, *Life and Labour: An Autobiography* (Sidgwick & Jackson, 1980)

Stewart, William, *J. Keir Hardie* (ILP, 1925)

Stockwood, Mervyn, *Chanctonbury Ring: An Autobiography* (Hodder & Stoughton, 1982)

Suggate, Alan M., *William Temple and Christian Social Ethics Today* (T. & T. Clark Ltd, 1987)

Tawney, R.H., *The Acquisitive Society* (G. Bell & Sons Ltd, 1921)

Tawney, R.H., *Religion and the Rise of Capitalism* (Penguin, 1926)

Tawney, R.H., *Equality* (Unwin Books, 1931)

Taylor, A.J.P., *English History 1914–1945* (Penguin, 1987)

Terrill, Ross, *R.H. Tawney and His Times – Socialism as Fellowship* (André Deutsch, 1973)

Thomas, George, *George Thomas, Mr Speaker: The Memoirs of The Viscount Tonypandy* (Century, 1985)

Thorpe, Andrew, *A History of the British Labour Party* (Macmillan, 1997)

Tressell, Robert, *The Ragged Trousered Philanthropists* (Lawrence and Wishart, 1995; new edition Paladin, 1991)

Tyler, Froom, *Cripps: A Portrait and a Prospect* (G.G. Harrap & Co., 1942)

Vernon, Betty D., *Ellen Wilkinson 1891–1947* (Croom Helm, 1982)

Vulliamy, Colwyn E., *Charles Kingsley and Christian Socialism* (Fabian Society Tract No 174, 1914)

Weiler, Peter, *Ernest Bevin* (Manchester University Press, 1993)

Weinbren, Daniel, *Generating Socialism: Recollections of Life in the Labour Party* (Sutton Publishing, 1997)

Wheen, Francis, *Tom Driberg: His Life and Indiscretions* (Chatto & Windus, 1990)

Wilkinson, Alan, *Dissent or Conform? War, Peace and the English Churches 1900–45* (SCM Press, 1986)

Wilkinson, Alan, *Christian Socialism: Scott Holland to Tony Blair* (SCM Press, 1998)

Williams, Francis, *Ernest Bevin* (Hutchinson, 1952)

Wilson, Harold, *The Labour Governments 1964–1970: A Personal Record* (Weidenfeld and Nicolson, and Michael Joseph, 1971)

Wilson, Harold, *Memoirs: The Making of a Prime Minister 1916–1964* (Weidenfeld and Nicolson, and Michael Joseph, 1986)

Winter, J.M., *Socialism and the Challenge of War: Ideas and Politics in Britain, 1912–18* (Routledge and Kegan Paul, 1974)

Wolffe, John (ed.), *Evangelical Faith and Public Zeal – Evangelicals and Society in Britain 1780–1980* (SPCK, 1995)

Wood, Ian S., *John Wheatley* (Manchester University Press, 1990)

Wright, Anthony, *R.H. Tawney* (Manchester University Press, 1987)

Wright, D.G., *Democracy and Reform 1815–1885* (Longman, 1989)

Wright, Tony and Carter, Matt, *The People's Party* (Thames and Hudson, 1997)

Wrigley, Chris, *Arthur Henderson* (GPC, 1990)

Index

INDEX

GOD'S POLITICIANS

sleaze 212
Slovenia 206
slums 75
Smith, A. 8, 216
Smith, C. 208
Smith, G. 56
Smith, I. 174
Smith, J. 205, 206–14,
219–20, 232
Snowden, P. 25, 35, 64–5,
67, 77–80
Great Depression
103–4, 115
National Government
105, 107
pacifism 130
second government 98
Wilson 167
Social Democratic
Federation (SDF)
25–6, 32–3, 35, 44,
100, 111
Social Democratic Forum
18
Social Democratic Party
(SDP) 186–8, 198,
210
social justice 1–23, 38
Socialism 6, 15–20, 36, 38
Attlee 126
Benn 194, 196
Bondfield 100
budgets 77
Catholic Church 70,
72–5
Cold War 145
Cripps 136, 138
Crosland 157–8
CSL 111–12
education 96
equality 119
ethics 59, 165, 167, 171
Field 200
first government 66, 68
Heffer 190, 192
Henderson 63–4
House of Lords 156

ILP 116
journalism 71
Lansbury 106, 110–11,
113
Manning 138, 139–40
money markets 178
National Government
108
radical policy 47
rationing 128
reflection 228
revisionism 155, 164
Russia 62
SDP 187
Smith 213
Snowden 78–9
Soper 152
Tawney 86–7, 89, 105
values 185
violence 33
vision 46
Wilson 172, 176
working class 132
World War I 36
Socialist Christian League
154–5
Socialist League 132,
133
Socialist Sunday Schools
19, 38, 40
Socialist Ten
Commandments 20
Society of Graphic and
Allied Trades
(SOGAT) 202–3
Society of Labour
Lawyers 217
Society of Socialist Clergy
154–5
Somerville, H. 74
Soper, D. 118, 145,
149–58, 162–4, 171
Soskice, F. 178–9
South Africa 36, 163, 174,
195
Soviet Union 206
Spain 123, 141–2

Spanish Civil War 133,
141–2, 160, 190–1
Spanish Medical Aid
Committee 142
Spurgeon, C.P. 9
Stalin, J. 134–5, 147–8
stamps 197
Stansgate, Lord 197
Statement of Principles
19
Stead, W.T. 15, 58
Steel, D. 184, 210
Steels, R.R. 35
Stepney Council 114
Stewart, D. 209
Stockwood, M. 155, 159,
162, 196
Stokes, R.R. 126
Straw, J. 208
strikes 49–50, 61, 175–6
breaking 30
General 232
miners 188–9
SOGAT 202–3
Wilson 177
Student Christian
Movement 150
Suffrage Bill 113
suffragettes 36, 40–1,
49–50, 101, 113
swinging sixties 166
Swithinbank, I. 130

Taff Vale railway dispute
26–7, 48
tariffs 68
Tatchell, P. 188
Tawney Lectures 208, 212
Tawney, R.H. 6–7,
86–105, 134
CSM 155
equality 232
SDP 187
Smith 212–13
Socialism 105
theology 151, 152
Wilson 176

266